THE
DESKTOP PUBLISHER'S
LEGAL HANDBOOK

By
Daniel Sitarz
Attorney-at-Law

**NOVA PUBLISHING COMPANY
CARBONDALE, ILLINOIS**

Manufactured in the United States.

Library of Congress Catalog Card Number 88-18002

ISBN 0-935755-02-0

Library of Congress Cataloging-in-Publication Data
    Sitarz, Dan, 1948-
    The Desktop Publisher's Legal Handbook
    (Legal Self-Help Series) Includes index.
    1. Press Law--United States--Popular Works.
    2. Desktop Publishing--United States. I. Title
    II. Series
    KF2750.Z9S58 1989 343.73'0998 88-18002
    ISBN 0-935755-02-0 (pbk.) 347.303998

This publication is designed to provide accurate and authoritative information in regard to the subject matter covered. It is sold with the understanding that the publisher and author are not engaged in rendering legal, accounting or other professional services. If legal advice or other expert assistance is required, the services of a competent professional person should be sought.

> - From a Declaration of Principles jointly adopted by a Committee of
>   the American Bar Association and a Committee of Publishers.

DISCLAIMER

Because of possible unanticipated changes in governing statutes and case law relating to the application of any information contained in this book, the author, publisher, and any and all persons or entities involved in any way in the preparation, publication, sale or distribution of this book disclaim all responsibility for the legal effects or consequences of any document prepared or action taken in reliance upon any information contained in this book. No representations, either express or implied, are made or given regarding the legal consequences of the use of any information contained in this book. Purchasers and persons intending to use this book for the preparation of any legal documents are advised to check specifically on the current applicable laws and statutes in any jurisdiction in which they intend the document to be effective.

NOVA PUBLISHING COMPANY
CARBONDALE, ILLINOIS

● TABLE OF CONTENTS ●

PREFACE

This book is part of Nova Publishing Company's continuing series on Legal Self-Help. These self-help legal guides are prepared by licensed Attorneys who feel that public access to the American legal system is long overdue.

Many areas of law are easily understood and applied by the average person in today's world. In the past there have been attempts on the part of the organized Bar and other lawyer organizations to prevent "self-help" legal information from reaching the general public. These attempts have gone hand-in-hand with efforts to leave the law cloaked in antiquated and unnecessary legal language which, of course, one must pay a lawyer to translate.

Law in American society is far more pervasive than ever before. There are legal consequences to virtually every public and most private actions in today's society. Leaving knowledge of the law within the hands of only the lawyers in such a society is not only foolish but dangerous as well. A free society depends, in large part, on an informed citizenry. This book and others in Nova's Legal Self-Help Series are intended to provide the necessary information to those members of the public who wish to use and understand the law for themselves.

However, in an area as complex as publishing law, encompassing topics as diverse as copyright law, constitutional freedoms, and legal contracts, it is not always prudent business practice to attempt to handle every legal situation which arises without the aid of a

11

competent attorney. Although the information presented in this book will begin to give its readers a basic grounding in the areas of law covered and, thus, enable them to better cope with many day-to-day legal problems, it is not intended that this text entirely substitute for experienced legal assistance.

Regardless of whether or not a lawyer is ultimately retained in certain situations, the legal information in this handbook will enable the reader to understand the framework of publishing law as it relates to the new computer "desktop" publishing industry.

To try and make that task as easy as possible, technical legal jargon has been eliminated whenever possible and plain English used instead. Naturally, plain and easily-understood English is not only perfectly proper for use in all legal documents but, in most cases, leads to far less confusion on the part of later readers. When it is necessary to use a legal term which may be unfamiliar to most people, the word will be shown in *italics* and defined when first used. For reference, at the end of this book there is a glossary of other legal and publishing terms which may be encountered in various publishing law contexts.

INTRODUCTION

In the last several years, computer publishing technology and mass production of computer equipment have combined to create a technological atmosphere in the information industry unlike any before. The world is on the verge of an enormous increase in access to the means to produce mass communication materials. Unlike other waves of the technological/information revolution, the wave of desktop publishing will not crest for many years to come. At a time when many observers feared that giant business concerns and media conglomerates were beginning to gain unprecedented and, in many cases, unregulated control of the worldwide flow of information, affordable desktop publishing technology has unleashed a powerful counter-measure to the centralization of information dissemination.

Printing technology advances in the last few decades has already fostered an enormous increase in the number of publishing concerns in the U.S. In the last 40 years, the number of publishers has increased some 60 fold, to over 21,000. In the coming decades, this astounding increase is expected to accelerate. Although the top 15% of these publishers continue to exert a top-heavy influence over the publishing industry, controlling over 90% of the books in print, the proliferation of small publishers is a sign of a renewed health for the industry.

The number of new books printed each year is also increasing at a rapid pace. Now standing at nearly 100,000 new books produced annually, the amount has been nearly doubling every decade since World War II. This increase also is expected to accelerate and continue far into the future. In addition to these dramatic increases in book production, specialized magazine publications have grown at an even greater rate in recent years. Newsletters, journals, pamphlets, brochures, catalogs; in short—all print media—have experienced rapid growth and will continue to grow in the future. In addition to the recent desktop publishing phenomenon, these increases are also attributable to technological advances in traditional printing technology and increased specialization in the publishing industry. On the horizon are even more rapid increases in the quantity and quality of mass communication publications. The full impact of the desktop publishing revolution has yet to be felt.

The tremendous potential of low-cost computer publishing is virtually untapped. Much of the initial first wave of the computer publishing revolution has been in the area of internal corporate publishing and small organization newsletter production. Both of these areas have been fertile ground for testing and refining the technology required to effectively produce high-quality, low-cost, and easily-formatted computerized publishing and will continue to be a major segment of the desktop publishing revolution far into the future. However, it is with the next wave of desktop publishing that the true potential of this technology will emerge.

The formation of small, even one-person, publishing concerns will create an opportunity of unprecedented scope for people to communicate and exchange ideas on a wide-scale. Although it was initially hoped that personal computers would usher in a grassroots worldwide age of information flow and communication, this has been true only to a limited extent. Despite the enormous growth of the personal computer market and its many applications in both the home and in business, the world is still a long way from having the personal computer become a common household furnishing on par with the television or radio. In spite of the relative proliferation of personal computers, for a long time into the future the vast majority of people will continue to gather their basic information from two main sources: television and the written word (in the form of newspapers, books and magazines).

Cable television has opened the TV channels, to a limited extent, to many new voices and perspectives, all of which combine to bring a much richer mix of culture and knowledge to the airwaves. However, the prohibitive cost of gaining access to the cable airwaves continues to be a significant hurdle for anyone desiring to enter the arena of television information dissemination. Although there are presently exciting advances in the use of computers, digital and laser optical recording, and video cassette recorders which will make state-of-the-art recording technology available at a much more affordable cost, the additional expense of disseminating the recorded information over the airwaves will keep widespread access to cable television programming out of the reach of most people. This is due to both the nature of the broadcast industry and the cost of the actual broadcast production facilities, back-up support, and personnel necessary to produce and air a high-quality video recording.

In the field of print media, however, the future is here. For relatively small sums of money, people are now able to effectively duplicate, in terms of quality of production, the results obtained by the massive publishing giants. Using laser technology, computerized type faces, and scannable graphics on today's enormously powerful personal computers, typeset-quality printing and graphics can be produced literally on a desktop. Of course, the quality of the writing, graphics and layout will still depend on the skill and expertise of the operator. But, the potential is now available for anyone to single-handedly produce printed information which is packaged in a marketable form. And, given the open nature of the marketplace for print information as opposed to the relatively restricted flow of the airwaves, printed communications are considerably easier to distribute at an affordable price.

It is the legal consequences and potential legal problems of these enormous future waves of information flow that this book attempts to address. As the technology of computer publishing becomes more affordable, more "user-friendly", faster, and able to produce ever higher quality results, more and more people will be drawn into the arena of public and private dissemination of information and ideas. This publishing revolution will allow more people than ever before to have access to the means to communicate and publish via print on a wide-scale basis. Additionally, as more and more of the world's citizenry become literate, the proliferation of print information will accelerate at a rate unknown in the past.

The technology to foster this publishing revolution is currently available, as is technical guidance on writing, graphics, typesetting, layout and all of the other facets of traditional publishing. What this book makes available is the legal and business expertise necessary for desktop publishers to safely and effectively enter the field of computer publishing. An awareness of the legal requirements of a publishing business, regardless of how small such a business might seem, is a very real prerequisite to any successful venture in desktop publishing. Whether the desk-top publications produced are simple 4-page newsletters for a small company or full-length books for worldwide distribution, there are certain general legal principles and practices which all who enter the field of publishing should understand.

As a business, desktop publishing has much in common with any other small business enterprise. Although certain general business issues will be touched upon, it is the unique legal and business characteristics of desktop publishing which will be the focus of this book.

Chapter 1 of this guide provides a brief overview of the various situations encountered in desktop or computer publishing which require a knowledge of the law and an understanding of specific legal requirements.

Chapter 2 contains an explanation of U.S. copyright law and how it relates to desktop publishing.

Chapter 3 details how to properly register a claim of copyright.

Guidelines and forms for obtaining permission to use copyrighted material are contained in Chapter 4.

Various non-copyright registrations are detailed in Chapter 5. Although not legal requirements, these registrations are considered standard in the publishing industry.

In Chapter 6, a comparison is made of the advantages and disadvantages of the five main business structures from which to operate a desktop publishing concern: the sole proprietorship, the partnership, the limited partnership, the corporation and the "S" corporation.

Chapter 7 elaborates on the choice of business structure in the area of taxation and the tax consequences of how the computer publishing business is formed and operated.

In Chapter 8, basic contract law fundamentals for use in a computer publishing business are outlined. In addition, sample book publishing contract clauses are set forth and explained.

The legal pitfalls of defamation and libel are outlined in Chapter 9. Additionally, legal defenses to defamation actions and how to avoid libel are covered.

Closely related to libel, but requiring a different perspective, are the problems of invasion of privacy from the context of a desktop publishing business. This topic is discussed in Chapter 10.

Chapter 11 contains an overview of various other concerns for the desktop publisher, including unfair trade practices, censorship, and obscenity law.

Appendix A contains a listing of useful copyright publications and circulars, while Appendix B includes various legal forms for use in copyright situations. Appendix C contains copyright registration forms and instructions, and Appendix D incorporates various sample desktop publishing contracts.

Finally, there is a bibliography and a glossary of pertinent legal and publishing terms.

This book is intended both to advise the computer publisher of the necessary legal requirements for operating a publishing business and to alert the desktop publisher to the various areas of law which any publisher must approach with caution. With a clear understanding of the law, unnecessary legal complications can be avoided and the business of desktop publishing can proceed unhindered by legal problems.

CHAPTER 1

THE LAW AND DESKTOP PUBLISHING

Regardless of what form desktop publishing takes, be it a simple newsletter for internal corporate distribution or a large fully-typeset book for bookstore sales, there are certain serious legal consequences that can arise from the very act of publishing. Computer desktop publishing, as a business, is much like any other business concern. There are the basic problems of financing, personnel training, management, advertising, and all of the other general obstacles which any successful enterprise must overcome. However, the desktop publisher also enters a different arena: the arena of communications and information dissemination. The communications business has evolved certain specialized rules and laws in an effort to make the marketplace of ideas and information as open as is mandated by the First Amendment of the U.S. Constitution and as fair as is required by a general sense of justice.

There are two general sets of legal principles and rules which apply specifically to publishing. Both of the general areas of publishing law have evolved from provisions contained in the U.S. Constitution; the first from provisions of the Constitution providing for Copyright and the second from various interpretations of the First Amendment to the Constitution.

The first area of relevant law may be generally characterized as legal protections for the publisher. These protections are centered around the copyright laws of the U.S. A publication's copyright is the foundation of many of the contractual rights involved in publishing. Failure to abide by copyright regulations can result in the loss of certain legal rights obtained by copyright and copyright registration. Infringement upon another's copyright can render the infringer liable for large monetary fines and judgements and possibly a prison term.

The second general set of legal principles relates to restrictions on publishing. These range from legal restrictions against publishing obscenities to legal rules against invasion of privacy. In general, these publishing restrictions stem from exceptions to the First Amendment right of a free press. A violation of any of the restrictions in this second set of legal rules is normally a civil infraction and is generally punishable by a monetary fine.

COPYRIGHT PROTECTIONS

The first area in which a desktop publishing business differs markedly from other general business concerns is in the realm of copyright. Provided for by the U.S. Constitution and an Act of Congress, the protections of copyright for the printed word and other forms of expression are, in many ways, the framework of the publishing industry. Although often taken for granted, frequently overlooked and nearly universally misunderstood, copyright protection is the foundation of literally all written commercial information that enters the marketplace.

Understanding the copyright process and what is protected by copyright and, equally important, what is not protected is central to successful publishing. Even if the materials produced are relatively simple business publications, knowledge of the fundamentals of copyright law is essential both for protection of the work itself and for avoidance of infringement upon another's copyright.

Related to this is the area of rights to the copyrighted material. Who may do what with the material and where, when, and how may they do it is an area which is generally covered by a publishing contract of some form or another. A grasp of the basics of contract law and an understanding of particular publishing industry terminology and practices is fundamental for dealing with others in the information industry.

GENERAL BUSINESS LAW

Additionally, a desktop publisher should have a basic understanding of some general business law in order to successfully launch a publishing venture. As with any business, contracts will form an integral part of any legal transactions with other parties. The general nature of contracts and the specific idiosyncrasies of publishing contracts will be detailed.

In addition to the law of contracts, the choice of a business structure, be it a *sole proprietorship* (a business owned by one person), a *partnership* (a business owned by two or more persons or organizations), or a *corporation* (a business owned by one or more shareholders) is an important initial decision which must be made when launching a desktop publishing business.

The tax aspects of the formation of a publishing business, as with any business, must also be considered. In order to maximize tax savings and thus, insure the greatest potential for success, the organization of the record-keeping and accounting aspects of the business must be done with an eye on the latest tax laws.

RESTRICTIONS ON PUBLISHING

Publishing in any form in the United States operates under the umbrella of protection of the First Amendment of the U.S. Constitution. The framers of the Bill of Rights could think of no clearer way to state their contention that the freedom of the press in this country should be absolute than with the chosen words of the First Amendment: "Congress shall make no law . . . abridging the freedom . . . of the press."

Although this sounds like an absolute restriction on any form of regulation of the press or publishing, certain restrictions have been held to apply to the right to print anything one chooses to. These restrictions are generally in the nature of *legal civil liability* (being subject to a lawsuit for damages) for printing or publishing something which infringes on another person's rights.

■   LIBEL

Into this category of restrictions falls *libelous publishing* (printing or publishing falsities which harm, in some way, the reputation of another person).

Libel is a very illusive concept which is constantly being redefined by the courts. Many statements and references which seemed perfectly harmless to the publisher have been the subject of libel suits. A classic example is the innocuous statement in a newspaper that a woman had given birth to a new baby. This innocent reference gave rise to a lawsuit by the mother for defamation of character since, unknown to the newspaper, the woman's husband had been overseas for over 12 months prior to the child's birth. A general understanding of the elements of libel is key to avoiding a costly lawsuit from an irate reader.

■   THE RIGHT OF PRIVACY

Closely related to defamation and libel but a relative newcomer to the rights of the public, the right of privacy has four basic tenets which apply to desktop publishing. First, there are   restrictions against using another's image   for commercial gain without reimbursement.   This is referred to as *misappropriation*.   This restriction generally applies in the area of commercial advertising. Second, the public disclosure of embarrassing private facts, even if true, is restricted, to some extent. Publications which place someone in a false light by distortion of the truth are also subject to liability. And finally, intrusive reporting or the actual physical invasion of the solitude of a person is a recognized violation of a person's right of privacy which may be enforced by the courts.

■   OBSCENITY/ NATIONAL SECURITY/ TRADE SECRET/
    UNFAIR TRADE PRACTICE RESTRICTIONS

Also related to this area of restrictions on publications are the various
limits which the courts have placed on the publishing of erotic
materials.   Yet another area of publishing which may fall subject to
government restrictions is the publishing of sensitive national security
information or secrets.   Related to this is the potential for civil
liability stemming from the publishing of information which is the
breach of a commercial trade secret agreement.   Unfair competition
and unfair trade practices are also pertinent to the area of publishing.

Although many of these areas may seem esoteric and on the fringes
of law from the viewpoint of the standard publisher, in order to avoid
any possible exposure to lawsuits and legal entanglements which
would effectively destroy a fledgling desktop publishing concern or
damage the parent organization of the publication, an understanding
of these areas of publishing law is highly recommended.   The lines
that have been drawn by the courts in their decisions as to how far to
extend the restrictions on publishing without infringing on the rights
of a free press are anything but clear.   Many large and knowledgeable
publishers, backed by teams of lawyers, have fallen into serious legal
difficulties by underestimating the potential for lawsuits from angered
readers.

Each of these various topics will be dealt with in detail in the
following chapters.   The goal of this book is to provide a basic
understanding of how a desktop publishing business can avoid
unnecessary legal entanglements and effectively use the laws and
regulations that are in place.

There may, of course, be situations in which it will be prudent or even
necessary to consult with an attorney regarding decisions concerning
much of what is discussed in this book.   Many of the areas of law
which confront the publishing industry are complex and constantly in
flux.   Generally, the small size of the publishing company or the
limited scope of its publications will have little or no bearing on
whether the same laws will apply to its operations as to some of the
industry giants.   Readers are encouraged to use the information in

this book as a basis to understand the general framework of publishing law as it relates to computer desktop publishing. With an overall understanding of the issues in publishing law, those involved in applying desktop publishing technologies to practical uses will be better able to recognize and avoid situations which may have a potential for legal complications.

CHAPTER 2

U.S. COPYRIGHT LAW

Copyright protection is one of the most misunderstood legal fields in America, even by many attorneys. Although most people feel that they have a rough general understanding of what copyright is and what it protects, most are totally unfamiliar with how one might go about obtaining such protection and what the real benefits of copyright protection are. With the recent explosion of desktop computer publishing technologies, vast numbers of people are now creating copyrightable material every day without any notion of how to obtain the fullest extent of copyright protection available.

In the past few years, the rapid advancements in computer technology combined with the mass production of personal computers and their peripherals have made available to the American public the tools of instant creativity. The relative ease of creating and publishing a written product of communication on a personal computer and the evolution of simplified document-processing hardware and software has unleashed an unprecedented wave of creative expression. People who never before would have thought themselves capable are producing and publishing creative works with the aid of a computer.

Very little of this enormous bulk of computer-produced creative work currently has copyright registration and, thus, full copyright protection. Much of it should. With the advent of desktop publishing technology, the business risks associated with the distribution of non-copyright-registered material are being assumed by many small business publishers without the requisite knowledge of what those risks entail. Although this book will deal specifically with the copyright registration of published material, it should be understood that copyright registration is available for all original written works, whether published or unpublished (including simple print-outs of matter produced on a word processor and even information never printed out but existing only as stored data on a hard or floppy disk), as well as non-written communications, such as musical or artistic creations and movies or videotapes.

WHAT IS COPYRIGHT PROTECTION?

The exclusive right to ownership of a creative work is one of the prime motivating factors for the creator. This motivation for creation of scholarly and artistic works was important enough to have been recognized and specifically protected by the Constitution.

The availability of copyright protection in the United States is based on a provision of the U.S. Constitution. In Article I, Section 8, Congress is given power to "Promote the Progress of Science and the useful Arts by securing for limited Times to Authors and Inventors the exclusive Right to their respective Writings and Discoveries."

Based on this broad grant of power, Congress has provided a complex system of copyright and patent protection. The general protection provided to the holder of a copyright is clear: it is the right to control any copies of his or her work and to prevent any unauthorized use of the work.

The current Copyright Act (The Copyright Act of 1976) was a major revision of copyright law. It brought copyright protection totally

26

under the umbrella of federal jurisdiction for all actions arising after January 1, 1978, when the Act first took effect. The bulk of the information contained in this book will relate to copyright situations involving material which was created after the current Copyright Act took effect.

Considerable confusion has resulted from the various levels of copyright protection available. Copyright protections and the various rights that accompany it are divided into three basic levels:

- Copyright protections and rights by *creation*;

- Copyright protections and rights by *publication*;

- Copyright protections and rights by *registration*.

Each of these levels of copyright protection has slightly differing rights and benefits which attach to it. After a work is created, in order to achieve the fullest set of rights and protections, a work should be *published* (for Copyright law, published means "distributed to the public for sale or rental") and registered with the Copyright Office. These matters are explained in detail below.

Copyright protection is available to the authors of "original works of authorship". This very broad definition includes literary, dramatic, musical, artistic, and other intellectual works, whether published or unpublished. Under the new Copyright Act, copyright protection exists *immediately* from the time the work is created in a fixed form and the copyright is, generally, the property of the author (See below, however, for "works-for-hire" and joint works). Specifically, the owner of the copyright has the <u>exclusive</u> right to do or authorize others to:

- make any copies of the copyrighted work;

- prepare derivative works based on the copyrighted work (for example: translations or adaptations of a work to another medium) ;

27

- distribute copies of the copyrighted work to the public for sale or rent/lease;

- perform the copyrighted work publicly (in the case of plays, movies, or similar "performance" works);

- display the copyrighted work publicly (in the case of movies, art, photographic, or similar works).

A violation of any of these rights is illegal under the Copyright Act and can subject the violator to a suit for copyright infringement and, possibly, criminal penalties. However, there are exceptions to these broad protections which allow certain limited uses of copyrighted material without either permission of the copyright holder or payment of royalties. "Fair Use" and "Compulsory License" are two such exceptions which will be explained later in this chapter.

For the desktop publisher, the first three of these exclusive rights are the most important and will form the backbone of any publishing concern: the right to produce (publish) copies of the work, the right to prepare derivative works from the original, and the right to distribute any copies for sale.

The right to publish a work for profit is comprised of two of these rights: the right to reproduce a work and the right to distribute copies of a work for sale. For print material, these rights are a straight-forward matter and are the basis of most of the contractual rights stemming from copyright. The owner of the copyright may subdivide this broad "right to make and distribute copies" into many different rights, such as "the right to make English-language copies for distribution and sale only in North America". The division of these subsidiary rights are dealt with in detail in Chapter 6: Basic Desktop Publishing Contracts.

The "right to prepare derivative works from the original" is the other important copyright issue which must be understood by the desktop publisher. A *derivative* work is defined, for copyright purposes, as a work which is based upon an original pre-existing work. Thus, a derivative work would include a translation of a work, a movie version of a particular work, and a condensation of a work. It would also include editorial revisions of the original work and any modifications of the original work. This right, then, is the right to vary, alter, modify, or adapt the original copyrighted material.

WHO IS THE OWNER OF THE COPYRIGHT?

While much of what may be produced in a desktop publishing format will be created personally by the individual publisher, often the work may be produced by an employee or by another person on a contract basis. In general, it is the actual author/creator of the work who owns the copyright. However, in the case of a work created by an employee within the scope of his or her employment (defined as a *work-for-hire*), it is the employer who is presumed to be the author and owner of the copyright. This presumption can be altered by a written agreement between the employer and employee indicating that certain works created by the employee within the scope of his or her employment will be owned solely by the employee. A sample "Agreement for Employee to be Copyright Owner" is contained in Appendix B. There is also a generally recognized exception to the work-for-hire rule which allows teachers and professors to retain the copyright to materials which may, normally, be considered to be prepared within the scope of their employment.

In addition, in the case of specially commissioned works to be used in a collective work, an agreement may be made that the work also be considered a "work for hire", giving the ownership of the copyright to the person or entity which has commissioned the work. Such an agreement, however, must be in written form and signed by the actual author of the work. This type of arrangement will be used in many contract-type situations when an author is specifically requested by the publisher and contracted to produce a particular work for inclusion in a collection (for example: a contributing article in a magazine). A sample "Work-for-Hire Agreement" is included in Appendix B.

If two or more authors jointly produce a creative work and their intention was to create an inseparable whole work, then all authors are jointly and equally co-owners of the work. This arrangement can be altered if there is a written agreement to the contrary. However, if there was no intention to create such a whole work, each author may copyright his or her individual contribution. For example, a work may have a separate copyright for the written text and a separate copyright for the illustrations.

Copyright of each separate contribution to a periodical or other collective work is distinct from copyright in the collective work as a whole and is owned by the author of the contribution, unless there is an agreement otherwise.

Simple ownership of a book or manuscript does not give the owner the copyright. It is the creator who has the ownership of the copyright, unless such copyright is effectively transferred.

Of course, ownership of the copyright can be transferred to another and separate rights under the copyright can be parceled out to different parties. (Please see below under "Transferring the Copyright").

Copyright protection is available to minors and for all unpublished work regardless of the nationality of the author or where the author resides. For published material to be eligible for copyright protection it must, on the date of first publication, either:

- have at least one author who is a resident or citizen of the U.S. or of another country which has a copyright treaty in force with the U.S; or

- be first published in the U.S. or in a country which is a party to the Universal Copyright Convention.

Initially then, unless the copyright is transferred, the ownership of the copyright is:

- The author or creator of the work;

    - <u>Unless</u> the author was an employee <u>and</u> the work was created within the scope of his or her employment <u>and</u> no written agreement otherwise exists;

    - <u>Or</u>, the author was specially commissioned to create the work as part of a collective work and signed a written agreement to do so as a "work-for-hire".

- The joint authors or creators of the work, if there was a mutual intention to create a joint work.

WHAT WORKS ARE ELIGIBLE FOR COPYRIGHT PROTECTION?

General copyright protection exists immediately for all original works of authorship as soon as they become fixed in a tangible form of expression. The work does not have to necessarily be in a written form. It is only required that the form of expression be, somehow, directly perceptible. This may be with the aid of a machine or device (for example: a computer, a movie projector, microfilm reader, etc.). If a work is prepared over a period of time, whatever exists on a particular date constitutes the "work" as of that date.

Copyrightable works include the following general categories:

- Literary works;

- Musical works, including any accompanying words;

- Dramatic works, including any accompanying music;

- Pantomimes and choreographic works;

- Pictorial, graphic, and sculptural works (including cartoons and comic strips);

31

- Motion pictures and other audiovisual works;

- Sound recordings.

These general categories should be broadly interpreted. For example, computer programs are generally considered to fall under the heading of "literary works", as are computer databases. Any commercial and business textual publications are considered "literary" works and include advertising text, catalogs, directories, and even indexes. Maps, advertising artwork, cartoons, logos, schematics, and architectural blueprints are copyrightable as "pictorial" or "graphic" works. Video games and other machine readable audiovisual works are considered to be in the same category as motion pictures and may be copyrighted.

There is some overlap of these categories due to the nature of evolving technology. For example, to obtain full copyright protection for a video game, it may be necessary to register the copyright for the pictorial images and the accompanying music, sound and text as a work of performing art. The underlying computer program may then need to be separately registered as a non-dramatic literary work. Finally, it may be necessary to register the design of a semiconductor computer chip separately if it is unique to the particular work.

A *compilation* of material is considered to be a separate work formed by assembling pre-existing work together in an original way. If the pre-existing work is previously copyrighted, the compilation is considered a *derivative* work. If the pre-existing work is not copyrighted, the original compilation is defined as a *collective* work. Note that only the author's contribution to a compilation is copyrightable by that author. If pre-existing work by others is assembled into a compilation, permission to use such material must be obtained prior to publication.

WHAT IS NOT ELIGIBLE FOR COPYRIGHT PROTECTION?

What is protectable by copyright can be as important as what is not copyrightable. The following categories are not generally eligible for copyright protection:

- Works that have not been fixed in a tangible form of expression. For example, an improvisational speech that has not been written or recorded;

- Titles, names, short phrases, slogans, familiar symbols or designs. (These type of words and symbols may be eligible for Trademark or Servicemark protection. For more information regarding possible trademark or servicemark registration, write: Commissioner of Patents and Trademarks, Washington, DC 20231);

- Format, arrangement, typography, lettering, or coloring of a work;

- Mere listings of ingredients or contents;

- Ideas, procedures, methods, systems, processes, concepts, principles, discoveries, or devices, as distinguished from a description, explanation, or illustration. This is a difficult distinction to grasp. In general, it is the specific expression of an idea or principle which may receive copyright protection, and *not* the idea itself. Other expressions of the same idea or system may be copyrighted without being considered an infringement of the original copyright, as long as the expression of that idea is different. For example, a particular economic theory is not copyrightable. What is copyrightable are the specific words used to express the theory. Another expression of the same theory in different words would not be an infringement of copyright. An idea cannot be copyrighted.

- Works consisting *entirely* of information that is common property and containing no original authorship. This category includes standard calendars, height and weight charts, tape measures and rulers, and lists or tables taken from public documents or other common sources.

- Blank forms and similar works which are designed to record rather than to convey information;

PUBLICATION OF COPYRIGHTED MATERIAL

Publication is no longer the key to copyright protection as it was under the previous Copyright Act. However, particularly for the desktop publisher, publication remains an important factor in copyright protection. *Publication*, for copyright purposes, means the distribution of copies of a work to the public by sale or rental.

Publication of a work creates certain significant consequences. These consequences are as follows:

- When published, all published copies should bear a notice of copyright (see "Notice of Copyright" below).

- All works that are published in the United States with such notice of copyright are subject to mandatory deposit requirements with the Library of Congress (see below under: Deposit Requirements).

- Publication of a work can affect the limitation on the exclusive rights of copyright owners.

- The year of publication is important for determining the duration of copyright for anonymous works, pseudonymous works, and works-for-hire.

- Registration deposit requirements are different for published works.

NOTICE OF COPYRIGHT

Whenever a work is published for distribution to the public, a notice of copyright should be placed on all copies. This notice is required even on works published outside of the United States. Failure to comply with this notice requirement can result in the loss of certain additional rights which are otherwise available to the copyright owner.

The use of the copyright notice is the responsibility of the copyright owner and does not require the permission of nor registration with the Copyright Office.

A notice of copyright should contain the following three elements:

1. The symbol © (the letter C in a circle), or the word "Copyright", or the abbreviation "Copr." It is recommended that the © symbol and the word "copyright" always be used in order to bring the copyrighted work under the full terms of the Universal Copyright Convention and, thus, obtain copyright protection in many foreign countries.

2. The year of first publication of the work. In the case of compilations of previously copyrighted material, the year of the first publication of the compilation is sufficient.

3. The name of the owner of the copyright, or a recognizable abbreviation of the name.

The copyright notice for an individual will appear as: © Copyright 1988 John Smith. For a company which owns the copyright, the notice will be: © Copyright 1988 Smith Publications, Inc..

For a book, this copyright notice, traditionally, should appear on either the title page of the work or on the *verso* or reverse of the title page. For a magazine or other periodical, the notice should appear as part of or adjacent to the masthead of the periodical or adjacent to a prominent heading at or near the front of the particular issue.

Individual contributions to a compiled work which has an overall copyright may be granted individual copyrights. For each individual contribution to a magazine, periodical, or collective work to be considered to have a separate copyright, the separate notice of copyright must appear either:

- Under the title of the separate contribution on the same page, or;

- Adjacent to the individual contribution, or;

- Anywhere on the first page of the separate contribution as long as it is clear that the notice of copyright applies to that particular contribution.

Although other positions are technically acceptable for the location of the copyright notice, it is wise to follow the accepted industry standards and locate the copyright notice where most people will look for it.

If the work is unpublished (that is, has not yet been prepared for distribution to the public), it is still advisable to include a form of copyright notice on any copies that leave one's control. This is to avoid any possibility of inadvertent publication without notice.

In the past, errors or omission of the copyright notice may have had the effect of completely destroying copyright protection for the work and placing the material in the public domain. This, of course, could be disastrous, as works in the *public domain* are available for anyone's use without permission or payment of any royalty fee.

Under the current law, there is a grace period for correcting any errors or omissions to the copyright notice on anything published after January 1, 1978. In general, the omission of the copyright notice or an error in the notice does not invalidate the copyright *if*:

- Copyright registration of the work has been made before the publication without notice, or;

- Copyright registration of the work is made within 5 years after the publication without notice, and;

- A reasonable effort is made to promptly add the correct notice to all copies that are distributed to the public in the United States after the error or omission is discovered.

If a work contains a preponderance of material that is taken from a U. S. Government publication which is in the public domain, the notice of copyright must also contain a statement identifying those portions of the work that are from the U. S. Government publication.

Please note that the copyright notice requirements for phonorecords of sound recordings are different than those required for printed matter. Please see Appendix A for the proper Copyright Circular if you need further information on this matter.

THE MANUFACTURING CLAUSE

The Manufacturing Clause of the Copyright Act, which required that copies of all non-dramatic literary works written in English be manufactured in the United States, expired on July 1, 1986.

Thus, it is no longer legally necessary to include a statement on the copyright page of a book detailing that the book was "manufactured in the United States", as was previously required. Many publishers, however, continue to include such a statement out of custom.

HOW LONG DOES COPYRIGHT PROTECTION LAST?

For anything copyrighted after January 1, 1978, protection lasts as follows:

- For an individual author: the author's life plus 50 years.

- For a "jointly" authored work: 50 years after the last surviving co-author's death.

- For works-for-hire, anonymous works and pseudonymous works: 75 years from publication (generally as determined by the date shown on the notice of publication for the first publication) or 100 years from creation, whichever is shorter.

For works copyrighted prior to January 1, 1978, the work was given an initial copyright term of 28 years. During the last year (the 28th year) of this first term, the copyright was eligible for renewal for another 28 year term. The new Copyright Act has made the renewal term 47 years for those works whose renewal term would have expired between 1962 and 1978 and for those works initially registered between 1950 and 1978. The current law, thus, makes those works created after 1909 but prior to January 1, 1978 eligible for a total of 75 years of copyright protection, if timely renewals were and are filed.

If the work was published and registered prior to January 1, 1978, the maximum copyright term is 75 years. Therefore, as of January 1, 1989, all works copyrighted prior to January 1, 1914 are in the public domain. Of course, many works copyrighted after that date are also in the public domain due to failure to renew the copyrights, but an investigation of the copyright status of each individual work is necessary for this determination.

For works that were created but not published or registered prior to January 1, 1978, the length of the copyright term is equivalent to that of works created after January 1, 1978, with one addition: for works in this category, the copyright term will extend to at least December 31, 2002.

All copyright terms, whether under current or prior law, expire on December 31st of the last year of the copyright. If a renewal is available for works created prior to 1978, such renewal must be made within the last year of the initial copyright term or the copyright is lost forever.

Once a copyright in a work is lost or expires, the work enters the public domain and is free to use without permission or payment.

TRANSFERRING A COPYRIGHT

Any or all of the five separate rights inherent in a copyright may be transferred by the owner of the copyright. The rights under copyright may also be subdivided by the owner. However, to be valid, the transfer of exclusive rights must be in writing and signed by the owner of the rights to be transferred. A transfer of rights on a non-exclusive basis does not have to be in writing. *Exclusive* rights are those rights which only the present owner of the particular right may exercise.

A written document which effectively transfers an exclusive right under copyright must contain the following:

● A description of the work;

● A description of the rights transferred;

● A statement showing intent to transfer the rights;

● The name of the one making the transfer;

● The date of the transfer;

● The signature of the one making the transfer.

A sample "Assignment and Transfer of Copyright" form is contained in Appendix B. It may be used when all exclusive rights in a copyright will be transferred to another party.

A copyright is a personal property right and, as such, may be given as a gift, left to someone in a will, or pass as personal property to the next of kin where there is no will. All of the rights which may be transferred from the copyright of an original work must originate with the creator (or employer if a work-for-hire) of the work. It should be noted that the ownership of a copyright is distinct from the ownership of any actual copies of the work in question.

Lifetime transfers of copyright are generally made by contract. Any such contractual transfers should be recorded with the Copyright Office. In fact, the documents relating to any transfer of copyright (for example: a will, deed, power of attorney, mortgage, or contract) should be recorded with the Copyright Office. While the transfer will be valid without this recordation, such recording does provide certain legal advantages and may be required to validate the transfer against third parties to the agreement. In addition, the documents of any transfer of copyright ownership must be recorded with the Copyright

Office prior to the institution of any lawsuit for copyright infringement. For further information regarding Recordation of Transfers of Copyright, write:

> Renewals and Documents Section
> Examining Division
> Copyright Office
> Library of Congress
> Washington, DC 20559

TERMINATING A COPYRIGHT TRANSFER

There is a unique aspect of copyright law relating to any contract which transfers the creator's original exclusive copyright. Under current law, any transfer of copyright ownership by the creator of an original work can be unilaterally terminated during a five year period beginning 35 years after the date of transfer by serving written notice on the person or entity to whom the ownership rights were originally transferred to. The notice must be filed between 25 and 33 years after the original transfer of copyright. For works with a copyright term and a renewal term registered prior to January 1, 1978, the right of termination of any transfer can only be exercised after 56 years have elapsed since the original copyright date.

The right to terminate a transfer of copyright ownership is irrevocable and the creator need not pay for the return of the copyright ownership. This right of termination allows the original author or the author's surviving spouse, children, or grandchildren another chance to use the work for commercial gain. However, a work-for-hire is not subject to this right of termination. This provision was added to the current Copyright Act in an attempt to rectify the injustice of an author giving up all rights to a work for far less than its potential future worth.

The right to terminate a copyright transfer is a unique and important right. There are complicated and decisive deadlines which must be strictly adhered to in order for a termination of transfer to occur. It is recommended that an attorney well versed in copyright law be retained for assistance in terminating a copyright transfer.

EXCEPTIONS TO FULL COPYRIGHT PROTECTION

As mentioned earlier, there are several situations in which exceptions are granted to total copyright protection. Congress has felt that it is necessary to allow use of copyrighted material under certain circumstances without payment of a fee and without actual permission of the owner of the copyright.

■   FAIR USE

The most important exception is termed the "Fair Use" exclusion. Essentially, the *Fair Use* doctrine allows for the reproduction of copyrighted material for purposes such as the following without permission or payment of a fee and without it being considered an infringement of copyright:

● 	Teaching (including multiple copies for classroom use);

● 	Criticism and comment;

● 	News reporting;

● 	Scholarship or research.

When determining in a particulai case whether infringement has taken place, the following factors are also considered:

● 	The purpose and character of the use of the work, including if the work was used for commercial gain or merely for educational purposes;

● 	The nature of the copyrighted work;

● 	The amount of the portion of the work used in proportion to the entire work;

● 	The effect of the use on the potential market or value of the copyrighted work.

41

Thus, a teacher may make complete photocopies of magazine articles and pass them out to a class without having to purchase many individual copies of the entire magazine. Similarly, a book reviewer may use direct quotes from a book in a review without seeking prior permission of the copyright owner. However, the commercial use of a single strategic phrase from a short musical lyric may be considered a copyright infringement.

The "Fair Use" exception to copyright protection is intended to provide reasonable limited access to and use of material which otherwise would require actual permission to use or copy. The scope of this exception is limited in nature and should seldom be relied upon to provide protection for the use of copyrighted material in a publication without the permission of the copyright owner. A discussion of copyright permission requirement is contained in Chapter 4. For the forms necessary for obtaining the permission to use copyrighted material, please see Appendix B.

- ### COMPULSORY LICENSE

The "Compulsory License" exception to copyright protection relates to the use of musical material and has little bearing on desktop publishing. In general, it provides that once a recording of a musical work has been publicly distributed in the U.S., anyone else may obtain a "compulsory license" to make and distribute records of the same work without the express permission of the copyright owner of the original. Royalties for such use must still, however, be paid to the owner of the original copyright of the musical work.

INTERNATIONAL COPYRIGHT PROTECTION

There is no "international" copyright as such. Protection against unauthorized use of material in a particular country depends upon the individual national laws of that country. However, most foreign countries do provide protection for creative material under specific international copyright conventions and treaties.

The United States is a member of the Universal Copyright Convention. This provides copyright protection in all member nations if the work is produced by a citizen or resident of a member nation and bears the proper notice of copyright within the member nation. The acceptable notice of copyright for this protection is the same as required by the United States (if the © symbol is used): the copyright symbol, the name of the copyright owner, and the year of first publication. It is recommended that the word "copyright" also be used.

In addition, if international copyright protection of the fullest extent is desired, the statement "All rights reserved" should be included directly after the notice of copyright. This essentially brings the work under the protection of the Buenos Aires Convention, extending protection to much of Central and South America.

If a particular work is to be published specifically for distribution in a foreign country, make certain that the country is a member of the Universal Copyright Convention or the Buenos Aires Convention prior to publication, since copyright protection in certain nations may depend on facts existing at the time of *first* publication. Be advised that some countries offer little or no protection for foreign works. See Appendix A for the proper Copyright Office Circular for determination of specific foreign copyright protection.

COPYRIGHT REGISTRATION

In general, copyright *registration* is a legal formality which places the basic facts of each specific piece of copyrighted material on public record. Under the new (1976) Copyright Act, registration is voluntary, not mandatory. The copyright exists as soon as the work is created in a fixed form. However, actual copyright registration has many important advantages which are not available to non-registered material. These are as follows:

● The formal registration of a copyright establishes a verifiable public record of the copyright claim.

● Registration secures for the copyright owner the right to file an "infringement of copyright" lawsuit. This right is unavailable without formal copyright registration.

43

- If registration is made before publication or within 5 years of publication of the work, registration provides *prima facie* (legally sufficient on its face) evidence of the validity of the copyright. This makes it far easier to prove one's case in any subsequent lawsuit involving infringement of the copyright.

- If registration is made within 3 months after publication of the work or is made before any infringement of the work has taken place, the owner of the copyright becomes entitled to additional statutory damages of up to $50,000.00 and the payment of attorney's fees and legal costs of a suit in any subsequent successful court action for copyright infringement. Without timely registration, only an award of actual damages is available to the copyright owner. (See below: "Copyright Infringement").

- If published material is publicly distributed without the necessary copyright notice, copyright registration must be obtained in order to avoid loss of all copyright benefits.

Under the earlier Copyright Act, copyright was obtained only upon publication with a notice of copyright or by registration. Under the new Act, copyright is immediate upon creation, but, as was noted above, publication and registration confer other important benefits on the copyright owner.

A work may be registered at any time within the life of the underlying copyright. If a work has been registered prior to publication, it is not necessary to re-register the work upon publication.

For the desktop publisher, it is clearly advantageous to register the copyright claim for any particular work which has any commercial value within the 3-month period after publication in order to secure the additional legal rights which accompany prompt registration. The cost of registration is minimal ($10.00 at present) and the benefits conferred are substantial.

Detailed procedures for copyright registration are contained in Chapter 3. Copies of the required forms for registering a copyright are located in Appendix C.

DEPOSIT REQUIREMENTS

Although formal copyright registration is voluntary under the new Copyright Act, there is a mandatory "publication" deposit requirement on any work which has been published in the United States with a notice of copyright, even if the work is not submitted for copyright registration. Thus, the owner of the copyright (in general, the author), or the owner of the right of first publication (generally the publisher if specified by contract) has a legal duty to provide the Copyright Office with 2 copies of the copyrighted work within 3 months of the date of first publication. Failure to provide this "publication" deposit can give rise to stiff fines (possibly over $2,500.00) and other penalties, but does not affect the copyright protection.

In addition, there is a mandatory "registration" deposit requirement (detailed in Chapter 3). However, if the work has been submitted for copyright registration, the copy or copies of the work submitted to the Copyright Office for the voluntary "registration" deposit will satisfy the mandatory "publication" deposit requirement and a further deposit is unnecessary.

COPYRIGHT SEARCHES

It may, on occasion, become necessary to conduct a search of Copyright Office records to determine the copyright status or ownership of a particular piece of work. Unlike the situation in Patent law, copyright searches are not legally necessary prior to any publication and are not ordinarily made to determine whether a similar work has already been copyrighted. They are useful, however, to determine the copyright ownership of a particular work or the "public domain" status of a work.

The records of the Copyright Office are open to the public for inspection and searches. In addition, most large library collections in the U.S. contain copies of the <u>Copyright Office Catalog of Copyright Entries</u> which is a good starting point for a copyright search. This is essentially the entire Copyright Card Catalog of the U.S. published in book form.

However, on request, the Copyright Office will conduct a search at the rate of $10.00 per hour. As the Copyright office workers are much more adept at understanding the methods of classification, it is probably more prudent to let them handle any extensive or complex searches. The Reference and Bibliography Section of the Copyright Office will, upon request, estimate in advance the cost of a search. A report on the search will be prepared upon completion.

The Copyright Office will not, however:

- Comment on the merits, copyright status, or ownership of particular works, or on the extent of copyright protection afforded to particular works;

- compare copies of works for similarities;

- give opinions as to the validity of copyright claims;

- advise on questions of copyright infringement.

If you do need additional assistance beyond what you can obtain from the Copyright Office and from this book, a bibliography of books on copyright is contained at the end of this book.

ADDITIONAL INFORMATION ON COPYRIGHT

The Copyright Office publishes a broad range of material regarding the intricacies and details of copyright law and regulations. Surprisingly, for a governmental bureaucracy, most of the Copyright Office Circulars are prepared in easily-understood language.

A list of the most useful Copyright Office Circulars is contained in Appendix A.

COPYRIGHT INFRINGEMENT

Since 1978, when the current Copyright Act took effect, copyright protection has fallen under exclusive federal jurisdiction. This means that for all actions occurring after January 1, 1978, the federal courts are the place to go for relief. As was noted earlier in this chapter, under the current Copyright Act, the right to file a lawsuit alleging that someone has infringed upon a valid copyright is one of the benefits of copyright registration. Without having registered the copyright, there is no legal recourse available if someone is making and even profiting from unauthorized copies of a particular work.

However, since it is possible to register a copyright long after its creation and even long after its publication, it is possible to register a copyright even after it has been infringed upon. The obvious danger in waiting to register a copyright until after an act of infringement occurs is that the other party may have registered first, thereby obtaining for themselves an earlier copyright registration and, hence, earlier verifiable proof of copyright.

Infringement, in general, is defined as a violation of any of the five exclusive rights of copyright, those being:

* The exclusive right to make copies,

* The exclusive right to make derivative works,

* The exclusive right to distribute copies to the public,

* The exclusive right to perform the work publicly,

* The exclusive right to display the work publicly.

There are two levels of copyright infringement: civil copyright infringement and criminal copyright infringement. The legal owner of the copyright (whether it is the original author, or one who has obtained ownership by purchase, gift, will, or other legal means), has the right to file a lawsuit for any civil infringement that takes place while they own the copyright. However, the documents relating to any transfer of ownership of the copyright must be recorded with the Copyright Office prior to filing any infringement lawsuit. In addition, the U.S. Justice Department may bring a criminal action against a willful violator of copyright law.

■ CIVIL COPYRIGHT INFRINGEMENT

In order to prove a case of civil copyright infringement, it is necessary to prove certain items. First and probably easiest to prove is one's ownership of the copyright. This is shown by documents of copyright registration and by recorded documents of copyright transfer. Next, it must be shown that the infringer had access to the material that it is alleged was copied or used in an unauthorized manner. If the work has been published and available to the public, an inference of access is relatively easy.

Finally, it must be shown that the infringer copied the copyrighted material. This may be a word-for-word copy or it may be a "substantially similar" paraphrase of the material in question. In most infringement cases, it is this final issue of "substantial similarity" which becomes the central issue in the case. The courts have applied various tests to determine such similarity. Essentially, both the structure of the work and the literal expression of the work are examined. If there is a definite structural similarity between the two works, then the specific expressions used are further compared. If, in structurally similar works, a similarity of expression is also present (even though in the nature of paraphrasing) copyright infringement will be held to have taken place.

Civil suits for infringement must be filed within three years after the act of infringement. The possible civil remedies available for infringement are quite broad and, if invoked, are quite effective in preventing further commercial damage to the true copyright owner. The remedies available are fourfold:

■ Injunction

First, one may seek a temporary or permanent injunction against the infringer in order to prevent further use and/or distribution of the material which is in violation of copyright law. Such an injunction is, if obtained, quite a powerful tool. It will be valid in all 50 states and may be enforced by any U.S. District Court. State boundaries are not relevant in the enforcement of a copyright injunction.

■   Impoundment

A second remedy available is to have the items claimed to be in violation of copyright laws impounded by federal marshalls. Such an order for impoundment is also a very powerful tool. The court may additionally order the impoundment of any items which were used to produce the offending material, such as plates, masters, tapes, or negatives. Finally, the court has the power to not only impound these items but also to have them destroyed or otherwise disposed of.

■   Monetary Damages

Next, and in addition to the above two remedies, an infringer of copyright is liable for monetary damages to be paid to the true copyright owner. These monetary damages may take two forms:

1.   The *actual damages* or losses due to the copyright infringement and the profits of the infringer due to the infringement, or;

2.   Statutory damages as provided by law. Statutory damages are available instead of actual damages only if elected by the one infringed against and if chosen prior to a final verdict in any infringement case, as long as the owner of the copyright had registered the copyright prior to the infringement. Federal law provides for statutory damages of up to $10,000.00 if the infringement was merely negligent and up to $50,000.00 if the act of infringement was willful. The actual amount of statutory damages awarded is up to the discretion of the court. Often the election of

statutory damages will result in a greater damage award for the party seeking relief.

- ■   Legal Costs and Fees

Finally, an infringer who has lost a lawsuit may also be liable for the legal costs and attorney's fees of the successful claimant if the infringement took place after the copyright was registered with the Office of Copyright.

- ■   CRIMINAL COPYRIGHT INFRINGEMENT

In addition to the above, an infringer who willfully infringes upon a copyright for commercial advantage or financial gain may be prosecuted for criminal copyright infringement.

Criminal infringement is a felony and a conviction may carry with it a prison term of up to five years and a fine of up to $250,000.00. These penalties are in addition to any possible money damages awarded in a civil infringement suit.

Copyright infringement is a very serious offense and is treated as such by federal law. It is dealt with essentially as the theft of a valuable property.

CHAPTER 3

COPYRIGHT REGISTRATION PROCEDURES

Although copyright registration is not mandatory, as explained in the previous chapter, it is highly recommended because of the various legal benefits which it provides to the copyright owner.

The registration procedures are fairly simple and straightforward. However, the instructions must be followed explicitly or the registration will not be accepted by the Copyright Office.

To register a work, the following three elements must be sent *in the same package* to:

> The Register of Copyrights
> Copyright Office
> Library of Congress
> Washington, DC 20559

1.   A properly completed appropriate application form (use a typewriter or a black pen);

2.   A nonrefundable filing fee of $10.00 per application in the form of check, money order, or bank draft payable to the Register of Copyrights. The fee payment should be stapled to the application form;

3.   A deposit copy or copies of the work being registered. The "registration" deposit requirements are as follows:

- If the work is *unpublished* (not yet distributed to the public for sale or rental): one copy;

- If the work is published in the U.S. after January 1, 1978: two copies of the best edition (the *best edition* means the edition with the highest quality production. For example: hardcover if both soft and hardcover editions are published. If there are differences in the *content* of editions, separate copyrights must be obtained for each such edition.);

- If the work was first published in the United States before January 1, 1978: two complete copies of the work as first published;

- If the work was first published outside the U.S.: one copy as it was first published;

- If the work is a contribution to a collective work: one copy of the best edition of the collective work.

As noted in the previous chapter, this "registration" deposit will satisfy the mandatory "publication" deposit requirements.

WHO FILES THE APPLICATION

The Certification Blank on the Application for Registration forms (Space #10) requires that a person legally entitled to submit the

52

application verify the correctness of the information in the application. Only the following persons are legally entitled to submit an application form for copyright registration:

- The Author. This is considered to be either the actual creator of the work, or the employer of the creator, if the work was created by an employee or as a work-for-hire.

- The Copyright Claimant. This may be the author or it can be a person that has obtained ownership of all rights of the copyright which originally belonged to the author. The claimant will need to show on the application how he or she came to be the owner of the copyright (for example, by assignment of copyright).

- An Owner of Exclusive Rights. Any of the five rights that make up a total "copyright" can be transferred and owned separately. This is true even if the transfer is limited in time or in place. The copyright owner of an "exclusive right in copyright" has the authority to apply for a registration of the particular claim in copyright. This is true even if another person or entity has ownership of other exclusive rights in the same work.

- An authorized agent of the author, copyright claimant, or owner of exclusive rights. This allows anyone who is authorized to act on behalf of the copyright owner to apply for registration. The agent may be another individual or it may be some type of organization (for example: a partnership or corporation).

There is no requirement that copyright registrations be prepared or filed by an attorney.

TYPES OF APPLICATION FORMS

There are various types of Copyright Registration Application Forms designed to cover all of the different kinds of creations which may be registered. The following is a listing of each form and a discussion of when and by whom it should be used. Appendix C contains copies of all listed copyright registration forms and detailed instructions for their completion.

NOTE:

Please note that the Copyright Office will NOT accept photocopied versions of these application forms. Only the <u>original</u> officially printed application forms will be accepted.

Additional copies of the forms and instructions may be obtained free of charge by writing to:

> The Copyright Office
> Information and Publications Section
> Library of Congress
> Washington, DC 20559

You may also order forms directly from the Copyright Office HOTLINE: (202)287-9100.

There are five different application forms for basic original registration:

Form TX: The most widely used registration application form. This form should be used for original registrations of all published or unpublished non-dramatic literary works. This includes books, pamphlets, computer programs, manuscripts, poetry, directories, catalogs, advertising copy, compilations of written works, etc.

Form SE: This form should be used for all original registrations of serials, works issued or intended to be issued in successive parts bearing numerical designations, or works to be continued indefinitely. This category includes periodicals, magazines, newspapers, newsletters, annuals, journals, etc. Please note that each individual issue of a series or magazine is a separate copyrightable item and a separate application for registration must be filed for each issue.

Additionally, note that the claimant registering a serial copyright is claiming copyright for all portions of the work which have either been actually authored by the claimant, or created by an employee-for-hire of the claimant, or which have been transferred to the claimant. Portions of the collective work which have not been transferred to the claimant may be registered individually by the author/owner of the copyright of the individual contribution. Thus, a magazine article may be registered by the owner of the magazine as part of the copyright for the entire issue if the copyright was acquired by the magazine by virtue of a contract or employer/employee relationship; or the article may be registered by the author separately in his or her own name using Form TX.

Form PA: This is the correct application form to be used for original registration of published or unpublished works of the performing arts. This includes musical and dramatic works, plays, motion pictures, and other audiovisual works.

Form VA: Use this form for original registration of works of the visual arts (for example: pictorial, graphic or sculptural works, prints, art work, technical drawings, maps, blueprints, etc.). If the predominate nature of the publication is visual art as opposed to literary, Form VA should be used. For example: Form VA should be used to register a copyright claim for a book consisting of photographs with minor captions.

Form SR: This is the form for original registration of published or unpublished sound recordings. The author of sound recordings is the performer, the record producer, or both.

Most works will fall into one of these five categories. If it is felt that the publication contains material that may fall into two or more categories, choose the category which is most appropriate to the work as a whole.

In addition to the original registration application forms, there are three supplemental application forms for various situations which may arise. These are as follows:

Form RE: This is the form to be used for claims to renew copyrighted works for a second term under the prior Copyright Act (1909). Use this form only for renewal of copyright on works which have an original copyright of 1977 or earlier. Be aware that the renewal must be made during the last year of the original 28-year copyright term or it will not be effective and the copyright will be lost forever.

Form CA: This is the proper form to be used for any corrections or to provide additional information for an earlier registration of copyright with the Copyright Office. It may be used for a work with a copyright in any year, either before or after 1978. Please see "Corrections and Additions to Registration" below.

Form GR/CP: This form should be used as an additional application to register a group of contributions to a periodical in addition to the original application under Forms TX, PA, or VA. If the group of contributions was registered under Form SE, do not file a Form GR/CP.

EFFECTIVE DATE OF REGISTRATION

Upon completion of the appropriate application form, send the three required elements (the application form, the fee and the deposit copies) to the following address:

> The Register of Copyrights
> The Copyright Office
> Library of Congress
> Washington, DC 20559

When all three elements have been received in acceptable form and in one package, the Copyright Office will process the registration. However, the registration becomes effective immediately upon receipt by the Copyright Office of the three required items. This is true regardless of how long it may actually take to process the application.

The application will not be processed without the deposit copy or copies. Unpublished deposits alone will also be returned. Published deposits without the application and fee will be transferred to the Library of Congress to fulfill the mandatory "publication" deposit requirements, but will not be registered.

Upon completion of processing the applicant will receive a Certificate of Copyright Registration from the Copyright Office. As long as 4 months may elapse before actual receipt of this Certificate. This important document is the official certified record of the copyright registration.

CORRECTIONS OR ADDITIONS TO COPYRIGHT REGISTRATION

Corrections or additions to original copyright registration can be made at any time after the original registration is completed. These changes must be submitted on Form CA. The changes then become a supplement to the original registration.

Typically, changes or additions will fall into the following categories:

- A correction of information which was incorrectly listed on the original application form;

- Additional information which should have been given, but was omitted on the original application;

- Changes that have occurred since the original registration;

- Explanations which clarify previously submitted information.

Supplemental registration is NOT appropriate in the following instances:

- If there have been any changes in the actual content of the work itself. If there have been changes in content, the proper procedure is to make application for a new basic copyright registration for the revised version of the work;

- As a substitute for recording a transfer of copyright ownership;

- As a substitute for renewal registration.

CHAPTER 4

COPYRIGHT PERMISSION GUIDELINES

In addition to understanding the necessity and procedures for the registration of copyright claims, the desktop publisher should have a thorough grasp of the instances in which written permission to use works copyrighted by others is required. Unless it falls under the limited Fair Use exception, the use of copyrighted material without the permission of the owner is an infringement of the copyright, regardless of how innocent the use may have been.

Sample forms for requesting such consent when permission is warranted are included in Appendix B.

The following guidelines will enable the publisher to determine when written permission to use material is necessary.

MATERIAL AVAILABLE FOR USE WITHOUT PERMISSION

In order to avoid copyright infringement situations in publishing, there are five sources of material for publication that are safe for usage without the permission of the copyright owner.

■ **MATERIAL CREATED BY THE PUBLISHER**

The first of these, obviously, is original material which the publisher has personally created and the copyright of which, therefore, is already owned by the publisher. For the desktop publisher, this category may encompass much of the material used.

■ **MATERIAL CREATED BY AN EMPLOYEE OR AS A WORK-FOR-HIRE**

The second body of safely used material is that which was created by an employee-for-hire of the publisher within the scope of the employment or which was specifically commissioned for inclusion in a collective work and for which a written contract clearly specifies that the work is to be considered a work-for-hire. The copyright to any material which is prepared for publication by an employee of a publishing concern as part of his or her job is owned by the employer, unless there is a written contract otherwise.

■ **SUBSIDIARY RIGHTS MATERIAL**

The publisher is free to publish any previously copyrighted material for which he or she has obtained the necessary subsidiary rights to publish. Of course, the publication of such material must fall within the parameters of the contractual rights which the publisher has obtained. For a discussion of subsidiary rights, please see Chapter 8: Desktop Publishing Contracts.

■ **FAIR USE MATERIAL**

This category of material, as noted in Chapter 2, includes the use of material which is exempted from full copyright protection by law. The "fair use" of such material must be determined carefully by the publisher on a case-by-case basis following the guidelines laid down by Congress. Please refer to the discussion in Chapter 2 for these guidelines. Most commercial use of material for publication will require the consent of the copyright owner and will not fall under the "fair use" exemptions. If it is decided that specific material will fall under the "fair use" exception to copyright, a credit line must be included. A credit line should contain the same information as shown on the copyright notice for the work from which the "fair use" material was excerpted (for example: © Copyright Jane Doe 1980).

■   PUBLIC DOMAIN MATERIAL

The final group of material which may be used without permission of the creator is material in the public domain. As noted earlier, material in the public domain consists of material for which the copyright has expired, material for which the copyright was lost (by an error or oversight on the part of the copyright owner), and federal government publications.

Any such public domain material may be used freely by anyone without the permission of the creator and without payment of any type of royalty fee.

■   Material with Expired Copyright

For material with an apparently expired copyright, it is wise to be certain that the copyright owner has not applied for a copyright renewal under applicable laws. For instance, the copyright for a book with a copyright date of 1942 would have expired on December 31, 1970 unless the owner chose to renew the copyright for another 28-year period. In turn, under the Copyright Act of 1976, the potential second 28-year copyright term has been extended to 47 years. Without an actual search of copyright records, it is often difficult to determine if a copyright has been renewed since further publication and public distribution of the copyrighted material is not required for the renewed copyright to be valid. A search of copyright records, however, will show those works for which the one-year renewal period (the last year of the initial 28-year copyright term) has expired without a valid renewal being registered.

■   Material With Lost Copyright

Material for which the copyright was lost has become much more difficult to identify under the current Copyright Act. Under the previous Act, failure to include a copyright notice in the published work could cause the copyright to be lost. Current law provides a grace period of up to five years before the copyright is lost.   This seriously complicates the determination of whether or not a work without a copyright notice indeed has copyright protection.   To avoid possible infringement difficulties, it is best to assume that a work without an actual copyright notice is protected unless the work is clearly a federal government publication.

■   Government Publications

Generally, federal government publications are in the public domain and are not subject to copyright. This broad range of material includes any material prepared and produced by federal government officials or employees as part of their official duties. This includes speeches and statements by elected or appointed federal government officials if those statements are made in the context of their duties as a federal government official. Materials prepared by state, county, or municipal government employees or officials are entitled to full copyright protection.

There are, however, a few minor exceptions to these broad rules. Materials prepared by federal government officials or employees outside of their official duties are fully copyrightable by the individual author and are not part of the public domain. Similarly, any personal statements, writings or speeches by a federal government official which are clearly outside of their duties as a government official are subject to copyright.   This category may include campaign speeches, autobiographies, and any other personal works.

Additionally, a government publication which has been prepared by a private person or organization under a federal government grant or contract may be copyrighted by the creator. If so, the work must contain a copyright notice. Use of such a copyrighted work requires the written permission of the owner.

MATERIALS WHICH REQUIRE WRITTEN PERMISSION

Other than the above five categories of material which may be used without written permission or payment of any royalty fee, use of any other material for publication will require the written consent of the owner of the copyright. A copyright owner may charge the party desiring to use such material a "permission" or "royalty" fee for the use of material and may attach any stipulations or conditions to the use of such material. Such conditions may include one-time only use, proper acknowledgement of the copyright owner, geographical restrictions on use (U.S. use only, for example), or any other restriction on the use of the copyrighted material.

The following rules cover most situations in which written permission is required:

- The use of any advertising copy prepared by another, whether written, graphic or photographic, requires the permission of the owner of the copyright. For national advertising, it may be difficult to determine the actual ownership of the advertising. Contact the advertising department of the producer or manufacturer of the product depicted for information regarding the advertising agency that created the work.

- The use of any portion of a poem, play, or musical lyric requires the written permission of the owner of the copyright. Although these works are subject to "fair use" exemptions, the interpretive nature of such works makes the "fair use" rules difficult to apply. If the usage of the portion of the work is for commercial gain (rather than for scholarship or research), a single word of a poem, play, or song may be considered such an integral part of the work that use without permission may be copyright infringement.

- The use of photos, drawings, cartoons, or maps, if these items were prepared by others and are not part of a federal government publication will require the written consent of the owner. For photos actually taken by the publisher, the consent of any person depicted in a photo must be obtained. A standard "Model Release" form is included in Appendix B for such consent.

- The use of charts or graphs will require the permission of the creator or owner of the copyright, if they are not public domain material. The facts from which any chart or graph is prepared may be used to prepare another chart if the facts are available from other sources and the new chart or graph is not a recognizable copy of the concept of the original.

- The use of verbatim portions of newspaper or magazine articles will, generally, require the written consent of the owner of the copyright. In many cases, the publication itself owns the copyright if the article was prepared by a staff writer or reporter. Permission must be obtained for use of any material from syndicated columns, individually copyrighted articles and articles which are published under the "byline" of the author. Brief portions of newspaper articles containing factual statements may be used under "fair use" guidelines. Independently verifiable facts which may be part of a newspaper or magazine article may be used without permission of the copyright holder. After the passage of approximately 6 months, it can be assumed that brief use of textual material in a newspaper article that is not published under a "by-line" is available under "fair use" guidelines.

- Any use of the textual portions of a book, journal, or magazine which is over 100 words in length, whether cumulative or consecutive, generally requires the consent of the owner of the copyright. If the excerpts of text are edited in any way by deletions or additions, the owner's permission must be obtained for such editing changes. The amount of text that can be used without permission is dependent on the proportion that text is to the entire work. If 50 words is one-fourth of a short magazine article and those 50 words are the thrust of the article, permission should be obtained. On the other hand, 100 words of description in a 500 page novel could possibly be used without permission if it is not central and integral to the novel. The safest way to proceed, of course, is to always obtain permission. If permission is not granted, the material may not be used.

• The use of direct quotes from dictionaries, encyclopedias, reference works, etc. will normally require the permission of the owner of the copyright.

PERMISSION FORMS

Included in Appendix B are three forms which may be used for obtaining written permission to use copyrighted material. The "Request for Permission Form" is intended to be used for written material. The "Photographic Request Form" should be used for obtaining the permission of the photographer to use certain photographs. This form may also be altered for use in securing permission to use artistic works or works of graphic art. The final form, the "Model Release Form" should be used to secure the permission of any person depicted in a photograph that will be used for commercial publication.

Note that the permission forms state that a credit line will be used when the material is published. It is very important that this agreement be adhered to in order not to infringe upon the copyright of the person granting permission.

Completed copies of the necessary permission and release forms for all items which are published should be kept on file for the duration of the publication's life.

Often the easiest method to secure permission to use particular material is to write directly to the publisher of the material, rather than attempt to locate the creator. Book and magazine publishers can often reach the creator of a work which they have published much more easily than an individual can and may have the right or authority to grant permission for minor usages.

When using the permission forms, be certain that the exact usage of material for which permission is sought is clearly specified. If the context of the work to be used is important, it may be wise to include a photocopy of the original work with the portions for which permission is requested clearly marked. The forms may be adapted for particular situations as long as the owner of the copyright whose permission is sought can clearly ascertain the extent of the request for consent.

Often a fee will be requested for permission to use material. The fee is usually negotiable and depends upon the amount of material to be used. For print material, a permission fee of $10-$30/page is within a normal range. For photographic or graphic arts material, the fees can be considerably higher, depending upon the particular usage requested.

CHAPTER 5

NON-COPYRIGHT REGISTRATIONS

In addition to copyright registration, there are several other voluntary registrations of published material which are beneficial for the desktop publisher to obtain. These non-copyright registrations will confer no additional legal rights on a published work and are not required. They are for cataloging and marketing convenience. They are, however, recognized as standard throughout the publishing industry and are widely used by bookstores, librarians, and readers for access to registered publications.

LIBRARY OF CONGRESS CATALOG NUMBER (LCCN)

The Cataloging in Publication Division of the Library of Congress is responsible for assignment of the Library of Congress Catalog Number to each publication. The Library of Congress Catalog Number is useful for indexing, cataloging and research purposes and should be obtained by most publishers if the proposed publication is in book form. The Cataloging Division of the Library of Congress is a separate and distinct branch from the Copyright Office. Copyright registration and deposit will not confer a Library of Congress Catalog Number on a publication. In order to obtain a LCC Number, write for the publication: "Procedures for Securing Preassigned Library of Congress Catalog Card Number" and copies of "Request for Pre-assignment of Library of Congress Catalog Card Number" (Form #607-7). The publication and forms are available from:

> CIP Office
> Library of Congress
> Washington, DC 20540

Library of Congress Catalog Numbers are available only for books which are considered acceptable to add to the Library of Congress collections or for which there is an anticipated demand for Library of Congress cataloging information. Generally, this means the book must be at least 50 pages long and not one of the following: a textbook, a publication of a vanity press (subsidized press), laboratory manuals, privately printed poetry books, religious materials for Bible students, teacher's manuals, coloring books, workbooks, brochures, publications designed for customers, question and answer books, and any other material that would not be generally considered a "library" book.

LIBRARY OF CONGRESS CIP PROGRAM

This is another program administered by the Library of Congress but is separate from the Library of Congress Catalog Number program. Again, only books are eligible for this program. This program prepares an advance catalog card containing all Library of Congress cataloging information and makes such cards available to libraries. This allows libraries to review cataloging data in advance of publication. In addition, the information on the catalog card is provided to the publisher in advance of publication for inclusion on the copyright page of the book.

The information contained on the CIP program data sheet includes: the author's name, the book title, the Library of Congress subject headings, the Library of Congress classification number, the Library of Congress Catalog Number, the Dewey Decimal System Classification Number, and the International Standard Book Number (see below).

In order to participate in this program, publishers should write for copies of the following:

- Library of Congress Cataloging Data Sheets;

- CIP-Information for Participating Publishers;

- CIP-Publisher's Response forms.

The Data Sheets must be prepared on official multi-part forms. Copies may be obtained from:

> Library of Congress
> Cataloging in Publication Program
> Washington, DC 20540

Participation in the CIP Program is initiated by the publisher submitting a galley proof of the particular work and the appropriate Data Sheet. If accepted for cataloging, within two weeks professional cataloging data will be returned to the publisher to be printed on the copyright page of the book. After the book is published, a deposit copy must be sent to the Library of Congress Cataloging in Publication Division. This deposit copy requirement is in addition to any copies sent to the Copyright Office for "publication" or "registration" deposit purposes.

If a publisher participates in the CIP program, separate Library of Congress Catalog Number application need not be made. The CIP process will include assignment of a Library of Congress Catalog Number

INTERNATIONAL STANDARD BOOK NUMBER (ISBN)

This is a non-governmental program for providing a uniform system of identifying publications. It is administered by the R. R. Bowker Company, the largest private book cataloging company in the United States and the publisher of the authoritative "Books in Print" series as well as many other industry-standard cataloging reference works. The ISBN number is used for ordering, indexing, and cataloging purposes by the book trade and by most libraries. It is the most useful "number" assigned to a book for purposes of marketing the book.

Participation in this program is highly recommended to the desktop publisher who will be publishing more than a single book. To participate, request a copy of "Title Output Information Request Form" and a copy of the "ISBN User's Manual" from:

>International Standard Book Numbering Agency
>245 W. 17th St.
>New York, NY 10011

Each publisher is assigned a publisher prefix identifier number and is issued a list of book identifier numbers for assignment to each individual book. Each separate book cover-type edition is considered a separate publication requiring a different ISBN. For example, a hardcover edition of a book requires a different ISBN than a softcover edition of the same book.

The ISBN should be printed on the copyright page and the back cover of the book and, if possible, the spine of the book.

STANDARD ADDRESS NUMBER (SAN)

The Standard Address Number is also a program for publishers administered by the R. R. Bowker Company. Application for this program may be requested when applying for the ISBN program.

This program provides a separate seven-digit "address" number for every firm in the publishing industry: libraries, wholesalers, printers, publishers, distributors, etc. Use of the SAN is encouraged to speed processing of orders and ease billing and shipping errors.

ADVANCE BOOK INFORMATION PROGRAM (ABI)

Although not a numbering system, the Advance Book Information program is another beneficial project handled by the R. R. Bowker Company. Participation in this program allows a book to be listed in the Bowker publications: "Books in Print" and "Forthcoming Books". These volumes are the standard industry source books for information regarding available and forthcoming titles.

To participate in this program, obtain copies of "Advance Book Information Guide" and "Advance Book Information" multi-part application forms from:

Advance Book Information Program
R. R. Bowker Company
245 W. 17th St.
New York, NY 10011

INTERNATIONAL STANDARD SERIAL NUMBER (ISSN)

Desktop publishers who publish serial works, like newsletters, magazines, annuals, or yearbooks should also investigate the ISSN program. This program is administered by the Library of Congress as part of the National Serial Data Program. For serial books, the ISSN number is used in conjunction with the ISBN number, with the ISSN number identifying the serial and title and with the ISBN number identifying the specific book within a series. For magazines and newsletters, the ISSN number uniquely identifies the periodical. For further information on the ISSN program and a copy of the "Serial Data Sheet for Publishers", write:

National Serials Data Program
Library of Congress
Washington, DC 20540

The ISSN number is traditionally included on the top right hand corner of the cover, on the masthead of the periodical, or on the page which includes the publisher's name and second-class mailing information. It should also be included in any advertisements or brochures for the publisher.

UPC BAR CODES

Although not technically a registration program, machine-scannable UPC (Uniform Product Code) bar codes are becoming an industry-wide practice and should be included on the covers of any book or magazine intended for bookstore sales.

Film masters of book industry bar codes for inclusion on camera-ready copy prior to printing are available at a reasonable cost from several sources. In addition, several desktop publishing typesetting programs have bar code typesetting fonts available for direct preparation by the publisher.

One such source for the finished camera-ready bar codes is:

> Book Industry Bar Codes
> 5311 North Highland
> Tacoma, WA 98407

Although none of the above registration and cataloging programs are required for any desktop publication, they are a substantial benefit to the potential reader or buyer of any publication. The combination of the government cataloging systems and private numbering programs has provided readers, bookstores, distributors, wholesalers, and librarians with a comprehensive system by which to locate and identify any book or periodical, as well as a method by which to conveniently locate the publisher.

CHAPTER 6

DESKTOP PUBLISHING BUSINESS ENTITIES

For the desktop publisher who works outside of the confines of another organization and who desires to begin a separate publishing business, a thorough understanding of the choices of business operational entities is necessary.

There are five specific methods under which to operate a small publishing firm. The types of structure are those available to any business:

- The Sole Proprietorship;

- The Partnership;

- The Limited Partnership;

- The Corporation;

- The "S" Corporation.

Although other types of business structures, such as the unincorporated association, are available, it is the above five types of business configurations that are best suited to the formation of a publishing enterprise.

Which of these forms of business organization is chosen can have a great impact on the success of a desktop publishing business. The structure chosen will have an effect on how easy it is to obtain financing, how taxes are paid, how accounting records are kept, whether personal assets are at risk in the publishing venture, the amount of control the "owner" has over the business, and many other aspects of the business.

Keep in mind that the initial choice of business organization need not be the final choice. It is often wise to begin with the most simple form, the sole proprietorship, until the business progresses to a point where another form is clearly indicated. This allows the business to begin in the least complicated manner and allows the owner to retain total control in the important formative period of the business. As the publishing business grows and the potential for liability and tax burdens increase, circumstances may dictate a re-examination of the business structure. The advantages and disadvantages of the five choices of business entity are detailed below.

THE SOLE PROPRIETORSHIP

A sole proprietorship is both the simplest and the most prevalent form of business organization. An important reason for this is that it is the least regulated of all types of business structures. Technically, the *sole proprietorship* is the traditional unincorporated one-person business. For legal and tax purposes, the business is the owner. It has no existence outside the owner. The liabilities of the business are personal to the owner and the business ends when the owner dies. On the other hand, all of the profits are also personal to the owner and the sole owner has full control of the business.

■ **DISADVANTAGES**

■ Risk of Personal Liability

Perhaps the most important factor to consider before choosing this type of business structure is that all of the personal and business assets of the sole owner are at risk in the sole proprietorship. If the demands of the creditors of the business exceed those assets which were formally placed in the name of the business, the creditors may reach the personal assets of the owner of the sole proprietorship. Legal judgements for damages arising from the operation of the business may also be enforced against the owner's personal assets. This unlimited liability is probably the greatest drawback to this type of business form. Of course, insurance coverage of various types can lessen the dangers inherent in having one's personal assets at risk in a business. For the publisher, even libel insurance is available. However, as liability insurance premiums continue to skyrocket, it is unlikely that a fledgling small business can afford to insure against all manner of contingencies and at the maximum coverage levels necessary to guard against all risk to personal assets.

■ Difficulty in Financing

A second major disadvantage to the sole proprietorship as a form of business structure is the potential difficulty in obtaining business loans. Often in starting a small business there is insufficient collateral to obtain a loan and the sole owner must mortgage his or her own house or other personal assets to obtain the loan. This, of course, puts the sole proprietor's personal assets in a direct position of risk should the business fail. Banks and other lending institutions are reluctant to loan money for small publishing concerns due to the essentially speculative nature of the market for the product. Without a proven track record, it is quite difficult for a small publisher to adequately present a loan proposal based on a sufficiently stable cash flow to satisfy most banks.

- Lack of Continuity

A further disadvantage to a sole proprietorship is the lack of continuity which is inherent in the business form. If the owner dies, the business ceases to exist. Of course, the assets and liabilities of the business will fall to the heirs of the owner, but the expertise and knowledge of how the business was successfully carried on will often die with the owner. Small sole proprietorships are seldom carried on profitably after the death of the owner.

- ADVANTAGES

- Total Control

The advantage of the sole proprietorship as a business structure which appeals to most people is the total control the owner has over the business. Subject only to economic considerations and certain legal restrictions, there is a total freedom to operate the business however one chooses. In the context of a desktop publishing concern, this advantage translates to the ability to choose absolutely whatever one wishes to publish within legal bounds. Many people feel that this factor alone is enough to overcome the inherent disadvantages in this form of business.

- Simplicity of Organization

Related to this is the simplicity of organization of the sole proprietorship. Other than maintenance of sufficient records for tax purposes, there are no legal requirements on how the business is operated. Of course, the prudent businessperson will keep adequate records and sufficiently organize the business for its most efficient operation. But there are no outside forces dictating how such internal decisions are made in the sole proprietorship. The sole owner makes all decisions in this type of business.

As was mentioned earlier, the sole proprietorship is the least regulated of all businesses. Normally, the only license necessary is a local business license, usually obtained by simply paying a fee to a local registration authority. In addition, it may be necessary to file a notice with local authorities if the business is operated under an assumed or fictional name. This is necessary to allow creditors to have access to the actual identity of the true owner of the business, since it is the owner who will be personally liable for the debts and obligations of the business.

Finally, it may be necessary to register with local, state, and federal tax bodies for I.D. numbers and for the purpose of collection of sales and other taxes. Please see the following chapter for a discussion of the tax aspects of this form of business. Contact your local and state taxing authorities for information on registration and tax liabilities for sole proprietorships. Other than these few simple registrations, from a legal standpoint little else is required to start up a desktop publishing business as a sole proprietorship.

■ Tax Advantages

A final and important advantage to the sole proprietorship is the various tax benefits available to an individual. The losses or profits of the sole proprietorship are considered personal to the owner. The losses are directly deductible against any other income the owner may have and the profits are taxed only once at the marginal rate of the owner. In many instances, this may have distinct advantages over the method by which partnerships are taxed or the double taxation of corporations, particularly in the early stages of the business. The tax aspects of the business of publishing are discussed in the next chapter.

THE PARTNERSHIP

A *partnership* is a relationship existing between two or more persons who join together to carry on a trade or business. Each partner contributes money, property, labor, or skill to the partnership and, in return, expects to share in the profits or losses of the business. A partnership is usually based on a partnership agreement of some type, although the agreement need not be a formal document. It may even simply be an oral understanding between the partners.

A simple joint undertaking to share expenses is not considered a partnership, nor is a mere co-ownership of property that is maintained and leased or rented. To be considered a partnership for legal and tax purposes, the following factors are usually considered:

- The partner's conduct in carrying out the provisions of the partnership agreement;

- The relationship of the parties;

- The abilities and contributions of each party to the partnership;

- The control each partner has over the partnership income and the purposes for which the income is used.

■ DISADVANTAGES

■ Potential for Conflict

The disadvantages to the partnership form of business begin with the potential for conflict between the partners. Of all forms of business organization, the partnership has spawned more disagreements than any other. This is generally traceable to the lack of a decisive initial partnership agreement which clearly outlines the rights and duties of the partners. This disadvantage can be partially overcome with a comprehensive partnership agreement. However, there is still the seemingly inherent difficulty that many people have in working within the framework of a partnership, regardless of the initial agreement between the partners.

■ Risk of Personal Liability

A further disadvantage to the partnership structure is that each partner is subject to unlimited personal liability for the debts of the partnership. The potential liability in a partnership is even greater than that encountered in a sole proprietorship. This is due to the fact that in a partnership the personal risk for which one may be liable is partially out of one's direct control and may be accrued due to actions on the part of another person. Each partner is liable for all of the debts of the partnership, regardless of which of the partners may have been responsible for their accumulation.

Related to the business risks of personal financial liability is the potential personal legal liability for the negligence of another partner. In addition, each partner may even be liable for the negligence of an employee of the partnership if such negligence takes place during the usual course of business of the partnership. Again, the attendant risks are broadened by the potential for liability based on the acts of other persons. Of course, general liability insurance can counteract this drawback to some extent to protect the personal and partnership assets of each partner.

■   Lack of Continuity

Again, as with the sole proprietorship, the partnership lacks the advantage of continuity. A partnership is automatically terminated upon the death of any partner. A final accounting and a division of assets and liabilities is generally necessary in such an instance unless specific methods under which the partnership may be reformed have been outlined in the partnership agreement.

■   ADVANTAGES

■   Greater Credit Opportunities

A partnership, by virtue of combining the credit potential of the various partners, has an inherently greater opportunity for business credit than is generally available to a sole proprietorship. In addition, the assets which are placed in the name of the partnership may often be used directly as collateral for business loans. The pooling of the personal capital of the partners generally provides the partnership with an advantage over the sole-proprietorship in the area of cash availability .

■   Tax Advantages

As with the sole proprietorship, there may be certain tax advantages to operation of a business as a partnership, as opposed to a corporation.   The profits generated by a partnership may be distributed directly to the partners without incurring any "double" tax liability, as is the case with the distribution of corporate profits in the form of dividends to the shareholders. The tax aspects of partnerships are covered in the following chapter.

■   Potential Simplicity of Operation

For a business in which two or more people desire to share in the work and in the profits, a partnership is often the structure chosen.   It is, potentially, a much simpler form of business organization than the corporate form.   However, the simplicity of this form of business can be deceiving. A sole proprietor knows that his or her actions will determine how the business will prosper, and that he or she is, ultimately, personally responsible for the success or failure of the enterprise. In a partnership, however, the duties, obligations and commitments of each partner are often ill-defined. This lack of definition of the status of each partner can lead to serious difficulties and disagreements.

In order to clarify the rights and responsibilities of each partner and to be certain of the tax status of the partnership, it is good business procedure to have a written partnership agreement.   Although state law will supply the general boundaries of partnerships and even specific partnership agreement terms if they are not addressed by a written partnership agreement, it is more conducive to a clear understanding of the business structure if the partner's agreements are put in writing.   The drafting of a comprehensive partnership agreement is a complex activity, normally requiring the services of a competent lawyer. With proper guidance and the use of legal guidebooks it is, of course, possible to prepare the agreement oneself. Whether the agreement is prepared by a lawyer or the partners, the following matters need to be considered for inclusion in the agreement:

- The amount and type of capital or services to be contributed by each partner;

- The amount and type of property to be contributed by each partner, and provisions for the ownership of copyrights;

- The division of profits and losses of the partnership;

- Provisions for keeping accurate books and records;

- Provision for the management of the partnership;

- Methods for termination and dissolution of the partnership.

THE LIMITED PARTNERSHIP

The *limited partnership* is a hybrid type of business structure. It contains elements of both a traditional partnership and a corporation. The limited partnership form of business structure may be used when some interested parties desire to invest in a partnership but also desire to have limited liability and exercise no control over the partnership management.

A limited partnership consists of one or more general partners who actively manage the business of the partnership and one or more limited partners who are mere investors in the partnership and who have no active role in the management of the partnership. A general partner is treated much as a partner in a traditional partnership, while a limited partner is treated much as a shareholder in a corporation. The general partners are at personal risk in a limited partnership. The limited partners enjoy a limited liability equal to their investment as long as they do not actively engage in any management of the partnership.

- **DISADVANTAGES**
  - **Potential for Conflict**

  In as much as the business form is still a partnership, there is still a potential for conflict among the partners. This potential is somewhat mitigated in the limited partnership by the distancing of the limited partners from the actual management of the partnership. If the passive limited partners engage in any efforts to exert control over the management, they risk losing the benefits of limited liability that they enjoy.

  - **Increased Paperwork**

  Limited partnerships are formed according to individual state law, generally by filing formal Articles of Limited Partnership with the proper state authorities in the state of formation. They are subject to more paperwork requirements than a simple partnership but less than a corporation.

  - **Lack of Continuity**

  Similar to traditional partnerships, the limited partnership has an inherent lack of continuity. This may, however, be overcome in the case of the retirement or death of a general partner by providing in the Articles of Limited Partnership for an immediate reorganization of the limited partnership with the retired partner or the deceased partner's heirs or estate becoming a limited partner.

- **ADVANTAGES**
  - **Limited Liability for Limited Partners**

  The limited partners in such a business enjoy a limited liability, similar to that of a shareholder in a corporation. Their risk is limited to the amount of their investment in the limited partnership. The general partners remain at personal risk, the same as a partner in a traditional partnership.

■   Greater Opportunities for Attracting Investors

Since the limited partners will have no personal liability and will not be required to personally perform any tasks of management, it is easier to attract investors to the limited partnership form of business than to a traditional partnership. The limited partner will share in the potential profits and in the tax deductions of the limited partnership, but not in many of the financial risks involved.

THE CORPORATION

A corporation is a creation of law. It is governed by the laws of the state of incorporation and of the state or states in which it does business. In recent years it has become the business structure of choice for many small publishing businesses.

The *corporation* is an artificial entity. It is created by filing Articles of Incorporation with the proper state authorities. This gives the corporation its legal existence and the right to carry on business. Adoption of corporate *By-Laws*, or internal rules of operation, is often the first business of the corporation. In its simplest form, the corporate organizational structure consists of the following levels:

- Shareholders: who own shares of the business but do not contribute to the direct management of the corporation, other than by electing the directors of the corporation.

- Directors: who may be shareholders, but as directors do not own any of the business. They are responsible, jointly as members of the board of directors of the corporation, for making the major business decisions of the corporation, including appointing the officers of the corporation.

- Officers: who may be shareholders and/or directors, but, as officers, do not own any of the business. The officers (generally the president, vice president, secretary and treasurer) are responsible for the day-to-day operation of the business.

■ DISADVANTAGES

■ Lack of Individual Control

Due to the nature of the organizational structure in a corporation, a certain degree of individual control is necessarily lost by incorporation. The officers, as appointees of the board of directors, are answerable to the board for management decisions. The board of directors, on the other hand, is not entirely free from restraint, in that they are responsible to the shareholders for prudent business management. By allowing others to become involved in the ownership of a desktop publishing business, a certain amount of editorial and management freedom is lost.

■ Additional Recordkeeping and Paperwork

The technical formalities of corporation formation and operation must be strictly observed in order for a business to reap the benefits of corporate existence. For this reason, there is an additional burden to the corporation of detailed recordkeeping that is seldom present in other forms of business organization. Corporate decisions are, in general, more complicated due to the various levels of control and all such decisions must be carefully documented. Corporate meetings, both at the shareholder and director levels, are more formal and more frequent. These complications have the potential to overburden a small business struggling to survive.

■ Double Taxation

The profits of a corporation, when distributed to the shareholders in the form of dividends, are subject to being taxed twice. The first tax comes at the corporate level. The distribution of any corporate profits to the investors in the form of dividends is not a deductible business expense for the corporation. Thus, any dividends which are distributed have been subject to corporate income tax. The second level of tax is imposed at the personal level. The receipt of corporate dividends is considered income to the individual shareholder and is taxed as such. This potential for higher taxes due to a corporate business structure can be moderated by many factors. These are discussed in the next chapter: Taxation of a Publishing Business.

■ ADVANTAGES

■ Limited Liability

One of the most important advantages to the corporate form of business structure is the potential limited liability of the founders of and investors in the corporation. The liability for corporate debts is limited, in general, to the amount of money each owner has contributed to the corporation. Unless the corporation is essentially a shell for a one-person business or unless the corporation is grossly under-capitalized or under-insured, the personal assets of the owners are not at risk if the corporation fails. The shareholders stand to lose only what they invested. This factor is very important in attracting investors as the business grows.

■ Continuity

Unlike other business forms, a corporation can have a perpetual existence. Theoretically, a corporation can last forever. This may be a great advantage if there are potential future changes in ownership of the business in the offing. Changes that would cause a partnership to be dissolved or terminated often will not affect the corporation. For a publishing concern, this continuity can be an important factor in establishing a stable business image and a permanent relationship with others in the industry.

■ Free Transferability of Shares

Unlike a partnership, in which no one may become a partner without the consent of the other partners, a shareholder of corporate stock may freely sell, trade, or give away their stock unless formally restricted by reasonable corporate decisions. The new owner of such stock is then a new owner of the business in the proportionate share of stock obtained. This freedom offers potential investors a liquidity to shift assets that is not present in the partnership form of business. The sale of shares by the corporation is also an attractive method by which to raise needed capital.

■   Taxation

Taxation is listed both as an advantage and as a disadvantage for the corporation. Depending on many factors, the use of a corporation can increase or decrease the actual income tax paid in operating a publishing business. The tax aspects are discussed further in the following chapter.

THE "S" CORPORATION

The "S" corporation is a certain type of corporation that is available for specific tax purposes. It is a creature of the IRS. Its purpose is to allow small corporations to choose to be taxed like a partnership, but to also enjoy many of the benefits of a corporation.

To qualify as an "S" corporation, a corporation must not have over 35 shareholders, all of whom must be individuals; it must only have one class of stock; and each of the shareholders must consent to the choice of "S" corporation status.

The "S" corporation retains all of the advantages and disadvantages of the traditional corporation except in the area of taxation. For tax purposes, "S" corporation shareholders are treated similarly to partners in a partnership. The tax benefits of the "S" corporation are detailed in the following chapter.

CHAPTER 7

TAXATION OF A PUBLISHING BUSINESS

The choice of a business entity for a desktop publishing enterprise will often be a direct result of the perceived tax benefits available. While tax advantages are an important factor in this decision, they should not be allowed to overshadow the other important factors in the choice of a publishing structure. The ultimate success of the business will depend upon much more than any potential tax benefits one form of business may have over another.

Because tax laws are among the most volatile of all laws and have recently been the subject of sweeping legislative changes, the following discussion has been generalized to a certain extent to cover standard publishing business tax issues.

For each of the three major types of business form from which to operate a publishing business (the sole proprietorship, the partnership, and the corporation) there are differing tax situations. The specific tax differences for each business type are detailed below.

In addition, the tax aspects of the hybrid "S" corporation and general tax aspects of all publishing businesses, regardless of structure, are explained.

TAXATION OF THE SOLE PROPRIETORSHIP

In the sole proprietorship, the business itself does not pay any income taxes. It is the owner who is liable for the income taxes which result from sole proprietorship income. In addition, there is no tax effect if the owner takes money out of the business, or transfers money to and from the business. The sole owner of the business includes the profits or losses of the business in his or her individual income tax return and pays taxes accordingly. Any losses incurred in a sole proprietorship may be used to directly offset individual income from any other source.

For sole proprietorships, the profits or losses from the business are reported on Schedule C of IRS form 1040. The amount of profit or loss is then entered on the individual 1040 tax return. The sole proprietor is also likely to be liable for self-employment taxes, for which IRS Schedule SE must be filed. Additionally, the sole owner will often need to make estimated tax payments. Finally, for tax purposes, the sale of a sole proprietorship is treated simply as the sale of the individual business assets of the concern.

TAXATION OF THE PARTNERSHIP

A partnership is not a taxable entity. This is true even for the limited partnership. All partnerships must, however, file a tax return detailing its profits or losses for each tax year of its existence. The partnership tax return is filed on IRS Form 1065. The profits, losses, and individual distributive shares of certain business expenses of a partnership are divided and then passed on to the partners to be added to or deducted from the individual partners income on their separate tax returns.

Like the sole-proprietorship, any losses incurred by the partnership may be used by each partner (in his or her own proportionate share amount) to directly offset any other income. Beginning in 1987, newly-formed partnerships must use either the same tax year as the majority of its partners or a calendar tax year (January 1 to December 31), unless there is a clear business purpose for using a non-calendar tax year. An individual partner's income from the partnership is generally considered self-employment income and is, therefore, subject to self-employment tax.

TAXATION OF THE CORPORATION

In contrast to a sole proprietorship or a partnership, a corporation is a taxable entity. Unless the corporation has been formally dissolved, an annual corporate income tax return, generally IRS form 1120, must be filed. This is true even if the corporation has ceased doing business and disposed of most assets. In figuring corporate income, the corporation is generally allowed the same business deductions as a sole proprietorship. However, there are certain additional deductions to which a corporation is entitled. Except for an"S" corporation (see discussion below), the profits of a corporation are taxed both at the corporate level and at the shareholder level when the profits are distributed as dividends. The corporate tax rates currently range from 15% to 34%. Also, except for an "S" corporation, any losses generated by a corporation are not available to the shareholders to offset other income.

The use of a corporate business structure allows for many tax benefits. Reasonable compensation may be paid out to both directors or officers for corporate duties performed as long as such compensation is within normal industry standards. For a small corporation with a single group acting as shareholders, directors, and officers, this allows corporate profits to be taken out of the corporation without incurring the tax liability of dividends. In addition, corporate profits may be retained by a corporation in various ways without direct taxation.

TAXATION OF THE "S" CORPORATION

The "S" corporation is a hybrid type of business structure for tax purposes only. It allows the owner/shareholders to use a corporate business structure, but be taxed essentially as a partnership.

A corporation which has met all of the qualifying requirements may select "S" corporation status through the filing of IRS form 2553. Such a qualified corporation is generally exempt from federal income taxation. Its shareholders will then include on their individual income tax returns, their proportionate share of the corporation's income, deductions, losses, and credits. There are a few items of corporate income which remain subject to federal income tax, even for the "S" corporation. These include: excess net passive investment income, capital gains, built-in gains, and tax on certain aspects of investment credits.

GENERAL BUSINESS TAX ASPECTS

Regardless of the business structure chosen, there are certain aspects of taxation which are common to all small businesses. These include accounting and recordkeeping, depreciation of business property, expense deductions of qualified costs, tax treatment of inventories and various retirement plan alternatives. A basic understanding of these various tax aspects is necessary in order to organize a business in the most efficient and profitable manner.

■ ACCOUNTING/RECORDKEEPING

All businesses must keep accurate records. For a publishing business such records are particularly important to chart the financial progress of the business. Tax laws require that these records be permanent, accurate, complete, and available to clearly establish the income, deductions, and credits of the business. Specifically, travel expenses, entertainment expenses, and expenses relating to the business use of property must be clearly and fully substantiated by the business records.

In forming a publishing business, an accounting system must be chosen. Tax laws limit the choices to some extent. There are two basic accounting methods, cash or accrual.

■ The Cash Method

The cash method is available only if your publishing business will not have inventories of goods (books, for example) that are retained year-to-year for sale. This method of accounting is also not available to corporations (except "S" corporations), or partnerships that have been established with a corporation as one of the partners. In general, this method of accounting is "checkbook" accounting: income received is credited when received and expenses paid out are deducted when paid.

■   The Accrual Method

The accrual method of accounting is the usual choice for a publishing business and must be used if the business will operate with inventories of merchandise held for sale. Under this type of accounting system, all items of income are included in gross income when earned, regardless of when the actual payment is received. Similarly, items of expense are deductible when the business becomes liable for them, regardless of when the actual expense payment is made. The accrual method of accounting will generally give a clearer and more accurate picture of the financial status of a business and is the only accurate method which will reflect the economic health of a business which operates with an inventory.

■   TAX TREATMENT OF PUBLISHING BUSINESS
      EXPENSES

A publishing business will have many different types of costs and expenses during a year. There are those which are clearly continuing business expenses and can be deducted from gross income to arrive at the business net income. These are discussed below in the section on "Publishing Business Expense Deductions". In addition, if the business is operated with an inventory of merchandise which is sold for a profit, there is the "cost of goods sold" expense which is discussed below under "Inventories". Finally, there are those expenses which are counted as part of the investment in the business and are considered *capital expenditures*.

■   Capital Expenditures

Capital expenditure costs are not deducted in full in the year paid, but must be "capitalized", generally by some method of

91

depreciation. Thus, they are not fully taken into account each year to determine the actual annual profit or loss of the business, but are proportionately credited against income for a specific length of time.

There are three kinds of costs which must be capitalized:

1. The costs of starting the business are considered capital expenditures. Before the actual business operations are begun, nearly all of the business expenses are capital expenditures. Most of the costs which must be capitalized prior to starting a business are similar to those which will be deductible after the business is started. For example, pre-operation advertising, travel, utilities, repairs, and wages must be capitalized.

2. The costs of any assets which will be used in the publishing business for over one year must be capitalized. These include buildings, office furniture, copyrights, computer equipment, and any other property used in the business that has a useful life of over one year. The cost of the asset is the *basis* of the asset for tax purposes.

3. The costs of making any improvements to a business asset are also capital expenditures. Normal repairs to an asset, however, are deductible business expenses. The cost of an improvement to an asset is added to the "basis" of the asset.

Although capital expenditures are not deductible in the year made, the costs may generally be recovered through depreciation (the method used to recover capital expenses of most business costs) or amortization (the method used to recover business start-up expenses). *Depreciation* is an accounting and tax principle which divides the basis or cost of the business asset by the expected useful life of the asset and allows the business to recover the proportionate yearly cost of the asset as a yearly deduction against expenses.

In addition, rather than being treated as a capital expenditure, a specific amount (currently $10,000.00) of the cost of most tangible business equipment is deductible yearly as a business expense. This is known as an "election to expense depreciable assets placed in service during the tax year". Depreciation, amortization and the election to expense are all figured on IRS Form 4562.

There are currently three methods which the IRS has established to determine the correct amount of yearly depreciation allowance for property. Before the depreciation deduction can be computed, the correct set of rules must be chosen. The determination as to which set of depreciation rules applies depends upon many factors, including the type of property, the estimated useful life of the property, and the year in which the property was placed in service.

The Modified Accelerated Cost Recovery System (MACRS) will apply to most tangible business property placed in service after 1986. The Accelerated Cost Recovery System (ACRS) applies to most property placed in service between 1981 and 1986. There are extensive pre-1981 depreciation rules which apply to property placed in service prior to 1981 and to property that does not qualify for the other depreciation systems. If extensive depreciable property is used in the publishing business, consultation with a tax advisor is recommended.

■   Publishing Business Inventories

If the publishing business prints or has printed books or other items for sale which it retains as inventory, the actual cost to the publisher of the inventory items sold is deducted from the sale price of the goods to arrive at the net profit from the sale of the goods. To compute the cost of the goods sold, the actual cost of the goods (including the labor, material, and supplies which entered into the acquisition and production of the goods) and all costs of the goods required to be capitalized are added together. From this total, the year-end inventory cost is subtracted. The final figure is the cost of the goods sold during the year. The cost of the goods sold is then deducted from the gross sales receipts (minus any returns or allowances) to arrive at the net income from goods sold for the business. From this figure the allowable business expenses are deducted to arrive at the net profit of the business.

■ Publishing Business Expense Deductions

Most expenses of a publishing business that are neither inventory nor capital expenditures will be deductible. For accrual method businesses, such costs are deductible in the year in which the business first becomes liable for the payment, regardless of when the payment is actually made. For cash method businesses, the expenses are deductible in the year paid.

To be deductible, a business expense must be "ordinary and necessary". This phrase is generally interpreted rather loosely, even by the IRS, to mean "common and helpful". Following is a list of typical expense deductions for a small publishing concern:

- All compensation paid to employees, including salaries and wages, meals and lodging, employee health insurance, employee retirement plans, and educational assistance;

- The cost of any contract labor or services (graphics, typesetting, clerical, computer, printing, and marketing services etc.);

- Any expenses paid for rent and utilities for an office;

- The yearly amount of depreciation, amortization, or expense election for tangible and depreciable business property;

- Travel, entertainment and gift expenses: (Business meals and entertainment expense deductions are limited to 80% of the amount that would otherwise be deductible. Travel expenses are all normal costs of business-related travel away from home, other than commuting to work.);

- Interest paid on any outstanding business debts;

- The cost of any business liability insurance (including media liability, errors and omissions, or libel insurance) and 25% of the cost of medical insurance for the self-employed person and his or her family;

- The amount of any business taxes paid, including taxes on any business real estate;

- The full cost of any advertising expenses;

- The cost of any materials and supplies used in the business;

- Postage and telephone expenses;

- The amount of any charitable contributions made on behalf of the business;

- The cost of dues in trade or professional organizations and the cost of subscriptions to professional, technical or trade journals;

- The amount of educational expenses, if such education is to improve a business skill, and is not a qualification for a new job or business;

- Business-related legal fees and accounting expenses;

- The cost of repairs to any business property or assets.

PENSION AND RETIREMENT PLANS

There are a number of pension and retirement plans that are available under the tax laws to achieve a lower tax rate on funds set aside for retirement. There are three types of plans that are most desirable for the small publishing business: the IRA, the KEOGH plan, and the SEP plan.

■ THE INDIVIDUAL RETIREMENT ACCOUNT (IRA)

For the self-employed publisher, the IRA is the simplest form of retirement account available. Unless the self-employed person and/or their spouse are covered by a retirement plan through another employer or have an adjusted gross income of over $40,000.00, a yearly tax-deductible contribution to an IRA of up to $2000.00 is allowed per person. The money contributed to the IRA can earn interest each year and any tax on such interest is deferred until the money is withdrawn. Early withdrawals of money from an IRA result in a 10% penalty.

Most banks, financial institutions, or brokerages will assist with setting up an IRA.

■ THE KEOGH (HR-10) PLAN

For the self-employed publisher with net earnings from the business, a KEOGH retirement plan is available. Under this plan, annual contributions to a KEOGH account may be made for up to $30,000.00 or 15% of the compensation from the business, whichever is less. Compensation is generally considered to be the amount of individual income which is subject to self-employment tax.

There is a slight quirk in figuring the compensation since the contribution to the KEOGH must be taken into account. If the net profit from the publishing concern is $50,000.00, up to $7,500.00 (15% of $50,000.00) could be contributed to a KEOGH account. Then, of

96

course, the actual compensation will only be $42,500.00 which would appear to lower the amount of allowable contribution to $6,375.00 (15% of $42,500). The IRS offers an adjusted contribution rate to counteract this mathematical spiral. The actual contribution rate allowed a self-employed person is 13.0425%. At this contribution rate level, if the net earnings from the publishing business are over $15,350.00, the choice of a KEOGH plan will allow a greater amount of money to be set aside into a retirement account each year than would be possible under an IRA plan alone.

To set up a KEOGH account, a self-employed person may adopt their own program or use an IRS-approved program sponsored by a bank, insurance company, or investment company. An annual IRS form 5500 must be filed for KEOGH plans by the individual participant.

■ SIMPLIFIED EMPLOYEE PENSION PLANS (SEP)

This is the simplest method of setting up a retirement plan for any employees of a business. It allows the employer to contribute up to $30,000.00 or 15% of an employee's compensation to an individual retirement account. The individual retirement account to which the employer will contribute the pension funds is a separate SEP-IRA account which has been set up for the employee. The employee may continue to make his or her own contributions to an IRA account. Contributions to the SEP plan account, however, may cause limitations on the amount that may be placed in an individual IRA account.

The employer's contribution to a SEP plan can either be direct or be considered as having been taken out of the employee's pay. There is a $7,000.00 limit on the amount of contribution that can be taken out of an employee's salary. In addition, a self-employed person may set up a SEP-IRA account for his or herself. In this case, the contributions are limited to the lesser of 13.0425% of compensation or $30,000.00. Again, if the self-employed person's business has a net taxable profit of over $15,350.00, the choice of a SEP-IRA allows for a larger amount of retirement funds to be set aside each year than is possible with a basic IRA.

97

A SEP-IRA account or annuity may be established with a bank, insurance company, investment company or any other company qualified to sponsor an IRA.

TAXPAYER ID NUMBERS

All partnerships, corporations (including S corporations) and any sole proprietorships which pay wages to employees must obtain a Federal Employer Identification Number (FEIN). For sole proprietorships without employees, the owner's social security number is sufficient identification for tax purposes. For all other business structures, the FEIN number is used on all business tax forms and may be obtained by filing IRS form SS-4, Application for Employer Identification Number.

CHAPTER 8

DESKTOP PUBLISHING CONTRACTS

Every publishing business, whether it is large or small, must work within the framework provided by many types of legal contracts. A basic knowledge of the various elements of a contract is fundamental to understanding how to use contracts to effectively describe and record business agreements.

This chapter will explain the general requirements for a legally binding contract in all instances. These basic guidelines will provide the desktop publisher with a contractual framework to apply to many business situations. In the area of specific publishing contracts, each standard clause of a customary publisher/author contract will be presented and explained. The clauses have been simplified and drafted in plain English but are as legally valid and effective as the traditional difficult-to-understand clauses of the standard publisher/author contract. Finally, how to construct contracts to fit particular purposes will be explained. Appendix D contains several sample Publisher/Author contracts which have been prepared to suit various desktop publishing situations.

THE NATURE OF CONTRACTS

Initially, it should be emphasized that a contract need not be a long, complicated, and unreadable document, laced throughout with antiquated legal jargon. In fact, the best contracts are simple straightforward agreements which concisely spell out the understandings between the parties in plain English.

A *contract*, in the legal sense, is a legally enforceable set of mutual promises between two or more people. What this means is that if a contract exists, and if one of the parties to the contract does not fulfill his or her obligations under the contract, the other party can ask a court to force compliance. If there is no valid contract, a court will not enforce the agreement. For simplicity, the discussion below will assume that the contracts to be formed are between two people. However, please note that a contract may be formed between any number of people and between corporations or partnerships.

Contrary to popular understanding, in many cases a contract need not be in writing to be enforceable in court. However, it is strongly advised that all contracts for use in desktop publishing be put in writing. A contract is the blueprint for any business dealings. Its purpose is to carefully delineate the understandings between the parties. In order to do this properly and avoid future disagreements regarding what was intended, the contract terms must be set down in writing. Certain contracts must be in writing to be enforceable. Which contracts must be in writing is often difficult to determine. To be safe, all contracts in a business setting should be in writing and contain the following information at a minimum:

- The date of the agreement;

- An identification of the parties;

- An identification of the subject matter;

- The amount of money to be exchanged;

- The signatures of the parties.

100

In addition, a good contract should also provide an explanation of the various promises, terms, conditions, and warranties which apply.

A contract is an attempt to provide solutions to future problems in advance. In this regard, be aware that it is impossible to provide for all potential eventualities in a single legal document. A good contract covers the most predictable future events that may occur between the parties and may provide a method to resolve any future problems that are not specifically covered in the document. To be most effective, a contract should be a balanced agreement which provides benefits and responsibilities for both parties. Publishing is an uncertain business and both the author and the publisher take risks in an attempt to bring worthwhile publications to the public. A contract which spreads these risks in a fair and balanced manner between the two parties will be most beneficial for both sides.

There are three essential elements to a contract which must be present in order for a particular agreement to be a legally enforceable contract:

1.   That there is a mutual set of promises;

2.   That there is consideration (explained below) and;

3.   That there are no legal defenses to the contract.

■   MUTUAL SET OF PROMISES

The first element which is necessary for the formation of a legally valid contract is that there actually be mutual promises between the parties. This is legally defined as the offer and acceptance. When an offer of some type has been made and another person has accepted the terms of the offer, this element of a contract has been fulfilled. The standard is: Would a reasonable person agree that the words or conduct of the parties showed an intention to reach an agreement?

For example, if Publisher offers to publish Writer's book and provide a 15% royalty for any copies sold and Writer accepts this offer, there is a mutual set of promises. Writer has implicitly agreed to provide a finished book to Publisher along with some of the rights of publication. Publisher has agreed to print and distribute copies of Writer's book and pay a royalty fee for any copies sold. If the other two elements of a contract are satisfied, and either party fails to perform the agreed-upon promises, the other party can bring a lawsuit to force performance or ask for compensation for non-performance. Thus, if Publisher fails to publish the book or fails to pay the proper royalty, Writer may sue to force publication or may request monetary payment to compensate for the lack of publication or the failure to pay royalties. Alternately, if Writer fails to provide Publisher with a manuscript, Publisher can bring a lawsuit for compensation for lost income or lost investment.

■ The Offer

Generally, for an offer to be valid, it must be sufficiently definite in nature. All of the material terms must be clear and the parties must be identified. The details must be complete enough that a court could enforce the contract. In the above example, no specific amount of copies to be published was specified and, thus, a court will not enforce Writer's potential claim that Publisher did not publish enough copies of the book. The amount of royalty, however, was clearly specified and, thus, Publisher's failure to pay a 15% royalty would be an enforceable breach of the contract.

■ Acceptance of the Offer

For an acceptance of an offer to be valid, it must be made while the offer is still open, within a reasonable time, and it must be absolute. If the acceptance attempts to change any terms of the original offer, a valid contract is not formed. Going back to the above example using Publisher and Writer, if Writer had crossed out the 15% royalty provision and written in 20% instead, and then signed the contract, it would not be considered a valid acceptance. If Writer then returns the signed contract with the royalty change to Publisher, the modified Publisher's offer then becomes Writer's counter-offer, open for acceptance by the Publisher. If Publisher accepts the contract with the new royalty provision, a valid contract is then formed.

An offer is generally considered to be open for acceptance if:

- The person making the offer has not withdrawn the offer, or;

- The person to whom the offer is made has not refused to accept the offer, or;

- The person to whom the offer is made has relied upon the offer and begun performance and the one who made the offer should have expected this, or;

- The offer is a written offer by a business- or tradeperson involving the sale of goods, or;

- The offer is a valid option contract which provides for a specific time limit for acceptance.

■ CONSIDERATION

Consideration is a difficult legal concept. It means essentially that in order for a valid contract to exist there must be a mutually bargained-for exchange of something of value. This is normally:

- Either party promising to do something they have no legal obligation to do, or;

- Either party promising to refrain from doing something that they have a legal right to do.

If Writer agrees to write a book and allow Publisher to publish it, and if Publisher agrees to publish it and pay Writer a royalty, each has agreed to perform certain acts which they had no legal duty to perform prior to the contract. The performance of each act has a value. Therefore, there is consideration present and this element of a contract has been fulfilled.

103

Generally, there is no lack of consideration in a contract if there is an actual bargained-for agreement. The most important aspect of consideration then becomes whether or not the consideration is mutual. Mutuality means that both parties to the contract must be legally bound by the terms of the contract. If one party has a unilateral and unrestricted method by which to withdraw from or cancel the contract, there is no mutual "consideration" and the contract is not valid.

■   LEGAL DEFENSES TO CONTRACT FORMATION

There are various defenses to the formation of a contract. If the facts pertaining to the defense exist, the contract is not an enforceable agreement. For example: in most states, people under 18 are deemed too young to enter into legal contracts. Thus, a contract with a 16 year-old author will, under most circumstances, be unenforceable by the publisher. The following is a brief description of the most important defenses to contract formation.

■   Mistake

A mutual mistake by both parties regarding an important term of the contract renders the contract void. A mistake by only one of the parties, however, does not prevent the formation of a contract. If a particular important term of a contract is ambiguous, there may not be a contract unless both parties had the same general understanding of the ambiguous term.

■   Fraud, Misrepresentation, Duress

If any of these factors are present, it will generally be deemed that there was no valid agreement in the first place. Fraud is an intentional attempt to mislead. Misrepresentation may be either fraudulent or innocent. Duress is the use of force or coercion of some type in order to obtain an agreement.

■   Illegality of Contract

If the contract concerns performance of an illegal act, it is unenforceable. An example of an illegal contract in a publishing setting would be a contract to publish the life story of a criminal in a jurisdiction which has a "Son of Sam" type law which makes it a crime for a criminal to derive economic gain from the commercialization of their crime. New York presently has such a law in effect.

■   Lack of Capacity of Parties

Underage persons, insane persons and intoxicated persons are generally held not to have sufficient legal capacity to enter into valid contracts. For underage persons, however, in most jurisdictions, it is only the minor who has the right to rescind the contract once it is made.

■   Unconscionability

If a contract is conspicuously unfair or if one side to the contract is grossly and inequitably burdened by the contract, it may be determined that the contract is invalid.

THE PUBLISHER/AUTHOR CONTRACT

In the days when the publishing business was dominated by a relatively few giant publishing houses, authors had little choice than to agree to the standard contract terms offered by the publisher. Of course, those terms were highly favorable to the publisher. Today, partly as a result of the recent proliferation of new publishing outlets, authors enjoy a more equal bargaining position in contract negotiations. Although there are certain standard terms which are likely to be included in all publisher/author contracts, there is a wide variety of matters which are and should be open to negotiation between the parties. It is through negotiation that an agreement which is acceptable to both sides will eventually be reached.

The publisher is generally the party who will make the initial contract offer. Thus, it is the publisher who has the opportunity to construct a contract which will meet his or her most important needs. Careful consideration must go into the construction of the contract. However, the publisher must be flexible enough to allow for reasonable changes to be implemented at the request of the author.

What follows is a discussion of each of the important clauses which are generally included in a standard complex publisher/author book contract. The discussion of each clause will begin with a presentation of each publishing contract clause. The clauses have been drafted to be understandable and even-handed in application and do not unfairly favor the publisher, as many industry contracts do. After each clause, the issues involved and factors in the use of each clause will then be explained.

Not all of the following clauses are necessary for all publisher/author situations. Some will not be relevant in certain circumstances. Small publishers will wish to adopt a contract which may contain only a few of these clauses. The clauses outlined below touch upon virtually all of the major issues involved in any publishing situation. Thus, whether the publication contemplated is a magazine, a book, a journal, or merely a newsletter, a basic knowledge of all of the various legal issues involved in book publishing contracts will aid the desktop publisher in determining which contract provisions are relevant to a particular situation.

■ TITLE AND INTRODUCTORY CLAUSE

PUBLISHING CONTRACT

THIS PUBLISHING CONTRACT is made on _____ , 19_____ , between _____ (Full name of publisher), Publisher, residing at _____ (Address of publisher), and _____ (Full name of author), Author, residing at _____ (Address of author).

The contract title is a simplified description of the content of the document. For most purposes, "Publishing Contract" will suffice. However, more specific identification is acceptable. For example: "Textbook Publishing Contract".

The introductory clause specifies the effective date of the contract and is a brief identification of the parties to the contract and their addresses. This information is important and should be included in all contracts.

■ DELIVERY OF MANUSCRIPT CLAUSE

> The Author agrees to deliver an original and one copy of the Manuscript which is tentatively titled _____ (Tentative title of work), referred to as the Work, to the Publisher on or before _____, 19____.
>
> The Work is described as _____(Here provide a detailed description of the work, including subject matter, word length, outline if possible, and overall description).
>
> If the Author fails to deliver the Manuscript and any necessary related materials within _____ days of the Manuscript due date, the Publisher may terminate this contract and the Author agrees to repay any money advanced.

This clause and the following clause relating to the satisfactory nature of the delivered manuscript are the foundation of the typical publisher/author contract and are the root of most legal problems between publishers and authors. The most important aspect of the delivery of the manuscript clause is the due date. A publisher needs to coordinate many aspects of any publication and must rely upon a specific date for receipt of the manuscript. On the other hand, authors will often have valid reasons why they are unable to complete the manuscript on time. This conflict leads inevitably to certain problems. It is advisable to work closely with the author to attempt to set a reasonable initial due date.

The above clause sets a specific due date, then gives the Author some leeway before the Publisher has the right to cancel the contract (90 days is a typical period allowed for late delivery). Further extensions of time may be warranted depending on the circumstances surrounding the delay. The publisher should provide a written confirmation of any extension of the manuscript due date beyond what is provided for in the contract.

■ SATISFACTORY IN FORM AND CONTENT CLAUSE

> Within _____ days of receipt of the Manuscript, the Publisher agrees to notify the Author if the Publisher finds the Manuscript unsatisfactory in form or content. The Publisher also agrees to provide the Author with a list of necessary changes. The Author agrees to make the changes within _____ days. If the Publisher still reasonably rejects the Manuscript as unsatisfactory, the Publisher may terminate this contract and the Author agrees to repay any money advanced.

This particular clause is at the heart of the most difficult area in publisher/author relations. The publisher has a right to expect a publishable manuscript. The author desires compensation for the generally difficult task of creation of such a manuscript. The conflict arises when the two sides disagree on whether or not the manuscript fits the publisher's expectations. There are various alternatives to this clause, some of which give the publisher a virtually unrestricted right of rejection and some of which allow the author to only pay back the advance if he or she sells the rejected manuscript elsewhere. The above clause seeks a middle ground. It requires the publisher to request changes in the unsatisfactory manuscript (usually within 60 days) and allows the author to attempt to salvage a rejected work (again, usually within 60 days). A final rejection by the publisher must be made on reasonable grounds. This is a higher standard of rejection for the publisher to meet than mere good faith or personal taste, which was a previous industry standard highly favorable to the publisher.

■ **PERMISSIONS CLAUSE**

   ■ Author Responsibility

> With the delivery of the Manuscript, the Author also agrees to provide the Publisher with any necessary permissions to include material copyrighted by others. The Author is responsible for any payments necessary to obtain such permissions.

   ■ Publisher Responsibility

> The Publisher is responsible for obtaining any required permissions to include material copyrighted by others and for any payments necessary for such permissions.

One of these two clauses should be used if there is material to be incorporated into the publication which has been copyrighted by others. If the material is an integral part of the work, the author is normally expected to obtain the required permissions. However, it is often easier for the publisher to do so.

■ **ADDITIONAL MATERIAL CLAUSE**

> With the delivery of the Manuscript, the Author agrees to provide to the Publisher the following additional related items necessary for publication:_____ (Here detail any additional items required for the publication. For example: photographs, illustrations, drawings, charts, table of contents, prefix, forward, introduction, bibliography, appendices, glossary, index, etc).

This clause obligates the author to provide those additional materials which are essential to the publication of the work.

Often the publisher will agree to provide certain of these items if the publisher has greater access to the professionals who may be needed to prepare such material. Unless the amount of additional matter is substantial, the author is usually required to pay for all costs related to the preparation of such matter. However, publisher may provide the author with a "production grant advance" to cover the cost of such matter. This type of advance should be specified under the "Advances" clause below.

If the type of book is such that illustrations or photographs are substantial elements in the work, the illustrator or photographer may share in the actual publisher advance and royalties. For example, for a children's book consisting of large-type text and pictorial illustrations, the author and illustrator may agree to split the advance and royalties on a 50/50 basis. Agreements of this nature are generally negotiated between the creators of the work and then presented to the publisher for inclusion in the publishing contract.

■   GRANT OF RIGHTS CLAUSE

> The Author grants the Publisher the rights listed below, for the entire term of the copyright of the Work in _____ (Here detail the geographic limits of the rights granted. For example: the United States, North America, etc.):
>
> A. All Rights: All exclusive rights under the copyright;
>
> B. Book Trade Edition Rights: The exclusive right to print, publish, and sell hardcover or softcover editions of the Work for distribution through normal book trade channels;
>
> C. Mass Market Book Reprint Rights: The exclusive right to print, publish, and sell or license others to print, publish, and sell mass market softcover editions of the Work;

D. Book Club Rights: The exclusive right to license others to print, publish, and sell book club editions of the Work;

E. General Publication Rights: The exclusive right to print, publish, and sell or license others to print, publish, and sell condensations, abridgements, Braille editions, or selections from the Work for inclusion in anthologies, compilations, digests, newspapers, magazines, or textbooks;

F. Direct Mail Rights: The exclusive right to sell or license others to sell the work through direct mail or coupon advertising;

G. First Book Serialization Rights: The exclusive right, prior to initial publication, to publish or license others to publish the work or portions of the Work;

H. Dramatic Rights: The exclusive right to use or license others to use the work or portions of the Work in any stage presentation;

I. Movie Rights: The exclusive right to use or license others to use the work or portions of the work in any motion picture presentation;

J. Television or Radio Rights: The exclusive right to use or license others to use the work or portions of the work in any television or radio presentation;

K. Translation Rights: The exclusive right to translate or license others to translate the work or portions of the work into any foreign languages and print, publish, and sell such translations of the work;

L. Publicity Rights: The exclusive right to use the work or any portion of the work in any manner for the purposes of promoting sales of the work;

It is with this clause that the important determination is made regarding which "rights" the publisher will acquire. The duration of a publishing contract is typically for the entire term of the copyright, subject to the work being out-of-print (See below: " Out-of-Print Clause"). Under certain circumstances, of course, the duration of the contract may be limited to a specific time period. In addition, recall that the Copyright Act of 1976 allows for an author to terminate any exclusive grant of rights under a copyright after the passage of 35 years. (See Chapter 2: U.S. Copyright Law).

The primary right for a publisher is the "exclusive right to print, publish, and sell" a work. This primary right may, of course, be limited to a certain geographical area, for example: North America. It may also be limited to a certain type of publication, for example: hardcover books. Subparagraphs A and B in the above "Grant of Rights" clause are examples of exclusive primary rights. Payment for the grant of the primary right to publish is typically made in the form of an advance against royalties and future royalties on the sale of the work.

All other rights are considered secondary to the primary right to publish. The sale of hardcover books to a paperback publisher, the sale of a book to a book club, the sale of a manuscript to a television studio are all rights considered to be secondary to the initial publication of the work. The grant of secondary or *subsidiary* rights is generally open to considerable negotiation between the publisher and author. The subsidiary rights may be granted on an exclusive or non-exclusive basis. The author may not wish to grant the publisher certain of them at all. Payment for subsidiary rights may be either in the form of royalties (if the publisher exercises the rights), or as a percentage of licensing fees paid to the publisher (if the publisher *licenses* [authorizes] another to exercise the secondary rights). For a discussion of royalty fees, please see below under "Royalty Clause".

112

The publisher and author should give serious consideration to which of the author's rights are important for the publisher to control in order for the publication to have the best opportunity to become a success. It is often most beneficial for the publisher to control many of the subsidiary rights and attempt to market them to increase the publication's revenue. However, in some situations, the author may have valid reasons for desiring to retain control over certain subsidiary rights.

■ RESERVATION OF RIGHTS CLAUSE

> Any rights not specifically granted to the Publisher shall remain with the Author. The Author agrees not to exercise any retained rights in such a manner as to adversely affect the value of the rights granted to the Publisher.

This clause specifically allows the author to retain any rights not granted, but requires that the author not use those rights in any manner which would reduce the value the rights that he or she has sold to the publisher.

■ ADVANCE CLAUSE

> The Publisher shall pay to the Author as an advance against any money to be paid to the Author under this contract the amount of $_____ to be paid one-half upon signing this contract and one-half upon delivery of a satisfactory Manuscript. This amount is not repayable unless the Author fails to deliver a satisfactory Manuscript within the time allowed.

To an author, the advance is very important. It allows some payment for the work of creation prior to the future public sales of the book. For the publisher, however, it is a fact that many books never earn their advances.

The determination of an equitable author's advance should be part of the initial estimates on the projected sales of the first printing of a book. By determining the size of the first printing and the related production and promotional costs, a reasonable estimate can be made of the author's expected royalties. An advance of monies for a production grant, for the purchase of permissions, or for the preparation of additional material by the author may be added to the total amount or provided in a separate clause.

An advance against royalties should constitute a reasonable percentage of the expected author's royalties from a realistic sales figure from the first printing of the book. An advance of 50% of the expected first-run royalties would be considered fair. For example, a first run is to be 5000 books, and 75% sales are projected at a retail price of $10.00 per book. An author's estimated first-run royalties at a 10% royalty rate would be $3,750.00 (less a standard 20% reserve for returned copies) or $3,000.00. 50% of this figure would be $1,500.00 for the entire advance. This amount would typically be paid in two installments of $750.00 each.

The advance is paid out against future royalty payments. For example, if an advance of $1,500.00 is paid initially and a book earns a total of $2,500.00 in computed author royalties, the publisher would owe the author an additional $1,000.00 in payments, since the advance is considered an "advance royalty payment".

Additionally, the advance is the authors to keep regardless of the fact that the book may never earn enough royalties to cover the actual advance paid. In the above example, if the book only sells 1000 copies at $10.00 per copy for a total author's royalty of $1,000.00, but the author was paid an advance of $1,500.00, the publisher is not entitled to a rebate of the $500.00 overpaid in the advance. The author need only return the advance for failure to deliver a satisfactory manuscript within the time allowed.

■ ROYALTY CLAUSE

The Publisher agrees to pay the Author a royalty on the retail price of every copy sold by the Publisher (less any returns and a _____ percent reserve for returns), as follows:

A. _____ Percent (___%) up to and including _____copies;

B. _____ Percent (___%) up to and including _____copies;

C. _____ Percent (___%) for sales over _____copies;

D. _____ Percent (___%) of the amount received for sales by direct mail;

E. _____ Percent (___%) of the amount received for sales of _____ (elementary, junior high school, etc.) textbook editions;

F. _____ Percent (___%) of the amount received for sales on which the publisher granted a discount of greater than _____ percent to the purchaser;

G. _____ Percent (___%) of the amount received for any licenses of _____ rights granted by the Publisher under this contract.

Royalties are the central element of a publishing contract from the author's standpoint. It is with royalty payments that the struggles of creation are repaid. The royalty rates traditionally escalate upwards in a reflection of the publisher's lower publishing costs for more copies. Large publishing houses have created incredibly complicated royalty clauses in typical contracts that have been, in certain situations, grossly unfair to many authors. For the small publisher, it is more conducive to amicable publisher/author relationships to have an equitable and understandable royalty schedule.

There are typical royalty rates which are relatively standard in the publishing industry. These standard rates should not, however, be considered inflexible and should be tailored to fit each individual situation. The levels at which the royalties shift (or break points) may be adjusted for expected sales volumes. The actual royalty rates can be negotiated on either side of the standard rates. A 20% reserve for returns would be acceptable. The royalties are typically paid on the retail sales price of the book regardless of the discount which the publisher provides the distributor, unless the discount is greater than 50%. Some publisher's have begun to pay royalties on the basis of actual "net receipts" from the books sold. To be fair to the author, any "net receipt" royalty schedule should be adjusted upwards to account for this particular method of calculation.

Typical publishing industry royalty rates are as follows:

For Trade Books (Either hard- or soft-cover):

> 7.5% - 10% on the first 5,000 copies;
>
> 10% - 12.5% on the next 7,500 to 10,000 copies;
>
> 12.5% - 15% on all copies over 7,500 to 10,000.
>
> (There is often a differentiation made in contracts dealing with professional, scientific, or technical books as opposed to standard trade books. The trend, however, is to blend any distinctions between the different markets. For simplicity sake, a standard royalty schedule should be adopted.)

For Mass Market Paperbacks:

> 4% - 6% on the first 50,000 copies;

6% - 8% on the next 100,000 copies;

8% - 10% for all copies over 100,000.

For Direct Mail sales:

5% (This takes into account the substantial publisher's advertising and marketing overhead and, thus, lower profit margin involved in direct mail promotions).

For Textbooks:

10% for hardcover texts, 8% for softcover; perhaps with standard escalation clauses.

(Publishers of textbooks have traditionally attempted to obtain much lower royalty rates for authors of textbooks for various levels of schools. There is, however, no reasonable rationale for this practice).

For substantially discounted sales (generally over 50% discount, but may be specified to be sales at a discount of 60-70%):

Generally, the royalty rate is 2% to 5% lower than full retail sales royalties.

For Licenses of Rights:

For book club, mass market paperback, television, movie rights, etc: the industry standard payment ranges from 50% to 90%;

For First Serial Rights: 90%;

For Translation and Foreign Rights: 75%.

■ REVISIONS CLAUSE

> The Author agrees to proofread, correct, and promptly return all proofs of the work to the Publisher and to pay in cash for any changes required by the Author which are not the Publisher's or the printer's errors.
>
> The Author also agrees to provide necessary revisions of the Work in order to keep the Work up-to-date. Such revisions shall not be required more often than once every two years.

This clause obligates the author to verify that the proofs of the work as submitted for printing are acceptable and that any last-minute changes in the work, other than typographical errors, are the monetary responsibility of the Author. This avoids the situation where an author uses the proofs of a work to actually complete the work. The revisions portion of this clause is often necessary for non-fiction books of a timely nature which require frequent up-dating. Keeping a book current is beneficial to both the publisher and the author.

■ ALTERATIONS CLAUSE

> The style, format, design, layout, advertising, promotion, and price of the published work shall be in the sole discretion of the Publisher. However, no editorial changes in the manuscript which materially alter the meaning of the text will be made without the consent of the Author, unless the Publisher reasonably believes that the Work or portions of the Work are in violation of any of the Author's Warranties regarding the Work.

Total discretion is traditionally allowed the publisher in deciding how to actually publish the work. If an author is of sufficient stature or expertise, there may be some negotiation

118

on some of the items involved in the actual layout of the book, for instance, cover design.

On the other hand, any changes in the actual content of the work should be cleared with the author. It is the author's name and reputation, after all, which will be most associated with the work. The provisions of this clause allow the creator of the work to retain control over the material aspects of his or her creation, but allow the packaging of that creation to be in the hands of the publisher.

■   PROMOTION AND PUBLICITY CLAUSE

The Author agrees to be reasonably available for promotion of the Work in the _____ (geographic) area for radio, television, and newspaper interviews. If the Publisher desires the Author to promote the book outside of this area and the Author consents, the Publisher agrees to pay the cost of transportation, meals, and lodging for the Author to attend any such promotional engagements.

Often, a large part of a book's promotion will depend upon the efforts of the author. The author should reasonably be available for such promotion in the immediate area of his or her residence. If the author and publisher agree on more extensive publicity, the publisher should generally shoulder the basic travel costs for the author.

■ AUTHOR AND PROMOTIONAL COPIES CLAUSE

> The Publisher agrees to provide the Author with _____ copies of the published Work free of charge and to sell the Author any amount of additional copies at a 50% discount.
>
> The Publisher may distribute a reasonable number of books for promotional purposes without cost and without payment of royalty to the Author.

This clause specifies how many free copies of a book will be available to the author, and how much the author will be charged for additional copies. The number of free copies provided is generally under 25.

The right to distribute review copies and other promotional copies for free and without an obligation to pay the author a royalty is an important right for the publisher to obtain. The distribution of review and promotional copies is often the most cost-effective method for book marketing promotion.

■ MEDIATION CLAUSE

> The Publisher and Author agree to attempt to compromise any dispute over any terms in this contract. If unable to mutually agree within a reasonable time, they agree to submit the dispute to a professional mediator whom they mutually select, with the cost of the mediation to be equally shared.

Through this clause, an attempt is made to avoid costly litigation if there are disagreements over any of the terms of the contract. The use of a mediator is often a valuable alternative to bringing in lawyers and going to court to settle differences. Often, by contractually providing for a method of mediation, a more reasonable approach to differences will be adopted by both sides to the agreement.

■   AUTHOR'S WARRANTIES CLAUSE

The Author warrants that: :

A. The Work is the sole creation of the Author;

B. The Author is the sole owner of the rights granted under this contract;

C. The Work does not infringe upon the copyright of any other work;

D. The Work is original and unpublished;

E. The Work is not in the Public Domain;

F. The Work is not obscene, or libelous, and does not invade the privacy of any person;

G. All statements of fact in the Work are true and based upon reasonable research.

Publishers must generally rely on the author's statements and representations regarding libel, invasion of privacy, truth, copyright infringement, and ownership of the work. Realistically, there is no convenient or efficient method by which a publisher can independently verify these matters. A breach of any of the author's warranties is covered in the next clause.

■   INDEMNITY AND INSURANCE CLAUSE

> If there is ever a claim based upon an alleged violation of any of the Author's warranties, the Publisher has the right to defend against the claim, but will not settle any claim without the reasonable consent of the Author. The Author agrees to indemnify the Publisher for 50% of any losses under any such claim, except for any claim of copyright infringement for which the Author agrees to indemnify the Publisher in full.
>
> Publisher agrees to arrange for Author to be a named insured under any publisher liability insurance policy.

Under this clause, the publisher reserves the right to "stand in the Author's shoes" in defense of the work. The right of the publisher to settle cases is restricted somewhat by requiring the author's consent, which must be reasonably given by the author. The author's liability for any breach of the above publishing contract warranties, other than copyright infringement, is limited to 50%.

The brief statement with regard to insurance coverage is intended to allow inclusion of the author under any publisher liability insurance coverage. For the small publisher, however, such insurance is generally a luxury. See discussion of libel insurance in Chapter 9: The Law of Libel and Defamation.

■   PUBLICATION CLAUSE

> The Publisher agrees that, within one year from the receipt of a satisfactory Manuscript of the Work, the work will be published at Publisher's sole expense. If Publisher fails to do so, unless prevented by conditions beyond Publisher's control, the Author may terminate this Contract.

This clause obligates the publisher to actually publish the work within a certain time. Violation of this portion of an agreement can give rise to a suit by the author for damages. It is often difficult to judge in advance the amount of lost royalty revenue an author may be entitled to for failure of a publisher to publish a work. At least one court has awarded an author the amount deemed necessary for the author to self-publish the work: an award of $11,000.00.

■ COPYRIGHT CLAUSE

> The Publisher agrees to register the copyright of the Work in the name of the Author in the United States and include a sufficient copyright notice on all copies of the Work distributed to the public.

This clause obligates the publisher to protect the author's important rights relating to the copyright of the work.

■ ACCOUNTING CLAUSE

> The Publisher agrees to provide the Author with a _____ accounting of all monies due. Payment of all royalties due shall be made within 30 days of such accounting.
>
> The Publisher agrees that the Author shall have the right, on 48-hour notice, to examine the Publisher's accounting books and records which relate to the Work.

Semi-annual statements are normal for large publishing houses. Monthly or quarterly statements may be more appropriate for smaller publishers. Payment, however, should then be somewhat delayed to allow for returns from wholesalers or bookstores.

Publisher's have traditionally allowed authors to examine their books, although in practice this is rarely done. Despite some publisher's questionable ethics, there is a proud tradition of scrupulous honesty in the publishing industry.

■ **COMPETITION CLAUSE**

> The Author agrees that during the duration of the contract he or she will not edit, prepare, publish, or sell any material based on the Work which would interfere with the Publisher's sale of the Work.

This provision prevents the author from making slight alterations in the work and selling the new "work" to a different publisher. In certain situation, it may be necessary to revise this clause to allow reasonably similar material to be created by an author who specializes in a narrow field of expertise.

■ **OUT-OF-PRINT CLAUSE**

> The Work will be considered "out-of-print" when the Publisher fails to sell _____ copies during any calendar year. When the work is out-of-print, all rights granted to the Publisher will revert to the Author, except those rights which the Publisher has already licensed to others.

This clause allows the author to regain control over the Work when the publisher has exhausted its interest in the work. The failure to sell 1000 copies of a typical book within a year would be a reasonable determination of "out-of-print" status. This figure, however, should be tailored for each individual book based on projected sales volumes. A written confirmation to the author of the reversion of the rights involved would be appropriate.

■   RIGHT-OF-FIRST-REFUSAL CLAUSE

The Author agrees to submit his or her next work to the Publisher before submitting it to any other publisher. The Publisher agrees to make a decision on publication of the new work within six months of receipt. If a decision is made to publish the new work, the Author and Publisher agree to negotiate a publishing contract for the new work. If the Author and Publisher are, in good faith, unable to arrive at an acceptable contract within 30 days from the decision-to-publish date, the Author is free to submit the manuscript elsewhere.

The publisher of a quality work may likely wish to obtain the right-of-first-refusal on the Author's next work and build upon the success of the first publication. The author may also wish to build a lasting relationship with the publisher and may benefit from such an agreement. The time limits and deadlines in this clause may be altered to fit the particular needs of the parties.

■   BOILERPLATE CLAUSE

This contract shall be interpreted according to the laws of the state of the Publisher's residence. This contract shall be binding upon the heirs, representatives, and assigns of the Author and Publisher, but no assignment of this contract will be binding on either party without the written consent of the other. Time is of the essence in this contract.

This contract is the complete agreement between the Author and Publisher. No modification or waiver of any terms will be valid unless in writing and signed by both parties.

These provisions are relatively standard and provide that the laws of the Publisher's state of residence will used to interpret any terms in the contract. Also agreed upon is that the contract be binding on representatives of either party. They also provide that for an *assignment* of the contract (for another to "step into the shoes" of one of the parties), a written consent must be provided.

Additionally, both sides agree that "time is of the essence" in the contract. This is legal shorthand for an agreement that the deadlines specified are important and must be abided by. The parties also agree that the contract is the entire understanding between them and that there are no oral promises otherwise. Finally, they agree that any changes to the contract must be in writing and signed by both parties before they are effective.

■ SIGNATURES

This Contract is signed by the parties on the date first written above.

Signature of Publisher
(Typewritten Name of Publisher)

Signature of Author
(Typewritten Name of Author)
(Author's Social Security Number)

The parties must both sign the same agreement for it to be effective. Any changes in the agreement must be initialed by both parties. If any of the changes are extensive, the document should be re-typed. The author's social security number is provided to the publisher for tax purposes.

ALTERATIONS TO CONTRACTS

As noted in the "Boilerplate" provisions of the above contract, any changes to a written contract should also be in writing. Alterations, however, do not need to be nearly as formal as the original contract. For minor changes, a simple crossing-out or marginal notation will suffice, as long as both parties date and initial the changes. For more extensive changes, a "letter agreement" is the standard vehicle. A letter agreement is simply a letter detailing the agreed-upon changes to the written contract which provides for the signature of both parties. The letter agreement should specifically refer to the contract by date and should clearly identify the changes to be made. A sample of a letter agreement is contained in Appendix D: Sample Desktop Publishing Contracts.

For parties other than individuals who will be signatories to a contract, certain changes are necessary. In the Introductory Clause which specifies the names and address of the contracting parties, the type of business entity and state of incorporation or operation should be specified. For example: "ABC, Inc., a Colorado corporation, whose address is . . .", or "EFG Company, a New York Limited Partnership, whose address is . . ."

In addition, when a business entity will be a party to the contract, the signature lines must also be modified. Rather than the form shown on the previous page, use the following format:

ABC, Inc., a Colorado corporation,
BY: _____
Signature of Corporate Officer
(Typewritten Name of Corporate Officer)
(Corporate Officer's title)

EFG Company, a New York Limited Partnership,
BY: _____
Signature of General Partner
(Typewritten Name of General Partner)

127

PERIODICAL CONTRACTS

A contract for the publication of material in a periodical will involve many of the same issues as a book publication contract. However, magazine contracts tend to be far less complex and much briefer. In fact, many are simple letter agreements which briefly outline the terms of the "contract". The main reason for this acceptable brevity in magazine contracts is that the sale of a magazine or journal article is, generally, a cash sale for one-time use and does not involve extensive grants of rights, advances, or royalty schedules.

Traditionally, payment for magazine articles is made either upon acceptance of the article for publication or upon actual publication of the article. Which of these choices is appropriate should be specified in the contract. Additionally, some publishers provide a "kill fee", normally a percentage of the agreed-upon price (often 25%), which is to be paid to an author whose work is initially contracted for, but subsequently dropped from publication for various reasons.

After the amount of payment terms, the "grant of rights" provision of a periodical contract is often the most important to the author. Many magazines purchase all rights to a particular article. However, the purchase of Exclusive First North American Serial Rights (the exclusive right to print, publish, and sell the article for the first time on the North American continent) is often more appropriate. Second serial rights provide the right to publish the material after it has appeared in print elsewhere and the author has retained the right to license further sales. This right is often referred to as "reprint rights".

There are certain other contract specifics which may apply to a magazine contract which are different from considerations which apply to a book contract. There may be a need for the publisher to edit an article to fit space requirements. The material may be of such a timely nature that the author may wish to limit the publisher's time limits for publication to a certain extent. Any requirements should be specifically tailored to the needs of the parties involved.

A Magazine Article Publishing Contract is contained in Appendix D: Sample Desktop Publishing Contracts.

CONSTRUCTING A CONTRACT FOR SPECIFIC PURPOSES

After a careful review of the various publishing contract clauses and a serious consideration of which are appropriate to the specific situation, a contract can be prepared. The mechanics for this are relatively simple. The initial determination of which clauses to include in the contract is the crucial step. The aid of a competent attorney should be sought if the publishing situation is complex or if the publisher feels that such assistance is necessary.

For publishers who feel confident of their grasp of contract law, the steps for constructing a finished contract are as follows:

1. Determine precisely which contract clauses are appropriate to the circumstances.

2. Make a photo-copy of each of the contract clauses which have been selected.

3. Make a careful determination of any additions or alterations to the clauses which are felt to be necessary.

4. Make any required changes in the clauses and insert any necessary information in the spaces provided. (For example: insert the Author's and Publisher's correct name and address; insert the appropriate royalty rate and advance amount, etc.).

5. Number each of the chosen contract clauses consecutively.

6. Refer to the various Publishing Contracts included in Appendix D for assistance in providing the proper format for the contract.

7. Type a completed final version of the entire contract on fresh clean paper and make several photo-copies of the typewritten original contract. Preparation of the original contract on a

word processor or computer will simplify later additions or corrections.

8.   Mail or present the original contract to the Author for negotiation, being fully aware that changes and alterations to the contract are to be expected in the normal course of business.

9.   If agreed upon, sign the contract where indicated and keep an original of the contract in a safe place.

CHAPTER 9

THE LAW OF DEFAMATION
AND LIBEL

The relatively unrestricted freedom to publish in the United States springs from the First Amendment of the U.S. Constitution which provides that Congress shall pass no laws which abridge the freedom of the press. The framers of the Constitution felt very strongly that this particular right, along with freedom of speech and freedom of religion, deserved the exalted position as the First Amendment to the Constitution. Freedom of the press was considered essential to guarding the liberty of the people by providing the citizens of the United States with a free and unrestricted flow of information.

The freedom of the press as protected by the First Amendment, however, has never been absolute in terms of the right to publish anything one chooses. There have always been certain restrictions on the freedom to publish.

One of the most important restrictions on the absolute right to publish whatever one chooses is the potential of being subject to a lawsuit for defamation. Although this potential exerts a definite "chilling effect" on the freedom of the press in the United States, by causing publishers to pre-screen virtually everything that goes into print for possible defamation, it has always been an important aspect of publishing law.

Defamation is the overall description of false statements which tend to damage another's character or reputation in some way. *Libel* is written defamation and can be defined as the written publication of false statements which tend to damage a person's personal or business reputation. *Slander* is the spoken version of defamation, and can be thought of as verbal defamation.

This relatively straightforward definition of the forms of defamation, however, may tend to overshadow the difficulty of actually deciding if a particular instance is *actionable defamation* (damage to one's reputation because of a false statement that is substantial enough to support a lawsuit). The law of defamation, and in particular the law of libel, is extremely complex and in a nearly constant state of change. Virtually every year, the U.S. Supreme Court alters some nuance of the law of libel. The Supreme Court is the final arbiter of libel law in this country, by virtue of applying federal constitutional law to the states. Be advised, however, that each of the 50 states has a slightly different definition for libel and that there is no standardized federal libel law. Fortunately, in all major respects, the definition of libel is very similar for all states. The following discussion approaches libel from a generalized nationwide standpoint.

There are no definitive rules which allow for an easy determination of a libelous statement in every situation. Rather, there are a set of guidelines which must be applied to arrive at a practical decision of whether or not to publish a particular statement. As these guidelines are outlined in the following pages, keep in mind that in situations that appear to be borderline, the aid of a competent lawyer is advisable. Many large publishing companies have erred in decisions about the publication of libelous statements with often disastrous consequences. Small publishers are in no way immune to libel lawsuits and may even be more susceptible than larger firms. With no in-house legal department and no huge assets with which to finance and defend a lawsuit, a small publisher or small company involved in producing business publications can easily be destroyed by a charge of libel.

The vast majority of lawsuits for libel that are filed are not successful. There are several reasons for this. Many such suits are filed as a matter of saving face. Even if the allegedly false and libelous statements are known to be true, a certain amount of dignity may be maintained by filing suit against the defamer. Another reason is that most lawyers and many judges do not fully understand the intricacies of the constitutional protections of the First Amendment. As a result, most libel cases that actually get to trial (very few) and are successful (fewer still) wind up getting overturned on appeal, usually based on an interpretation of federal constitutional law.

The unfortunate result of this state of affairs is that most publishers can win most libel cases only by spending enormous amounts of money on the legal help necessary to successfully defend cases all the way to the appellate and Supreme Court levels. Thus, quite a few libel cases that would not win in court are settled each year based on a determination that the settlement will be less expensive than the legal costs of winning in court. In any legal area, this would be a sad commentary on the state of the legal justice system. In the area of law relating to one of our basic freedoms, it is deplorable.

There is a legitimate concern among publishers about the publication of material which may be libelous. A healthy respect for the potential of being sued for damaging someone's reputation with the publication of a false statement is acceptable. Fear of legal costs involved in defending against frivolous libel lawsuits, however, should not be allowed to lessen the publication of spirited, even controversial, material. As the Supreme Court has noted, for our society to remain strong the forum of ideas must be kept as open and unimpeded as possible. A clear understanding of libel law by publishers will aid in allowing worthy material to reach publication and, thus, enter the marketplace of ideas.

THE ELEMENTS OF LIBEL

By examining the various elements in the definition of libel, it can be determined exactly what is necessary for a person to win a lawsuit for libel. All of the various elements of libel must be proven in order for the lawsuit to be successful. In addition, there must be no legal defenses available to counter a charge of libel. Various defenses to libel will be discussed later.

■ STATEMENT

Initially, it must be determined whether or not the statement in question is capable of conveying a defamatory meaning. Certain statements have, over the years, been held by courts to be defamatory on their face (*libel per se*) and, thus, able to support a lawsuit for libel. These statements are generally as follows:

- An accusation of a criminal act (However, proof of conviction of the crime is a defense.) ;

- An accusation of a contagious disease (For example: syphilis, AIDS, tuberculosis, etc.);

- An accusation of a morally loathsome act ;

- An accusation of deviant sexual behavior or unchastity;

- An accusation of membership in a group which advocates violence in the political spectrum (For example: the Communist Party, the KKK, etc.);

- An accusation of dishonesty in a profession or trade.

The above list are those statements which will automatically be considered defamatory if made about a private individual (see below under "Libel of Public vs. Private Persons"). In addition, libel in the form of one of the above charges will affect the need for the *plaintiff* (the party claiming damage to reputation) to prove actual damage to reputation (see below under "Injury to Reputation").

Of course, many other statements may give rise to a charge of libel if they are such that a reasonable reader would consider the statement as potentially damaging to one's personal or business reputation. Other statements of a defamatory nature must be examined in the context of the entire statement and may have several interpretations. For example, to state that Mr. X is married but is living with Mrs. Y may seem defamatory on its face, but other circumstances may show that it is not. The woman Mr. X may be living with could be his daughter, sister, or mother.

■ FALSITY

In order to support a lawsuit for libel, the statement made must be false. No matter how damaging the statement may be to someone's reputation, the truth of the statement is an absolute defense to a charge of libel (see below under "Defenses to Libel - Truth"). However, truth may not be a defense to legal charges other than libel. (See Chapter 10: "Invasion of Privacy").

■ PUBLICATION

Another element of libel which must be proven is that the statement was published. In this context, *publication* means that the statement was somehow communicated to a third party. If the communication was in writing or by broadcast media, the resulting defamation will be considered libel. If the communication was by way of person-to-person speech, the defamation is slander.

Another important aspect regarding publication is the "single publication" rule. Accepted by most courts, this legal rule allows only one lawsuit for libel to be brought against a particular issuance of a publication, regardless of how many copies of the publication were distributed. Each individual copy of an issue is not considered an individual act of libel. However, be advised that publishers may be sued for libel in any state in which they distribute the libelous material.

■   IDENTIFICATION

In order to support a lawsuit for libel, the person whose reputation has been allegedly damaged must be able to show that they were the specific and identifiable target of the statement. If the person is identified by name, there is usually no problem with this proof. If, however, a general description is used to identify the person, the proof becomes more difficult. It must be shown that a reasonable person would be able to readily identify the target of the statement based on the entire context of the statement.

In fiction, the use of a fictitious name to disguise a real person may still give rise to a lawsuit for libel if reasonable readers will be able to deduce who the real person is. A derogatory character sketch of a real person will not be protected by transparent fictionalization and the mere changing of the character's name if it is reasonably evident who the target is.

Also in fictional works, the use of a fictional name can result in a lawsuit by someone with the same name as the fictional character who may become wrongly identified by the public with the fictional character. This will be true even if the writer or publisher had no intention to defame the person whose reputation is damaged. The test again is that of a reasonable person: "Would a reasonable person believe that the fictional character was intended to be the actual real-life person?".

If a group is libeled, the size of the group and the inclusiveness of all members in the libelous statement will determine if a lawsuit is viable. In general, the larger the group the more difficult it is to show individual damage to the members of the group. A rule of thumb is, that if the group libeled has over one hundred members, no individual may sue. If the libelous statement is only directed toward "some" members of a group, a particular individual member will, generally, not be able to sue. If the group is small enough, however, even a libelous statement that is not all-inclusive may support a lawsuit.

For example, a statement that "all doctors are butchers" would not support a libel suit by any individual doctor. However, a statement that "all doctors at the Smallville Clinic are butchers" would support a libel action by any of the doctors at the Clinic. A statement that "some doctors at the Smallville Clinic are butchers" may or may not be libelous.

A corporation or partnership may sue in its individual name for damage to the business reputation of the entity. This rule applies regardless of how many partners or shareholders there may be.

Finally, it is generally agreed that a dead person cannot be libeled. However, posthumous publication of deceased person's statements which libel a living person can be the subject of a lawsuit.

■ INJURY TO REPUTATION

The person whose reputation is damaged by a libelous statement must generally be able to show just how and to what extent such damage occurred (see below under "Libel of Public vs. Private Persons"). As noted above, however, damage to reputation is generally assumed without need of proof for those forms of libel which are held to be damaging on their face: accusation of a crime, of contagious disease, unchastity, membership in violent political groups, etc. In other cases, the individual must show the actual damage incurred as a result of the libelous statement, be it loss of a job, loss of business, a divorce, etc. However, the courts have been rather lenient in the proof required to satisfy this phase of the elements of libel.

■ DEGREE OF FAULT

Traditionally, it was not necessary to show any fault on the part of the publisher of libelous statements. If the statement was false and defamatory and caused injury to reputation, the publisher was liable, regardless of any facts showing that the statement may have been published innocently or by mistake. Recent rulings by the U.S. Supreme Court have radically altered this aspect of libel law. The degree of fault required to be proven in a libel case now relates directly to who has been libeled.

LIBEL OF PUBLIC VS. PRIVATE PERSONS

Related to the various traditional elements of libel is the relatively recent development in libel law of a distinction between libel of a public official or figure and libel of a private person. This particular aspect of libel law arose in 1964 as a result of a U.S. Supreme Court decision in a case entitled New York Times vs. Sullivan. This court decision fundamentally changed much of libel law in this country by making it far more difficult to prove libel of a public official or figure.

In this landmark case it was held that for a public official to win a libel case, he or she must show convincingly not only that the libelous statement was false, but also that the statement was published with "actual malice". *Actual malice*, in this context, is not "malice" in the usual sense of the word, but rather is defined as actual knowledge of the falsity of the libelous statement or reckless disregard for whether or not the statement is true or false. In other words, publication with "actual malice" is the publication of material that the publisher knew was false or was aware of a high probability of its falsity. Failure to investigate sufficiently or reliance on a single source is not generally considered "actual malice". Deliberate editorial deletions of proof of the falsity may be sufficient to show such "actual malice".

A public official must first prove all of the traditional elements of libel and must then prove "actual malice" on the part of the publisher. The result of this two-fold process of proof for a public official plaintiff is to make it far more difficult for a public official to win a libel suit. The Supreme Court based this decision on the justifiable premise that the primary purpose of the First Amendment protection of freedom of the press was to allow a full, free and robust debate of public issues. The court felt that the threat of libel suits by public officials for criticism of official duties created a situation in which free debate of public issues was stifled.

The New York Times vs. Sullivan case has been followed by many other Supreme Court cases which have consistently set up this further element to the proof of libel: a determination of the status of the person who has been libeled. In order to decide what level of proof will apply to the case, it must be determined initially whether the person libeled is a public official, a public figure, or a private person.

If the person libeled is a public figure or a public official, they must be able to show both the falsity of the statement and "actual malice" on the part of the publisher. Additionally, for a public official or public figure, in no event may damages to reputation be presumed. Actual damages (for example, direct loss of a job, divorce, etc.) must be shown.

On the other hand, if the person libeled is a private person, actual damages to reputation may be shown based on mere proof of the falsity of the statement in question. In the realm of statements defamatory on their face (accusations of crime, unchastity, communicable disease, etc.) damages to reputation may still be presumed without proof for a private person. However, in light of other Supreme Court rulings, a private person must additionally show some degree of fault on the part of the publisher of the libelous statement. The amount of "fault" required depends on individual state law, but may be as little as inattention to detail or negligence in not checking sources more thoroughly.

To make matters even more confusing, recent cases by the Supreme Court have hinted that even for private figures, there may be different levels of proof necessary if the issues involved are matters of public or private concern or if the media or another private person is the defendant.

As is evident, these recent cases have clouded the issues surrounding libel to a great extent. To a small desktop publisher, the main issue raised by all of this is the need to determine the status of the person who may be the subject of a potentially libelous statement.

■   PUBLIC OFFICIALS

As noted, a public official has the greatest difficulty in establishing a case of libel, even if it is clear that the statement published is false.

Additionally, they must show that the publisher knew the statement was false or had very serious doubts as to the truth of the statement and published it anyway. This obviously is a very high standard of proof and was intended as such to encourage open discussion and even free-wheeling criticism of all public officials. The libelous statements which are held to this high level of proof must relate, in some fashion, to the official duties of the public officials. However, a person's qualification for public office includes much of their private life. Discussion of factors which may affect a person's ability to perform official government tasks is generally considered to be within the realm of the protections afforded publishers of libelous statements regarding public officials.

The following parties have been held to be public officials subject to this higher standard of proof for libel:

- Any elected government officials, at either the national, state or local level;

- Any candidates for elected office;

- Law enforcement officials and employees;

- Appointed or employed government officials or employees, provided the person has authority to determine matters of policy and has some access to the press. This last category is the most difficult to define. One way that it has been approached is: "Does abuse of the person's job or office have great potential for social harm?". If it does, the public has an interest in the job-holders qualifications and performance, and the person is considered a "public official". In this group the following have been held to be "public officials": public school teachers and coaches, official court reporters, county officials, public works employees.

■ PUBLIC FIGURES

The Supreme Court has also created two categories of "public figure" libel plaintiffs: "celebrity" public figures and "limited" public figures.

Celebrity public figures are held to the same high level of proof as are public officials. In this context, a *celebrity public figure* is any person who commands such public attention that they are as important as public officials in influencing public opinion or commenting on public issues. These persons are deemed to be public figures for all purposes. They are generally non-government persons with great media exposure. The reasoning for requiring a higher level of proof from this type of public figure is their ability to influence debate and their access to the media to refute falsities. Examples of persons who have been held to be "celebrity public figures" are Johnny Carson and Carol Burnett. Network news anchorpersons, former high public officials, famous actresses or actors, and others with high levels of media exposure would likely be held to be included in this category.

The second category of public figure is the *limited public figure*. These are persons who have voluntarily thrust themselves into the debate surrounding a particular public controversy. To determine if a party is a limited public figure, there must first be a determination that there is a legitimate public controversy and, second, that the person has voluntarily become involved in the debate surrounding the controversy. If it is determined that the person is a limited public figure, then such a person will also be held to the higher "public official" level of proof for those cases of libel concerning the particular controversy. The reasoning is that these people have assumed the risk of public criticism and comment on a particular issue by virtue of voluntarily entering the debate relating to controversial public issues.

Examples of limited public officials are:

- Publishers of political newsletters;

- Authors who seek public attention;

- Political activists;

- People who take public positions on controversial issues.

■ PRIVATE PERSONS

If the person libeled is a private person, individual states are allowed to determine what level of proof is necessary to sustain victory in a libel case. About half of the states have decided that *negligence*, or failure to use reasonable care, is the proper standard by which to judge whether the publisher of a libelous statement should be held accountable. A few other states have held that even private persons must show "actual malice" at the same level as required of public officials. The rest of the states have chosen standards of proof somewhere between those two levels.

However, even "private person" plaintiffs must show "actual malice" to be awarded punitive damages. *Punitive damages* are excess damages which are awarded above and beyond the amount required to compensate the plaintiff for his or her actual loss and are intended to punish the defendant and deter such conduct in the future..

Which persons are included in the "private person" category is determined by virtue of elimination: a private person is anyone who is neither a public official, celebrity public figure, nor limited public figure.

DEFENSES TO LIBEL

There are some very important and powerful defenses which a *defendant* (the person or party against whom a law suit is filed) to a libel suit may use. Some are complete defenses available in every instance, and some are partial defenses available only in certain situations or under specific circumstances. In all cases, the law tends to favor free speech and a free press, while allowing flagrant abuses of these rights to be severely punished.

■ TRUTH

The most important defense to libel is truth. Truth is an absolute defense to libel. The truth of each element of the statement need not necessarily be shown, merely the truth of that part of the statement which gives rise to the damage to the plaintiff's reputation. For example, to state truthfully that a woman had extramarital sex with someone not her husband, but misidentify the man, would not allow the woman to bring suit in libel, although it may allow the misidentified man to bring suit.

From the standpoint of a small publisher, the easiest way to avoid libel suits is to be certain that everything that is published is accurate and truthful. This, however, is not always a simple matter. When dealing with outside authors, outside sources, and even research material, it is sometimes difficult to be 100% certain that a particular statement is truthful.

Couching a statement in less than absolute terms is one method to avoid libel in borderline situations. For example, if a publisher would like to print this statement: "Company X has polluted the river", and is relying on unsubstantiated reports of such pollution, the statement could be tempered to read: "It has been reported that Company X has polluted the river". The truth of the first statement is dependant on actual proof that the river is polluted. The truth of the second statement can be shown by proof that a report claiming pollution of the river by the company exists.

The method to approach potentially libelous statements is to attempt to understand what would be necessary to prove the truth of the facts in the statement. If the statement "X is a bastard" is published, the proof necessary to win a libel lawsuit using the defense of truth would be a birth certificate showing X's father as unknown. With a prior understanding of how a potentially libelous statement may be defended, an informed decision on publication can be made.

■   FAIR COMMENT/OPINION

Statements of opinion are not subject to lawsuits for libel. This is one facet of the First Amendment freedom of speech and the press. To use the words of the U.S. Supreme Court: "Under the First Amendment, there is no such thing as a false idea". It is, however, necessary to understand that only statements that are entirely opinion are so protected. A publisher may publish a book review which states: "Mr. Z's book is the poorest book on this subject that I have ever read". Although this may truly damage Mr. Z's reputation and

143

cause actual damage to the sale of the book, it is not libelous because it is an opinion. However, to publish the following statement would, if unprovable, be libelous: "Mr. Z's book is a brazen copy of Ms. A's book".

The difference between these two statements stems from the difference in the type of materials necessary to prove the "truth" of the statements. Opinions are only capable of subjective proof. Did the book reviewer actually believe that the book was the poorest that he or she had ever read? Factual statements, however, are capable of objective proof. Is Z's book a direct copy of A's book?

How to decide in close situations whether a statement is fact or opinion or both is often difficult. It hinges on several factors: the common meaning of the language, the context, and the verifiability of the statement. In general, matters of personal taste , religious beliefs, moral convictions, aesthetics, political views, and social theories are matters of opinion. For example: calling Judge X "incompetent" would be considered opinion, where as calling Judge Z "corrupt" would be considered libelous.

The facts upon which an opinion is based must be set forth truthfully. A publisher must be careful in not overlapping the underlying facts and the statements of opinions based upon those facts. An example of this might be attempting to state, in the form of an opinion, that a person is guilty of criminal activity. Even though phrased as an opinion, the statement, if untrue, will still be subject to a suit for libel.

Political cartoons and reviews (including criticism of art, literature, drama, etc.) are traditionally held to be purely opinions. Be aware, however, that it is possible to include a false " statement" of fact in either.

■ ABSOLUTE IMMUNITY

Publication of certain items are afforded an absolute immunity from libel suits. This immunity is also termed an "absolute privilege" to publish certain information. The reasoning for this privilege or immunity is that the courts have felt that certain information should be freely available for publication without any fear of post-publication libel suits. This gives publishers an assurance that at least certain information may be freely used without any thought of the risks of liability. Without such an assurance, a certain amount of information useful to the public would not be published. To avoid this loss of dissemination of useful information, an absolute and unrestricted right to publish certain material has been established.

A truthful, verbatim publication of the following material can never be the subject of a lawsuit for libel:

- Statements made during the course of any judicial proceedings (by witnesses, judges, lawyers, or defendants);

- Statements made during legislative proceedings (by legislators or witnesses);

- Statements made by government executives during the discharge of their official duties.

The only restrictions on the use of this absolutely privileged material are that the publication must be accurate, balanced, and fair. Libelous portions of a privileged statement may not be used out of context. The reporting of such statements must be balanced and objective to take advantage of this privilege. In addition, this absolute privilege will be lost if the publication is done with "*malice*" in the usual sense of the word (if the publication was done to willfully harm a person or damage a person's reputation). Note that this legal use of the word "malice" differs substantially from the legal definition of "actual malice".

A similar absolute privilege is available for reports based on official governmental actions or records. This privilege is based on the need for the public to be informed of what the government is doing. Again, to claim this privilege it is necessary to carry a balanced, fair, and objective account of the contents of the record or of the particular government action. Examples of items within this privilege are as follows:

- Reports based on official court, police, or legislative records;

- Reports based on actual official government actions (for example: indictments, arrests, investigations).

A similar privilege exists in many states for fair and accurate reports of any public meeting relating to matters of public concern, even if the group conducting the meeting is a private group.

■ QUALIFIED PRIVILEGE

There is a qualified privilege to respond to a defamatory attack made by another. This "reply" is allowed even if the original speaker is defamed by the reply. The reply must apply to the original attack and not exceed the scope of the attack. For example, if during a political campaign, one candidate calls the other a "dirty Communist", the other candidate may reply, with immunity, that the first is a "filthy liar". The second may not, however, call the first a "deranged killer", since that reply has no bearing on the initial attack. A subsequent publisher of the "filthy liar" statement is protected by the speaker's qualified privilege of reply.

■ NEUTRAL REPORTAGE

This defense is similar to the absolute privilege defense but applies to public charges made about a government official. This relatively new defense stems from the New York Times vs. Sullivan dichotomy of public vs. private persons. Please note that it is not accepted in all states. It offers protection from libel for the publication of any public allegations of official wrongdoing made against any public official relating to matters of public concern or his or her official duties. The privilege remains intact even if it ultimately is shown that the charges were false. The reporting of the charges must, again, be balanced, fair, and objective.

■ SATIRE/FANTASY

It has been held that an item which is satirical in nature or is clearly written as a fantasy can not support a suit for libel. The use of this defense is rather difficult, in that it depends on a subjective determination of the satirical or fantastic nature of the allegedly libelous material.

Similar to the satire exception to libel is the exception for *rhetorical hyperbole*, or obvious extreme exaggeration. This exception stems from the fact that extremely exaggerated statements are not generally interpreted literally.

■ CONSENT

This relatively rare defense normally applies only in a situation where a person who has been previously libeled consents to the republication of the original libel for purposes of rebuttal or counter-attack. Consent for this republication should be obtained in writing.

■ STATUTE OF LIMITATIONS

A final defense available against a charge of libel is the statute of limitations. This law, present in some form in all states, requires that a lawsuit be brought within a certain specified time from the publication of the libel. For libel, the time period is usually one to two years, although some states allow up to four years. The statute of limitation is an absolute defense. If the suit is not filed within the prescribed time, it is automatically disallowed.

REPUBLICATION OF LIBEL

The fact that a libelous statement has been previously published in some other publication and that the publication in question is merely a "republication" is generally not a defense to a charge of libel. However, under recent Supreme Court rulings which require a degree of fault for all libel actions, republication may provide a form of defense. If a publisher acted reasonably (not negligently) in reliance upon a normally reliable source for the material, the second publisher may not be liable for the republication of a libelous statement.

Similarly, distributors, printers, wholesalers, book sellers, and others involved in non-editorial aspects of publishing and who have no control over the content of the matter will not be held accountable

147

for libelous statements. This is true unless they actually know or have good reason to know that the material is libelous.

RETRACTION OF LIBEL

The retraction of a libelous statement does not constitute an actual defense to a charge of libel. Rather, it may mitigate the actual damages and, thus, reduce the money amount of any eventual judgements against a publisher. The majority of states have required that a person libeled must give the publisher notice of the falsity of the statement and demand that a retraction be published before any lawsuit may be filed for libel.

LIBEL INSURANCE

Libel insurance is available. It is in most cases, however, prohibitively expensive and out of the reach of the small desktop publisher. It is known variously as "errors and omissions insurance" or "libel insurance". "Media liability insurance" also can be obtained to cover most legal problems that confront publishers including libel, copyright and trademark infringement, invasion of privacy, etc.

Some major publishers do carry libel insurance and extend the coverage to the writers and authors that they publish. Many that did carry such insurance a few years back have dropped coverage because of escalating premiums. A few have never carried such insurance maintaining that knowledge of libel insurance tends to make writers careless.

There are some very serious problems with libel insurance. First and foremost is the problem of upwardly spiraling premiums. This is due, in part, to the crisis confronting the entire insurance industry. It is also due to the huge potential liability for a seemingly minor misstatement of fact which may be difficult to foresee.

A related problem is the insurance industry trend to continue to raise the minimum amount of deductible for libel insurance. This up-front deductible in libel insurance is similar to an auto insurance deductible. The insurance coverage only kicks in after the deductible amount is reached. Required deductibles for large publishers have soared from $5,000 to $100,000 and even $1,000,000 in some cases.

The actual cost of libel insurance is determined by the potential exposure that a particular publisher may have to lawsuits. A publisher of cookbooks would probably be offered a relatively reasonable premium. However, a cookbook publisher has no real need for such insurance anyway. A publisher of newsletters containing caustic political commentary may have a need for such insurance, but find that the premiums are outrageous.

Traditionally, publishers have carried the expense of defending against libel suits based on material written by individual authors. This is the case even though most publisher/author contracts provide for the author to *indemnify* the publisher (agree that if there is a libel suit, the author will be liable and not the publisher). Although it is the author who is clearly in the best position to determine whether a particular statement is libelous, since he or she is far more intimate with the facts and the research in support of those facts, it is the publisher who is in a much better position to defend against a libel suit. The publisher's and the author's positions regarding both libel insurance and liability for libel should be spelled out carefully in the publisher/author contract. (See Chapter 8: Basic Desktop Publishing Contracts).

EVALUATION OF MATERIAL FOR LIBEL POTENTIAL

The following is an outline of a method for evaluating material regarding its potential for libel:

1. Is the statement in question derogatory? Look at the statement in the worst possible light and using the worst possible connotations. Derogatory statements are not necessarily libelous, but most libelous statements are derogatory.

2. Is the statement an opinion? This depends on a look at the context, the language, and the subjectiveness of the statement.

3.   Is the statement a statement of fact? If so, can the truth of the facts stated be easily proven by reliable sources and have the sources been independently verified?

4.   Is the statement contained in a work of fiction? If so, is the general character description such that a reasonable reader might identify a real person as that character. Or, is the fictional character's name the same or similar to an identifiable real person's name?

5.   If the statement is factual, to whom does the statement apply? Is the target a public official, a celebrity public figure, a limited public figure, or a private person?

6.   Are there any defenses available? Is the publication of the statement absolutely privileged, subject to a qualified privilege, neutral reportage, etc.?

7.   Finally, is the statement fair and accurate?

The decision to publish a particular statement can, in most cases, be made on the basis of a careful review of the tenets of libel law as they relate to the statement in question. However, in certain cases, it may be very difficult to determine if a statement is libelous. In those instances, the wisest course is to consult an attorney with extensive professional experience in the area of defamation law.

CHAPTER 10

INVASION OF PRIVACY

The business of publishing can result in a violation of an individual's right to privacy in a number of ways. Publication of embarrassing facts about a person's private life, distortions of the truth in a publication, and the unauthorized use of a person's name in a commercial publication can all give rise to legal action for invasion of privacy against a desktop publisher.

The constitutional right to privacy is not specifically stated as such in the U.S. Constitution. However, during the twentieth century such a right has developed based on various terminology in the Constitution. Some individual states do not recognize all of the various aspects of the right of privacy. In general, however, the right to privacy is an accepted right, both federally and on a state level.

The single "right of privacy" is actually a collection of four similar rights, all having to do with intrusions into the private lives of individual citizens. All four of these individual rights can confront a publisher in some manner. The four tenets of privacy law are as follows:

- Actual invasion of a person's physical privacy (a physical intrusion upon a person's solitude);

- Publicity or publication of material which places a person in a false light;

- Public disclosure of truthful, but embarrassing private facts;

- The misappropriation of a person's name or likeness for commercial purposes.

INTRUSION UPON PHYSICAL PRIVACY

An actual physical intrusion upon another's solitude or seclusion can result in a lawsuit for invasion of privacy. To be the subject of such a suit, the intrusion must be considered highly offensive to a reasonable person. The violation of this particular privacy right does not arise upon the publication of any material gathered, but rather from the actual physical act of intrusion. The actions of a reporter or researcher who is in the direct employment of a publisher will be attributed to the publisher/employer and the publisher will be held accountable. For publishers, this violation is most likely to arise because of an employee's actions in attempting to gather information directly from a person or place.

There are three separate actions which have been held to be unreasonable intrusions. All three have the similar elements of an offensive intrusion upon the physical domain of another.

■ CONCEALED SURVEILLANCE

This violation arises if a person, generally a reporter, gains access to a private residence or business by trickery and while inside obtains information by hidden camera, hidden recorder, or concealed transmission of conversations. There may not be a violation of this right if the reporter did not use subterfuge to gain the access, even if hidden cameras or hidden microphones are then used. If the actions secretly recorded are a violation of a public official's duties, there will be no valid claim of the violation of a privacy right.

Federal and state statutes also forbid wiretapping in certain instances. Most hold that a person's consent is required before tape-recording a phone conversation.

Avoidance of a violation of this right is straightforward: don't gather information for publication by trickery and hidden or secret recording devices or cameras.

■   TRESPASS

Claims of a violation of this facet of the right of privacy usually come in two forms:

●   An unauthorized taking of documents or material, or;

●   An unauthorized presence on private property.

There is no intrusion, however, if filming, broadcasting, or information gathering takes place from a place open to the public, even if such filming or broadcasting is made of a private person in a private residence.

Again, violations of this type are usually accomplished by overzealous reporters in hot pursuit of information.

■   VIOLATION OF CONSENT

This violation arises when a limited consent is granted to a person, usually a reporter, to be in a certain place and the limits on the consent are overstepped. An example would be the use of a name or photograph from an interview which was granted on the condition of anonymity.

■   BREACH OF CONTRACT

Although not specifically a "right of privacy" issue, a related claim of breach of contract may arise if a promise of confidentiality in an interview is violated and the confidential information obtained or the confidential informant's identity is published. The contract breached would be an implied contract to provide information only if confidentiality is assured.

FALSE LIGHT

This aspect of privacy law can be explained as the negligent or intentional publication of material which places the target in a false light and which is offensive to a reasonable person.

This right is relatively similar to libel and tends to compensate victims of derogatory publications. Similar to libel, more proof of fault is usually required if the person injured is a public figure or a public official.

There are important differences, however, from libel. A false light injury need not be a damage to reputation. It may simply be an embarrassment. Additionally, whereas truth is an absolute defense to a charge of libel, literal truth will not necessarily defeat a charge of using the truthful statement out of context and in a manner which distorts the truth. Finally, in libel law, the attainment of "limited public figure" status and its attendant rise in the level of proof necessary to be successful requires a voluntary entrance into a public controversy. In a "false light" suit, even a person involuntarily thrust into the public limelight will be held to be a public figure and must satisfy the higher "actual malice" test of proof.

A violation of this particular facet of privacy law will usually arise in three situations:

- **DISTORTION OF MATERIAL**

Distortion of material takes place when published material conveys a false impression based on an editorial distortion of the material itself or the context in which the material is presented. Cases under this aspect of privacy law often develop from the use of photographs used in an inaccurate way or from intentional editing of material which alters the actual meaning of the material. The distortion must generally be substantial and offensive. Minor inaccuracies and insignificant mistakes will not be grounds for a lawsuit for distortion of material.

■ FICTIONALIZATION

This arises where published material contains a fictional portrayal of a real person which places the real person in a derogatory false light. Ironically, this claim may arise based on the very attempt to disguise the identity of a real person if the manufactured fictional characteristics of a person are unflattering. If the targets are public officials or public figures, there is generally a higher threshold of proof necessary. Criminals are often the target of fictionalized accounts of their crimes. Most often, they are held to be voluntary public figures and no violation of any privacy right is found.

■ EMBELLISHMENT

Embellishment takes place when additional false information is added to an otherwise true publication and, as a result, a person is placed in a false light. The added false information must be of a substantial nature and, normally, must be embarrassing or objectionable to a reasonable person. Often, a violation of this facet of the right of privacy arises from the attribution of statements to a person which the person did not make.

PUBLIC DISCLOSURE OF PRIVATE FACTS

A violation of this particular facet of the right of privacy occurs upon publication of information regarding the true but private details of another's life, the disclosure of which is both highly offensive and not of public concern.

■ PUBLIC OFFICIALS/PUBLIC INTEREST

There is generally held to be a two-fold constitutional privilege to publish public-interest information which may include the publication of embarrassing private facts:

- The right to publish truthful facts relating to public officials and public figures, or;

- The right to publish truthful information about private individuals which is in the public interest.

A balancing test is generally employed by the courts to determine if the offensiveness of the disclosure of private facts is outweighed by the legitimate public interest in those facts. The disclosure of previous criminal records is often the basis for claims based on this right. Courts have held that the passage of sufficient time precludes the disclosure of past criminal records unless the person's past criminality has a direct relevance to present-day concerns. Note, however, that it is generally agreed that the criminal record of a public official is always available for publication without fear of violation of a privacy right.

■ PUBLIC RECORDS

The method with which the private facts were obtained may also play a factor in how a case is decided. Several key cases in this area have dealt with information published which was obtained from official records. In those cases, it has been held that there is an absolute privilege to publish information obtained from official records which are available to the public, regardless of how embarrassing or offensive the information in those records may be.

If, however, the private facts were obtained from unauthorized or confidential sources, or were obtained fraudulently or by theft, the scales tip in favor of the person whose private facts are disclosed.

MISAPPROPRIATION

Misappropriation occurs when the name or likeness of a person is used without consent for commercial purposes, most generally in an advertising context. This final aspect of the right of privacy differs from the other three previous aspects in one important regard: the injury to the plaintiff. In a misappropriation case the damage is not an embarrassment or an injury to a person's feelings or reputation, but rather an economic injury caused by failure to be compensated for the commercial use of one's name or likeness.

The use of a person's name or likeness is not subject to a suit for misappropriation if the use is related to the subject matter of the publication, is newsworthy and of public interest, and is not simply for commercial purposes. In a very close case, the name of the famous author, Ayn Rand, was referred to in the review of a minor book. The publisher subsequently used an excerpt from the review which contained the famous author's name in promotional material for the minor book. It was held that such use was acceptable since the name had been taken from a review and that, even though used in a commercial manner, a review is of public interest with regard to the book reviewed.

If the use of the name or likeness is related to the editorial content of the publication, courts have generally held that there is no misappropriation. For this reason, Joe Namath, the football player, lost his misappropriation suit against Sports Illustrated Magazine to prevent his cover photo from being used in subsequent Sports Illustrated advertising without compensation.

■ RIGHT OF PUBLICITY

Closely related is a similar right to control the publicity relating to one's name or likeness. This right of "publicity" differs from misappropriation in two respects: the right of publicity can survive a person's death and belong to the person's heirs and the right of publicity is only recognized as a right for persons whose names or faces have achieved a commercial value. The assertions by the Estate of the late Elvis Presley to control all uses of the name and likeness of Elvis are an example of this right.

EVALUATION OF MATERIAL FOR INVASION OF PRIVACY

After wading through the foregoing discussion of the intricacies of privacy law, one can begin to understand the genuine dilemma faced by publishers in certain situations. There is no precise and totally reliable method to gauge the potential for liability for violations of

157

the right of privacy in all instances. A sense of fairness will carry one far in resolving such decisions, but will not always be sufficient. Even courts have great difficulty with cases in this area because of the need to balance the public interest with private rights.

The following guidelines should be used as a framework from which to examine material for potential right of privacy problems.

1.   Would any of the facts in the publication be considered offensive to a reasonable person?

2.   Is the person to whom the facts relate a public official, a public figure (even involuntarily), or a private person?

3.   Are any of the facts in the publication taken out of context or otherwise distorted or embellished?

4.   Is the target of any material in the publication placed in an offensive false light?

5.   Is anyone's name or likeness used in the publication for commercial purposes without consent?

6.   Were any intrusive means used in gathering any of the material for publication?

7.   If a work of fiction, could a reasonable person conclude that any of the fictional characters are fashioned after real people?

8.   Are any embarrassing private facts used in the publication that are not in the public interest?

After a careful review of material for potential problems, if an invasion of privacy complication seems evident and there is a desire to go ahead with the publication of the material, consultation with an attorney skilled in privacy law is recommended.

CHAPTER 11

ADDITIONAL LEGAL CONCERNS FOR DESKTOP PUBLISHERS

There are a number of other legal issues that may confront a desktop publisher on occasion. Most are in the form of further restrictions on publishing because of potential legal liability. Although less frequent than libel and invasion of privacy situations, all of the following may be encountered at some time by a publisher. Each of the following legal issues can have serious ramifications if ignored. An in-depth discussion of each of these topics, however, is beyond the scope of this book. Each issue will be briefly outlined in an effort to alert the publisher to the potential for legal complications. If a proposed publication has aspects which may indicate a violation of any of the following restrictions or if violations by competitors are suspected, consultation with a competent lawyer is advisable.

INTENTIONAL INFLICTION OF EMOTIONAL DISTRESS

This charge may be successfully maintained against a publisher for outrageous and extreme behavior in intentionally publishing material with the desire to inflict emotional distress upon another. Evangelist

Jerry Falwell brought a claim of this nature against sexually-explicit Hustler Magazine for the publication of a personally-offensive parody of an interview with him. In order to be held liable in a suit of this type, a publisher must generally be said to have passed "all bounds of common decency" in the publication of material expressly for the purpose of causing emotional harm to another. This charge may be successful even when, for the same publication, a charge of libel has failed.

DEFECTIVE OR MISLEADING INFORMATION CONTAINED IN BOOKS

There have been legal attempts to find publishers liable for injuries caused to readers of books which may contain false or misleading information. Cookbooks with recipes for inedible foods, science books with defective or dangerous science experiments, and other books with errors or misleading information have been the subject of this type of suit.

Courts have generally found in favor of the publisher on the grounds that a book cannot be a "defective product", since the intended purpose of a book is to be read and the injuries for which compensation has been sought have resulted from actions other than reading the books in question. In at least one case, however, a court found liability. Penalties were imposed for the publication of a faulty government chart detailing airplane instrument landings, the use of which caused an airplane crash.

Similarly, legal actions for negligent misrepresentation based on inaccurate information in published works have seldom, if ever, been successful. A case of this nature might arise where a book contains faulty financial investment information which, if followed, would lead to a monetary loss. Again, courts have been reluctant to hold publishers liable for a reader's use of information contained in books on a theory that the primary purpose of a book is to be read.

DROIT MORALE

Droit Morale is the French legal term given to the "moral rights" of authors. France and other foreign countries have established an elaborate system of author's creative rights which reach far beyond mere ownership of the work. These rights include the right to withdraw one's work from the public view, the author's right to insist on or prevent his or her name from being attached to a work, and the right to prevent distortion or modification of a work which may tend to be prejudicial to the author's reputation or honor.

Droit Morale has not been adopted as such in the laws of the United States, although certain cases involving "unfair competition" have reached similar results. If the issues raised by any of the moral rights of an author are relevant to a particular publishing decision, those rights should be addressed in a publisher/author contract relating to the use of the work in question. See Chapter 8: Desktop Publishing Contracts.

UNFAIR TRADE PRACTICES/UNFAIR COMPETITION

A group of related legal doctrines, known collectively as unfair trade practices, cover a wide variety of business actions which may be considered wrongful or unjust.

Intentional malicious damage to another's business is one facet of this group of doctrines. In a publishing context, this may arise if one publisher publishes a similar item as another publisher and intentionally sells it at a loss in an attempt to drive the other publisher out of business.

Wrongful interference with another's business is another issue which may arise in publishing. The unsubstantiated threat of a copyright infringement suit to prevent a competitor from publishing an author's work would likely be considered a wrongful interference.

Titles may not be copyrighted and are treated by courts as the generic name of a publication. However, if a title has become so closely associated with a particular work that another's use of the same title would confuse the public, it would be considered an unfair trade practice for another to use the title.

Even though ideas may not be copyrighted, wrongful misappropriation of ideas is another possible area of legal liability for the publisher. A publisher is not free to steal substantial, clearly delineated, and original ideas from manuscripts which have been submitted and rejected. Nor is a publisher free to capitalize on a competitor's published research or facts, if the research relates to the rapid publication of newsworthy items and the initial publisher spent a great deal of time and money to obtain the facts first.

A legal claim of unfair competition in a publishing context is generally based on an attempt by one party to cash in on the success of another. The creation of such a similar work that a reasonable person would have difficulty determining the difference, even though there is no infringement of copyright, is one method of unfair competition.

Authors have been successful in using unfair competition suits to prevent their names from being attached to distorted versions of their work, to prevent their names from being attached to a work created by someone else, and to prevent attempts to confuse the public by unfair use of their names or reputations.

TRADE SECRETS

Another legal method by which ideas can be protected is by designation as a trade secret. Any material can potentially be a trade secret. Information may be protected as a trade secret as long as it is not widely known, provides a competitive edge to its holder, and has been the subject of substantial precautions against its disclosure by the one attempting to keep the information secret.

In publishing, trade secret difficulties most often arise when a publisher is confronted with a manuscript disclosing trade secrets which was prepared by an employee of the company which owns the trade secrets. If the employee signed a non-disclosure employment agreement, the employer can prevent the publication. Even without an express contract, if the employer expended substantial efforts to prevent disclosure the courts may find an implied contract not to disclose the information. This may be the case even in situations where the employee was the actual discoverer of the "trade secret".

OBSCENITY

The publication of obscene materials is not protected by the First Amendment of the Constitution. To reach this curious result, the Supreme Court has defined speech and written communications in such a way as to leave obscene materials out of the definition.

Beginning with an understanding that obscenity is not constitutionally protected, the question becomes: What exactly is obscene? The Supreme Court has defined obscenity as follows:

> A particular work is obscene if the average person, applying contemporary community standards, would find that the work, taken as a whole,

- appeals to the prurient interest, <u>and</u>;

- depicts or describes, in a patently offensive way, sexual conduct specifically defined by the applicable state law, <u>and</u>;

- lacks serious literary, artistic, political or scientific value.

What this particular legal definition means in practical terms has been the subject of endless debate and litigation. Essentially, it allows a work to be judged by contemporary standards in a localized area by normal adults. If an average person in a particular area would find the entire publication degrading, thoroughly sexually offensive, and with virtually no other value, the work is obscene and not protected by the Constitution.

Although this definition of obscenity has been abused by some prosecutors in certain areas of the country, as a rule, there is considerable freedom to publish erotic sexually-oriented material, particularly in written form. However, due to the subjective nature of this current legal definition of obscenity, it is quite difficult to predict in advance whether a particular work is obscene. For the publisher who desires to publish erotica, prior consultation with a lawyer is advised.

CENSORSHIP

There have always been attempts to censor books and material that certain members of society find offensive in some way, due to the material's sexual, political, scientific, or moral content. The use of obscenity laws, of course, is one method by which attempts are made to remove the offending material from public sale or distribution. Increasingly, the choice or rejection of textbooks and library books by local school boards has focused attention on the issues of government censorship.

The thrust of court decisions in this area is that local governing bodies do have wide discretion in choosing books for school classrooms and libraries, as long as such discretion is not exercised in an attempt to limit access to particular political, religious, or social ideas. In addition, attempts to remove books which are already in libraries or schools because of the personal tastes or beliefs of the government officials involved have been found to violate the First Amendment.

Outside of the realm of libraries and schools, courts have generally struck down any attempts by local, state, or federal officials to ban books (other than obscene ones) from sale or distribution in a specific geographic area due to on political, scientific, or moral content.

For the desktop publisher, the issue of censorship is likely to arise only if controversial materials are distributed to schools and school libraries.

PRIOR RESTRAINT AND NATIONAL SECURITY

Prior restraint is the governmental prevention of the publication of any material. This was common practice in England in the 18th century. This type of censorship is regarded by the Supreme Court as the most dangerous of all to free speech and a free press since it prevents the material subject to prior restraint from ever reaching the public view. Very few cases have allowed the government to engage in such pre-publication censorship. The government attempted and failed to stop the publication of the stolen Pentagon Papers on the grounds of damage to national security. Publication of the methods for building a hydrogen bomb was also the subject of a failed government attempt at pre-publication censorship. Numerous books by former CIA officials have also been involved in prior restraint cases. Although there have been court decisions which require the prior CIA approval of certain books, these cases have been decided on the grounds of an employer/employee contract of secrecy, and not on First Amendment/national security grounds.

The Supreme Court has not entirely closed the door to possible prior restraints, however. If it can be shown that a publication will cause "direct, immediate, and irreversible harm" to national security, the government could potentially prevent its distribution.

The thread running through all of these peripheral legal restrictions is that the legal limits placed upon publishing in this country are the avoidance of injury or harm to others. As with the exercise of any personal right, the right to publish must be balanced carefully against unwarranted injury to others. The courts have been vigorous in their defense of the right and freedom to publish in this country. In the area of political publications, there is virtually unrestricted freedom. This is in keeping with the original rationale for developing a democratic system of representative government which depends, to a great extent, upon an informed citizenry. The courts have also, however, been willing to punish publishers for the publication of material which has caused sufficient harm to another person. It is this difficult balancing of competing goals which is at the heart of the restrictions and freedoms of publishing.

It is hoped that the information contained in this book will enable those involved in the newest forms of publishing to continue in the tradition of their predecessors in providing a free flow of useful information to the public.

APPENDIX A

LISTING OF COPYRIGHT PUBLICATIONS

The following Circulars are available free of charge from:

The Copyright Office
Publications Section
Library of Congress
Washington, DC 2059

"Best Edition" of Published Copyrighted Works for the Collections of the Library of Congress--Circular 7b

Blank Forms and Other Works Not Protected by Copyright--Circular 32

Cartoons and Comic Strips--Circular 44

Computing and Measuring Devices--Circular 33

The Certification Space on the Application Form--Circular 1e

Copyright Basics--Circular 1

The Copyright Card Catalog and Online Files of the Copyright Office--Circular 23

Copyright Fees--Circular 4

Copyright for Sound Recordings--Circular 56

Copyright Law of the United States of America--Circular 92

Copyright Notice--Circular 3

Copyright Protection Not Available for Names, Titles, or Short Phrases--Circular 34

Copyright Registration for Automated Databases--Circular 65

Copyright Registration for Computer Programs--Circular 61

Copyright Registration for Motion Pictures including Video Recordings--Circular 45

Copyright Registration for Multimedia Works--Circular 55

Copyright Registration for Musical Compositions--Circular 50

Copyright Registration for Musical Compositions and Sound Recordings--Circular 56a

Copyright Registration for Secure Tests--Circular 62

Copyright Registration for Serials on Form SE--Circular 62

Deposit Requirements for Registration of Claims to Copyright in Visual Arts Materials--Circular 40a

Duration of Copyright--Circular 15a

The Effects of Not Replying Within 120 Days to Copyright Office Correspondence--Circular 7c

Extension of Copyright Terms--Circular 15t

Federal Statutory Protection for Mask Works--Circular 100

How to Investigate the Copyright Status of a Work--Circular 22

How to Open and Maintain a Deposit Account in the Copyright Office--Circular 5

Ideas, Methods or Systems--Circular 31

International Copyright Conventions--Circular 38c

International Copyright Relations of the United States--Circular 38a

Limitations on the Information Furnished by the Copyright Office--Circular 1b

Mandatory Deposit of Copies or Phonorecords for the Library of Congress--Circular 7d

Obtaining Copies of Copyright Office Records and Deposits--Circular 6

Publications on Copyright--Circular 2

Recordation of Transfers and Other Documents--Circular 12

Registration of Video Games and Other Machine Readable Audiovisual Works--Circular 49

Renewal of Copyright--Circular 15

Reproduction of Copyrighted Works by Educators and Librarians--Circular 21

Reproduction of Copyrighted Works for Blind and Physically Handicapped Individuals--Circular 63

Selected Bibliographies on Copyright--Circular 2b

Special Postage Rates for Deposit Copies Mailed to the Copyright Office--Circular 30

Supplemental Copyright Registration--Circular 8

Trademarks--Circular 13

Works-Made-For-Hire Under the 1976 Copyright Act--Circular 9

APPENDIX B

COPYRIGHT LEGAL FORMS

NOTE ON THE USE OF FORMS

On the following page are the first of many standard forms which are included in this book. Before use of these forms or any of the other forms included in this book, please note the following:

These forms have been created to cover a generalized set of conditions, which may or may not apply to the specific situation that presents itself. As much as possible, the forms have been written in plain English. If simple changes are necessary to adapt the language used to a particular use (for example: changing the parties involved from singular to plural, or changing the name of a party from an individual to a company name), these forms may be carefully altered. If further terms or paragraphs are necessary to clearly and fully state a particular position or agreement, these too may be cautiously added to the forms. However, if extensive changes are necessary to make the forms correspond to a publisher's specific needs, it is recommended that legal assistance be obtained. For the most part, clear and concise language will satisfy the conditions necessary for a legally binding contract *as long as* certain threshold legal conditions are met and stated in the contract. These basic and necessary legal conditions are detailed in Chapter 8, "Desktop Publishing Contracts".

In using any of the forms contained in this book, it is advisable to make a copy of the form, fill in the information in the spaces provided, and then retype the entire form onto a fresh, clean sheet of paper.

ASSIGNMENT AND TRANSFER OF COPYRIGHT

THIS ASSIGNMENT AND TRANSFER OF COPYRIGHT is made on _____ , 19 _____ , by (Full name of Owner of copyright _____), Owner, residing at (Address of Owner of copyright _____), to (Full name of Purchaser of copyright _____), Purchaser, residing at (Address of Purchaser _____).

The Owner is the sole owner of the full and exclusive copyright of a Work titled (Full title of copyrighted work _____), described as (Description of copyrighted work _____), a copy of which is attached and is considered a part of this document. The Purchaser desires to buy the entire interest of the Owner in the Work.

In consideration of $ (Full amount paid for the work _____), for which the Owner acknowledges receipt, the Owner assigns and transfers to the Purchaser and the Purchaser's heirs, assigns, and representatives, all of the Owner's rights and interest in the Work and its copyright throughout the world, including the right to any renewals or extensions of the copyright.

The Owner has signed this document on the date stated above.

_____
Signature of Owner of copyright
(Typewritten name of Owner of copyright)

State (or Commonwealth) of _____}
County (or Parish) of _____}

On _____, 19 _____, before me, a Notary Public, (Full name of Owner_____) signed the above document as a free act.

_____
Signature of Notary Public
(Typewritten name of Notary Public)
(Place of Notary registration and date of commission)

WORK-FOR-HIRE AGREEMENT

THIS WORK-FOR-HIRE AGREEMENT is made on _____, 19
_____, by (Full name of Owner _____), Owner, residing at
(Address of Owner _____), and (Full name of Creator
_____), Creator, residing at (Address of Creator
_____).

The Creator agrees to individually create the following Work for
the Owner, as a commissioned work-for-hire: (Full description of
the work commissioned _____), with the full understanding
that the entire Work and its full copyright will be owned by the
Employer.

The Employer agrees to pay the Creator $ (Full Amount to be
paid for the Work _____) for the Work and intends that the
work created be used in a collective work.

The Owner and Creator have signed this document on the date
stated above.

_____
Signature of Owner
(Typewritten name of Owner)

_____
Signature of Creator
Typewritten name of Creator

State (or Commonwealth) of _____}
County (or Parish) of _____}

On _____, 19 _____, before me, a Notary Public, (Full name
of Owner _____) and (Full name of Creator _____)
signed the above document as their free act.

_____
Signature of Notary Public
(Typewritten name of Notary Public)
(Place of Notary registration and date of commission)

174

AGREEMENT FOR EMPLOYEE TO BE COPYRIGHT OWNER

THIS AGREEMENT is made on _____, 19 _____, by (Full name of _____), Employer, residing at (Address of Owner _____), and (Full name of Employee _____), Employee, residing at (Address of Employee _____).

Employee, while employed by Employer, and while working within the scope of that employment, created an original Work, titled (Full title of Employee's work _____), described as (Full description of Employee's work _____), a copy of which is attached and is considered a part of this agreement.

For consideration, Employer agrees that Employee shall, for all purposes, be the owner of all rights, including the exclusive copyright, in the Work.

The Employer and the Employee have signed this document on the date stated above.

_____
Signature of Employer
(Typewritten name of Employer)

_____
Signature of Employee
Typewritten name of Employee

State (or Commonwealth) of _____}
County (or Parish) of _____}

On _____, 19 _____, before me, a Notary Public, (Full name of Employer _____) and (Full name of Employee _____) signed the above document as their free act.

_____
Signature of Notary Public
(Typewritten name of Notary Public)
(Place of Notary registration and date of commission)

REQUEST FOR PERMISSION

Permission is granted to: (Name of publisher seeking permission _____) for non-exclusive world rights in all languages for use of the following material in (Book or Magazine title _____) and any subsidiary use, promotional use, future revisions, and future editions of the same :

From: (Title of Book, Magazine and article, or other _____)

By: (Name of Author _____)

Material: From Page _____, Line _____, through Page _____, Line _____, beginning with the words "_____" and ending with the words "_____" , and consisting of a total of _____ words.

The following credit line and copyright notice must accompany the use of this material:

(Indicate credit line and copyright notice [for example: "Used by permission of Jane Doe, © Copyright Jane Doe 1989"] _____)

Permission is granted on _____, 19____.

_____
Signature of Owner of copyright
(Typewritten name of Owner of copyright)
(Address of Owner of Copyright)

PHOTOGRAPHIC PERMISSION

Permission is granted to: (Name of publisher seeking permission _____) for non-exclusive world rights to the following photograph[s] for use in (Book or Magazine title _____) and for subsidiary use, promotional use, future revisions and future editions of the same:

From: (Title of Book, Magazine and article, or other _____)

By: (Name of photographer _____)

Material: From Page[s] _____, described as _____ and consisting of a total of _____ photographs.

The following credit line and copyright notice must accompany the use of this material:

(Indicate credit line and copyright notice [for example: "Used by permission of Jane Doe, © Copyright Jane Doe 1989"] _____)

Permission is granted on _____, 19_____.

_____
Signature of Owner of copyright
(Typewritten name of Owner of copyright)
(Address of Owner of Copyright)

MODEL RELEASE

For consideration, permission is granted to: (Name of publisher seeking permission _____) for exclusive world rights, including copyright, and use of any photographs containing my image for use in (Book or Magazine title _____) and for subsidiary use, promotional use, future revisions and future editions of the same.

I waive any right to inspect or approve final use of such photographs and I waive any right to file any legal actions, including libel or invasion of privacy, based on any use of the photographs under this release.

I am over 21 and understand the content of this document.

Permission is granted on _____, 19_____.

_____
Signature of Model
(Typewritten name of Model)
(Address of Model)

APPENDIX C

COPYRIGHT REGISTRATION FORMS

NOTE ON THE USE OF COPYRIGHT REGISTRATION FORMS

On the following pages various Copyright Office Registration forms and their accompanying instructions are reproduced. These forms are for illustrative purposes only and are not intended to be used for actual submission to the Copyright Office. The Copyright Office will only accept original official Registration Application forms.

To order copies of any forms for submission, contact:

Copyright Office
Information and Publications Section
Library of Congress
Washington, DC 20559

Filling Out Application Form TX

Detach and read these instructions before completing this form. Make sure all applicable spaces have been filled in before you return this form.

BASIC INFORMATION

When to Use This Form: Use Form TX for registration of published or unpublished non-dramatic literary works, excluding periodicals or serial issues. This class includes a wide variety of works: fiction, non-fiction, poetry, textbooks, reference works, directories, catalogs, advertising copy, compilations of information, and computer programs. For periodicals and serials, use Form SE.

Deposit to Accompany Application: An application for copyright registration must be accompanied by a deposit consisting of copies or phonorecords representing the entire work for which registration is to be made. The following are the general deposit requirements as set forth in the statute:

Unpublished Work: Deposit one complete copy (or phonorecord).

Published Work: Deposit two complete copies (or phonorecords) of the best edition.

Work First Published Outside the United States: Deposit one complete copy (or phonorecord) of the first foreign edition.

Contribution to a Collective Work: Deposit one complete copy (or phonorecord) of the best edition of the collective work.

The Copyright Notice: For published works, the law provides that a copyright notice in a specified form "shall be placed on all publicly distributed copies from which the work can be visually perceived." Use of the copyright notice is the responsibility of the copyright owner and does not require advance permission from the Copyright Office. The required form of the notice for copies generally consists of three elements: (1) the symbol "©", or the word "Copyright," or the abbreviation "Copr."; (2) the year of first publication; and (3) the name of the owner of copyright. For example: "© 1981 Constance Porter." The notice is to be affixed to the copies "in such manner and location as to give reasonable notice of the claim of copyright."

For further information about copyright registration, notice, or special questions relating to copyright problems, write:

Information and Publications Section, LM-455
Copyright Office
Library of Congress
Washington, D.C. 20559

LINE-BY-LINE INSTRUCTIONS

1 SPACE 1: Title

Title of This Work: Every work submitted for copyright registration must be given a title to identify that particular work. If the copies or phonorecords of the work bear a title (or an identifying phrase that could serve as a title), transcribe that wording *completely* and *exactly* on the application. Indexing of the registration and future identification of the work will depend on the information you give here.

Previous or Alternative Titles: Complete this space if there are any additional titles for the work under which someone searching for the registration might be likely to look, or under which a document pertaining to the work might be recorded.

Publication as a Contribution: If the work being registered is a contribution to a periodical, serial, or collection, give the title of the contribution in the "Title of this Work" space. Then, in the line headed "Publication as a Contribution," give information about the collective work in which the contribution appeared.

2 SPACE 2: Author(s)

General Instructions: After reading these instructions, decide who are the "authors" of this work for copyright purposes. Then, unless the work is a "collective work," give the requested information about every "author" who contributed any appreciable amount of copyrightable matter to this version of the work. If you need further space, request additional Continuation sheets. In the case of a collective work, such as an anthology, collection of essays, or encyclopedia, give information about the author of the collective work as a whole.

Name of Author: The fullest form of the author's name should be given. Unless the work was "made for hire," the individual who actually created the work is its "author." In the case of a work made for hire, the statute provides that "the employer or other person for whom the work was prepared is considered the author."

What is a "Work Made for Hire"? A "work made for hire" is defined as: (1) "a work prepared by an employee within the scope of his or her employment"; or (2) "a work specially ordered or commissioned for use as a contribution to a collective work, as a part of a motion picture or other audiovisual work, as a translation, as a supplementary work, as a compilation, as an instructional text, as a test, as answer material for a test, or as an atlas, if the parties expressly agree in a written instrument signed by them that the work shall be considered a work made for hire." If you have checked "Yes" to indicate that the work was "made for hire," you must give the full legal name of the employer (or other person for whom the work was prepared). You may also include the name of the employee along with the name of the employer (for example: "Elster Publishing Co., employer for hire of John Ferguson").

"Anonymous" or "Pseudonymous" Work: An author's contribution to a work is "anonymous" if that author is not identified on the copies or phonorecords of the work. An author's contribution to a work is "pseudonymous" if that author is identified on the copies or phonorecords under a fictitious name. If the work is "anonymous" you may: (1) leave the line blank; or (2) state " anonymous" on the line; or (3) reveal the author's identity. If the work is "pseudonymous" you may: (1) leave the line blank; or (2) give the pseudonym and identify it as such (for example: "Huntley Haverstock, pseudonym"); or (3) reveal the author's name, making clear which is the real name and which is the pseudonym (for example: "Judith Barton, whose pseudonym is Madeline Elster"). However, the citizenship or domicile of the author **must** be given in all cases.

Dates of Birth and Death: If the author is dead, the statute requires that the year of death be included in the application unless the work is anonymous or pseudonymous. The author's birth date is optional, but is useful as a form of identification. Leave this space blank if the author's contribution was a "work made for hire."

Author's Nationality or Domicile: Give the country of which the author is a citizen, or the country in which the author is domiciled. Nationality or domicile **must** be given in all cases.

Nature of Authorship: After the words "Nature of Authorship" give a brief general statement of the nature of this particular author's contribution to the work. Examples: "Entire text"; "Coauthor of entire text"; "Chapters 11-14"; "Editorial revisions"; "Compilation and English translation"; "New text."

3 SPACE 3: Creation and Publication

General Instructions: Do not confuse "creation" with "publication." Every application for copyright registration must state "the year in which creation of the work was completed." Give the date and nation of first publication only if the work has been published.

Creation: Under the statute, a work is "created" when it is fixed in a copy or phonorecord for the first time. Where a work has been prepared over a period of time, the part of the work existing in fixed form on a particular date constitutes the created work on that date. The date you give here should be the year in which the author completed the particular version for which registration is now being sought, even if other versions exist or if further changes or additions are planned.

Publication: The statute defines "publication" as "the distribution of copies or phonorecords of a work to the public by sale or other transfer of ownership, or by rental, lease, or lending"; a work is also "published" if there has been an "offering to distribute copies or phonorecords to a group of persons for purposes of further distribution, public performance, or public display." Give the full date (month, day, year) when, and the country where, publication first occurred. If first publication took place simultaneously in the United States and other countries, it is sufficient to state "U.S.A."

4 SPACE 4: Claimant(s)

Name(s) and Address(es) of Copyright Claimant(s): Give the name(s) and address(es) of the copyright claimant(s) in this work even if the claimant is the same as the author. Copyright in a work belongs initially to the author of the work (including, in the case of a work made for hire, the employer or other person for whom the work was prepared). The copyright claimant is either the author of the work or a person or organization to whom the copyright initially belonging to the author has been transferred.

Transfer: The statute provides that, if the copyright claimant is not the author, the application for registration must contain "a brief statement of how the claimant obtained ownership of the copyright." If any copyright claimant named in space 4 is not an author named in space 2, give a brief, general statement summarizing the means by which that claimant obtained ownership of the copyright. Examples: "By written contract"; "Transfer of all rights by author"; "Assignment"; "By will." Do not attach transfer documents or other attachments or riders.

5 SPACE 5: Previous Registration

General Instructions: The questions in space 5 are intended to find out whether an earlier registration has been made for this work and, if so, whether there is any basis for a new registration. As a general rule, only one basic copyright registration can be made for the same version of a particular work.

Same Version: If this version is substantially the same as the work covered by a previous registration, a second registration is not generally possible unless: (1) the work has been registered in unpublished form and a second registration is now being sought to cover this first published edition; or (2) someone other than the author is identified as copyright claimant in the earlier registration, and the author is now seeking registration in his or her own name. If either of these two exceptions apply, check the appropriate box and give the earlier registration number and date. Otherwise, do not submit Form TX; instead, write the Copyright Office for information about supplementary registration or recordation of transfers of copyright ownership.

Changed Version: If the work has been changed, and you are now seeking registration to cover the additions or revisions, check the last box in space 5, give the earlier registration number and date, and complete both parts of space 6 in accordance with the instructions below.

Previous Registration Number and Date: If more than one previous registration has been made for the work, give the number and date of the latest registration.

6 SPACE 6: Derivative Work or Compilation

General Instructions: Complete space 6 if this work is a "changed version," "compilation," or "derivative work," and if it incorporates one or more earlier works that have already been published or registered for copyright, or that have fallen into the public domain. A "compilation" is defined as "a work formed by the collection and assembling of preexisting materials or of data that are selected, coordinated, or arranged in such a way that the resulting work as a whole constitutes an original work of authorship." A "derivative work" is "a work based on one or more preexisting works." Examples of derivative works include translations, fictionalizations, abridgments, condensations, or "any other form in which a work may be recast, transformed, or adapted." Derivative works also include works "consisting of editorial revisions, annotations, or other modifications" if these changes, as a whole, represent an original work of authorship.

Preexisting Material (space 6a): For derivative works, complete this space and space 6b. In space 6a identify the preexisting work that has been recast, transformed, or adapted. An example of preexisting material might be: "Russian version of Goncharov's 'Oblomov'." Do not complete space 6a for compilations.

Material Added to This Work (space 6b): Give a brief, general statement of the new material covered by the copyright claim for which registration is sought. **Derivative work** examples include: "Foreword, editing, critical annotations"; "Translation"; "Chapters 11-17." If the work is a **compilation**, describe both the compilation itself and the material that has been compiled. Example: "Compilation of certain 1917 Speeches by Woodrow Wilson." A work may be both a derivative work and compilation, in which case a sample statement might be: "Compilation and additional new material."

7 SPACE 7: Manufacturing Provisions

General Instructions: The copyright statute currently provides, as a general rule, that the copies of a published work "consisting preponderantly of nondramatic literary material in the English language" be manufactured in the United States or Canada in order to be lawfully imported and publicly distributed in the United States. If the work being registered is unpublished or not in English, leave this space blank. Complete this space if registration is sought for a published work "consisting preponderantly of nondramatic literary material that is in the English language." Identify those who manufactured the copies and where those manufacturing processes were performed. As an exception to the manufacturing provisions, the statute prescribes that, where manufacture has taken place outside the United States or Canada, a maximum of 2000 copies of the foreign edition may be imported into the United States without affecting the copyright owners' rights. For this purpose, the Copyright Office will issue an Import Statement upon request and payment of a fee of $3 at the time of registration or at any later time. For further information about import statements, write for Form IS.

8 SPACE 8: Reproduction for Use of Blind or Physically Handicapped Individuals

General Instructions: One of the major programs of the Library of Congress is to provide Braille editions and special recordings of works for the exclusive use of the blind and physically handicapped. In an effort to simplify and speed up the copyright licensing procedures that are a necessary part of this program, section 710 of the copyright statute provides for the establishment of a voluntary licensing system to be tied in with copyright registration. Copyright Office regulations provide that you may grant a license for such reproduction and distribution solely for the use of persons who are certified by competent authority as unable to read normal printed material as a result of physical limitations. The license is entirely voluntary, nonexclusive, and may be terminated upon 90 days notice.

How to Grant the License: If you wish to grant it, check one of the three boxes in space 8. Your check in one of these boxes, together with your signature in space 10, will mean that the Library of Congress can proceed to reproduce and distribute under the license without further paperwork. For further information, write for Circular R63.

9,10,11 SPACE 9, 10, 11: Fee, Correspondence, Certification, Return Address

Deposit Account: If you maintain a Deposit Account in the Copyright Office, identify it in space 9. Otherwise leave the space blank and send the fee of $10 with your application and deposit.

Correspondence (space 9): This space should contain the name, address, area code, and telephone number of the person to be consulted if correspondence about this application becomes necessary.

Certification (space 10): The application can not be accepted unless it bears the date and the **handwritten signature** of the author or other copyright claimant, or of the owner of exclusive right(s), or of the duly authorized agent of author, claimant, or owner of exclusive right(s).

Address for Return of Certificate (space 11): The address box must be completed legibly since the certificate will be returned in a window envelope.

FORM TX
UNITED STATES COPYRIGHT OFFICE

REGISTRATION NUMBER

_____

TX _____ TXU

EFFECTIVE DATE OF REGISTRATION

_____ _____ _____
Month   Day   Year

DO NOT WRITE ABOVE THIS LINE. IF YOU NEED MORE SPACE, USE A SEPARATE CONTINUATION SHEET.

1

TITLE OF THIS WORK ▼

PREVIOUS OR ALTERNATIVE TITLES ▼

PUBLICATION AS A CONTRIBUTION If this work was published as a contribution to a periodical, serial, or collection, give information about the collective work in which the contribution appeared. **Title of Collective Work ▼**

If published in a periodical or serial give: Volume ▼   Number ▼   Issue Date ▼   On Pages ▼

2

a

NAME OF AUTHOR ▼

DATES OF BIRTH AND DEATH
Year Born ▼   Year Died ▼

Was this contribution to the work a "work made for hire"?
☐ Yes
☐ No

AUTHOR'S NATIONALITY OR DOMICILE
Name of Country
OR { Citizen of ▶
{ Domiciled in ▶

WAS THIS AUTHOR'S CONTRIBUTION TO THE WORK
Anonymous?   ☐ Yes ☐ No
Pseudonymous?   ☐ Yes ☐ No
If the answer to either of these questions is "Yes," see detailed instructions.

NATURE OF AUTHORSHIP Briefly describe nature of the material created by this author in which copyright is claimed. ▼

NOTE

Under the law, the "author" of a "work made for hire" is generally the employer, not the employee (see instructions). For any part of this work that was "made for hire" check "Yes" in the space provided, give the employer (or other person for whom the work was prepared) as "Author" of that part, and leave the space for dates of birth and death blank.

b

NAME OF AUTHOR ▼

DATES OF BIRTH AND DEATH
Year Born ▼   Year Died ▼

Was this contribution to the work a "work made for hire"?
☐ Yes
☐ No

AUTHOR'S NATIONALITY OR DOMICILE
Name of country
OR { Citizen of ▶
{ Domiciled in ▶

WAS THIS AUTHOR'S CONTRIBUTION TO THE WORK
Anonymous?   ☐ Yes ☐ No
Pseudonymous?   ☐ Yes ☐ No
If the answer to either of these questions is "Yes," see detailed instructions.

NATURE OF AUTHORSHIP Briefly describe nature of the material created by this author in which copyright is claimed. ▼

c

NAME OF AUTHOR ▼

DATES OF BIRTH AND DEATH
Year Born ▼   Year Died ▼

Was this contribution to the work a "work made for hire"?
☐ Yes
☐ No

AUTHOR'S NATIONALITY OR DOMICILE
Name of Country
OR { Citizen of ▶
{ Domiciled in ▶

WAS THIS AUTHOR'S CONTRIBUTION TO THE WORK
Anonymous?   ☐ Yes ☐ No
Pseudonymous?   ☐ Yes ☐ No
If the answer to either of these questions is "Yes," see detailed instructions.

NATURE OF AUTHORSHIP Briefly describe nature of the material created by this author in which copyright is claimed. ▼

3

YEAR IN WHICH CREATION OF THIS WORK WAS COMPLETED This information must be given in all cases.
◀ Year

DATE AND NATION OF FIRST PUBLICATION OF THIS PARTICULAR WORK Complete this information ONLY if this work has been published.
Month ▶ _____ Day ▶ _____ Year ▶ _____ ◀ Nation

4

COPYRIGHT CLAIMANT(S) Name and address must be given even if the claimant is the same as the author given in space 2.▼

See instructions before completing this space.

TRANSFER If the claimant(s) named here in space 4 are different from the author(s) named in space 2, give a brief statement of how the claimant(s) obtained ownership of the copyright.▼

APPLICATION RECEIVED

ONE DEPOSIT RECEIVED

TWO DEPOSITS RECEIVED

REMITTANCE NUMBER AND DATE

DO NOT WRITE HERE
OFFICE USE ONLY

MORE ON BACK ▶ • Complete all applicable spaces (numbers 5-11) on the reverse side of this page.
• See detailed instructions.   • Sign the form at line 10.

DO NOT WRITE HERE

Page 1 of _____ pages

EXAMINED BY	FORM TX
CHECKED BY	

| ☐ CORRESPONDENCE
Yes | FOR
COPYRIGHT
OFFICE |
| ☐ DEPOSIT ACCOUNT
☐ FUNDS USED | USE
ONLY |

DO NOT WRITE ABOVE THIS LINE. IF YOU NEED MORE SPACE, USE A SEPARATE CONTINUATION SHEET.

PREVIOUS REGISTRATION Has registration for this work, or for an earlier version of this work, already been made in the Copyright Office?

☐ Yes ☐ No If your answer is "Yes," why is another registration being sought? (Check appropriate box) ▼

☐ This is the first published edition of a work previously registered in unpublished form.

☐ This is the first application submitted by this author as copyright claimant.

☐ This is a changed version of the work, as shown by space 6 on this application.

If your answer is "Yes," give: **Previous Registration Number** ▼   **Year of Registration** ▼

5

DERIVATIVE WORK OR COMPILATION Complete both space 6a & 6b for a derivative work; complete only 6b for a compilation.

a. Preexisting Material Identify any preexisting work or works that this work is based on or incorporates. ▼

b. Material Added to This Work Give a brief, general statement of the material that has been added to this work and in which copyright is claimed. ▼

See instructions
before completing
this space.

6

MANUFACTURERS AND LOCATIONS If this is a published work consisting preponderantly of nondramatic literary material in English, the law may require that the copies be manufactured in the United States or Canada for full protection. If so, the names of the manufacturers who performed certain processes, and the places where these processes were performed must be given. See instructions for details.

Names of Manufacturers ▼   **Places of Manufacture** ▼

7

REPRODUCTION FOR USE OF BLIND OR PHYSICALLY HANDICAPPED INDIVIDUALS A signature on this form at space 10, and a check in one of the boxes here in space 8, constitutes a non-exclusive grant of permission to the Library of Congress to reproduce and distribute solely for the blind and physically handicapped and under the conditions and limitations prescribed by the regulations of the Copyright Office: (1) copies of the work identified in space 1 of this application in Braille (or similar tactile symbols); or (2) phonorecords embodying a fixation of a reading of that work; or (3) both.

a ☐ Copies and Phonorecords   b ☐ Copies Only   c ☐ Phonorecords Only

See instructions.

8

DEPOSIT ACCOUNT If the registration fee is to be charged to a Deposit Account established in the Copyright Office, give name and number of Account.

Name ▼   **Account Number** ▼

9

CORRESPONDENCE Give name and address to which correspondence about this application should be sent. Name/Address/Apt/City/State/Zip ▼

Area Code & Telephone Number ▶

Be sure to
give your
daytime phone
◀ number

CERTIFICATION* I, the undersigned, hereby certify that I am the

Check one ▶

☐ author
☐ other copyright claimant
☐ owner of exclusive right(s)
☐ authorized agent of _____

Name of author or other copyright claimant, or owner of exclusive right(s) ▲

of the work identified in this application and that the statements made by me in this application are correct to the best of my knowledge.

Typed or printed name and date ▼ If this is a published work, this date must be the same as or later than the date of publication given in space 3.

_____ date ▶ _____

👉 Handwritten signature (X) ▼

10

MAIL CERTIFICATE TO

Name ▼

Number/Street/Apartment Number ▼

City/State/ZIP ▼

Certificate will be mailed in window envelope

Have you:
• Completed all necessary spaces?
• Signed your application in space 10?
• Enclosed check or money order for $10 payable to *Register of Copyrights*?
• Enclosed your deposit material with the application and fee?

MAIL TO: Register of Copyrights, Library of Congress, Washington, D.C. 20559.

11

* 17 U.S.C. § 506(e): Any person who knowingly makes a false representation of a material fact in the application for copyright registration provided for by section 409, or in any written statement filed in connection with the application, shall be fined not more than $2,500.

U.S. GOVERNMENT PRINTING OFFICE: 1987-181—531-60.006

August 1987—100,000

Filling Out Application Form SE

Detach and read these instructions before completing this form. Make sure all applicable spaces have been filled in before you return this form.

BASIC INFORMATION

When To Use This Form: Use a separate Form SE for registration of each individual issue of a serial, Class SE. A serial is defined as a work issued or intended to be issued in successive parts bearing numerical or chronological designations and intended to be continued indefinitely. This class includes a variety of works: periodicals; newspapers; annuals; the journals, proceedings, transactions, etc., of societies. Do not use Form SE to register an individual contribution to a serial. Request Form TX for such contributions.

Deposit to Accompany Application: An application for copyright registration must be accompanied by a deposit consisting of copies or phonorecords representing the entire work for which registration is to be made. The following are the general deposit requirements as set forth in the statute:

Unpublished Work: Deposit one complete copy (or phonorecord).

Published Work: Deposit two complete copies (or phonorecords) of the best edition.

Work First Published Outside the United States: Deposit one complete copy (or phonorecord) of the first foreign edition.

Mailing Requirements: It is important that you send the application, the deposit copy or copies, and the $10 fee together in the same envelope or package. The Copyright Office cannot process them unless they are received together. Send to: *Register of Copyrights, Library of Congress, Washington, D.C. 20559.*

The Copyright Notice: For published works, the law provides that a copyright notice in a specified form "shall be placed on all publicly distributed copies from which the work can be visually perceived." Use of the copyright notice is the responsibility of the copyright owner and does not require advance permission from the Copyright Office. The required form of the notice for copies generally consists of three elements: (1) the symbol "©", or the word "Copyright," or the abbreviation "Copr."; (2) the year of first publication; and (3) the name of the owner of copyright. For example: "© 1981 National News Publishers, Inc." The notice is to be affixed to the copies "in such manner and location as to give reasonable notice of the claim of copyright." For further information about copyright registration, notice, or special questions relating to copyright problems, write:

Information and Publications Section, LM-455
Copyright Office, Library of Congress, Washington, D.C. 20559

PRIVACY ACT ADVISORY STATEMENT Required by the Privacy Act of 1974 (P.L. 93-579)
The authority for requesting this information is title 17, U.S.C., secs. 409 and 410. Furnishing the requested information is voluntary. But if the information is not furnished, it may be necessary to delay or refuse registration and you may not be entitled to certain relief, remedies, and benefits provided in chapters 4 and 5 of title 17, U.S.C.
The principal uses of the requested information are the establishment and maintenance of a public record and the examination of the application for compliance with legal requirements.
Other routine uses include public inspection and copying, preparation of public indexes, preparation of public catalogs of copyright registrations, and preparation of search reports upon request.
NOTE: No other advisory statement will be given in connection with this application. Please keep this statement and refer to it if we communicate with you regarding this application.

LINE-BY-LINE INSTRUCTIONS

1 SPACE 1: Title

Title of This Serial: Every work submitted for copyright registration must be given a title to identify that particular work. If the copies or phonorecords of the work bear a title (or an identifying phrase that could serve as a title), copy that wording *completely* and *exactly* on the application. Give the volume and number of the periodical issue for which you are seeking registration. The "Date on copies" in space 1 should be the date appearing on the actual copies (for example: "June 1981," "Winter 1981"). Indexing of the registration and future identification of the work will depend on the information you give here.

Previous or Alternative Titles: Complete this space only if there are any additional titles for the serial under which someone searching for the registration might be likely to look, or under which a document pertaining to the work might be recorded.

2 SPACE 2: Author(s)

General Instructions: After reading these instructions, decide who are the "authors" of this work for copyright purposes. In the case of a serial issue, the organization which directs the creation of the serial issue as a whole is generally considered the author of the "collective work" (see "Nature of Authorship") whether it employs a staff or uses the efforts of volunteers. Where, however, an individual is independently responsible for the serial issue, name that person as author of the "collective work."

Name of Author: The fullest form of the author's name should be given. In the case of a "work made for hire," the statute provides that "the employer or other person for whom the work was prepared is considered the author." If this issue is a "work made for hire," the author's name will be the full legal name of the hiring organization, corporation, or individual. The title of the periodical should not ordinarily be listed as "author" because the title itself does not usually correspond to a legal entity capable of authorship. When an individual creates an issue of a serial independently and not as an "employee" of an organization or corporation, that individual should be listed as the "author."

Author's Nationality or Domicile: Give the country of which the author is a citizen, or the country in which the author is domiciled. Nationality or domicile **must** be given in all cases. The citizenship of an organization formed under United States Federal or state law should be stated as "U.S.A."

What is a "Work Made for Hire"? A "work made for hire" is defined as: (1) "a work prepared by an employee within the scope of his or her employment"; or (2) "a work specially ordered or commissioned for use as a contribution to a collective work, as a part of a motion picture or other audiovisual work, as a translation, as a supplementary work, as a compilation, as an instructional text, as a test, as answer material for a test, or as an atlas, if the parties expressly agree in a written instrument signed by them that the work shall be considered a work made for hire." An organization that uses the efforts of volunteers in the creation of a "collective work" (see "Nature of Authorship") may also be considered the author of a "work made for hire" even though those volunteers were not specifically paid by the organization. In the case of a "work made for hire," give the full legal name of the employer and check "Yes" to indicate that the work was made for hire. You may also include the name of the employee along with the name of the employer (for example: "Elster Publishing Co., employer for hire of John Ferguson").

"Anonymous" or "Pseudonymous" Work: Leave this space **blank** if the serial is a "work made for hire." An author's contribution to a work is "anonymous" if that author is not identified on the copies or phonorecords of the work. An author's contribution to a work is "pseudonymous" if that author is identified on the copies or phonorecords under a fictitious name. If the work is "anonymous" you may: (1) leave the line blank; or (2) state "anonymous" on the line; or (3) reveal the author's identity. If the work is "pseudonymous" you may: (1) leave the line blank; or (2) give the pseudonym and identify it as such (for example: "Huntley Haverstock, pseudonym"); or (3) reveal the author's name, making clear which is the real name and which is the pseudonym (for example: "Judith Barton, whose pseudonym is Madeline Elster"). However, the citizenship or domicile of the author **must** be given in all cases.

Dates of Birth and Death: Leave this space blank if the author's contribution was a "work made for hire." If the author is dead, the statute requires that the year of death be included in the application unless the work is anonymous or pseudonymous. The author's birth date is optional, but is useful as a form of identification.

Nature of Authorship: Give a brief statement of the nature of the particular author's contribution to the work. If an organization directed, controlled, and supervised the creation of the serial issue as a whole, check the box "collective work." The term "collective work" means that the author is responsible for compilation and editorial revision, and may also be responsible for certain individual contributions to the serial issue. Further examples of "Authorship" which may apply both to organizational and to individual authors are "Entire text"; "Entire text and/or illustrations"; "Editorial revision, compilation, plus additional new material."

3 SPACE 3: Creation and Publication

General Instructions: Do not confuse "creation" with "publication." Every application for copyright registration must state "the year in which creation of the work was completed." Give the date and nation of first publication only if the work has been published.

Creation: Under the statute, a work is "created" when it is fixed in a copy or phonorecord for the first time. Where a work has been prepared over a period of time, the part of the work existing in fixed form on a particular date constitutes the created work on that date. The date you give here should be the year in which this particular issue was completed.

Publication: The statute defines "publication" as "the distribution of copies or phonorecords of a work to the public by sale or other transfer of ownership, or by rental, lease, or lending"; a work is also "published" if there has been an "offering to distribute copies or phonorecords to a group of persons for purposes of further distribution, public performance, or public display." Give the full date (month, day, year) when, and the country where, publication of this particular issue first occurred. If first publication took place simultaneously in the United States and other countries, it is sufficient to state "U.S.A."

4 SPACE 4: Claimant(s)

Name(s) and Address(es) of Copyright Claimant(s): This space must be completed. Give the name(s) and address(es) of the copyright claimant(s) of this work even if the claimant is the same as the author named in space 2. Copyright in a work belongs initially to the author of the work (including, in the case of a work made for hire, the employer or other person for whom the work was prepared). The copyright claimant is either the author of the work or a person or organization to whom the copyright initially belonging to the author has been transferred.

Transfer: The statute provides that, if the copyright claimant is not the author, the application for registration must contain "a brief statement of how the claimant obtained ownership of the copyright." A transfer of copyright ownership (other than one brought about by operation of law) must be in writing. If any copyright claimant named in space 4 is not an author named in space 2, give a brief, general statement describing the means by which that claimant obtained ownership of the copyright from the original author. Examples: "By written contract"; "Written transfer of all rights by author"; "Assignment"; "Inherited by will." Do not attach the actual document of transfer or other attachments or riders.

5 SPACE 5: Previous Registration

General Instructions: This space applies only rarely to serials. Complete space 5 if this particular issue has been registered earlier or if it contains a substantial amount of material that has been previously registered. Do not complete this space if the previous registrations are simply those made for earlier issues.

Previous Registration:
a. Check this box if this issue has been registered in unpublished form and a second registration is now sought to cover the first published edition.
b. Check this box if someone other than the author is identified as copyright claimant in the earlier registration and the author is now seeking registration in his or her own name. (If the work in question is a contribution to a collective work, as opposed to the issue as a whole, file Form TX, not Form SE.
c. Check this box (and complete space 6) if this particular issue, or a substantial portion of the material in it, has been previously registered and you are now seeking registration for the additions and revisions which appear in this issue for the first time.

Previous Registration Number and Date: Complete this line if you checked one of the boxes above. If more than one previous registration has been made for the issue or for material in it, give only the number and year date for the latest registration.

6 SPACE 6: Derivative Work or Compilation

General Instructions: Complete space 6 if this issue is a "changed version," "compilation," or "derivative work," which incorporates one or more earlier works that have already been published or registered for copyright, or that have fallen into the public domain. Do not complete space 6 for an issue consisting of entirely new material appearing for the first time, such as a new issue of a continuing serial. A "compilation" is defined as "a work formed by the collection and assembling of preexisting materials or of data that are se-

lected, coordinated, or arranged in such a way that the resulting work as a whole constitutes an original work of authorship." A "derivative work" is "a work based on one or more preexisting works." Examples of derivative works include translations, fictionalizations, abridgments, condensations, or "any other form in which a work may be recast, transformed, or adapted." Derivative works also include works "consisting of editorial revisions, annotations, or other modifications" if these changes, as a whole, represent an original work of authorship.

Preexisting Material (space 6a): For derivative works, complete this space and space 6b. In space 6a identify the preexisting work that has been recast, transformed, adapted, or updated. Example: "1978 Morgan Co. Sales Catalog." Do not complete space 6a for compilations.

Material Added to This Work (space 6b): Give a brief, general statement of the new material covered by the copyright claim for which registration is sought. **Derivative work** examples include: "Editorial revisions and additions to the Catalog"; "Translation"; "Additional material." If a periodical issue is a **compilation**, describe both the compilation itself and the material that has been compiled. Examples: "Compilation of previously published journal articles"; "Compilation of previously published data." An issue may be both a derivative work and a compilation, in which case a sample statement might be: "Compilation of [describe] and additional new material."

7 SPACE 7: Manufacturing Provisions

General Instructions: The copyright statute currently provides, as a general rule, that the copies of a published work "consisting preponderantly of nondramatic literary material in the English language" be manufactured in the United States or Canada in order to be lawfully imported and publicly distributed in the United States. If the work being registered is unpublished or not in English, leave this space blank. Complete this space if registration is sought for a published work "consisting preponderantly of nondramatic literary material that is in the English language." Identify those who manufactured the copies and where those manufacturing processes were performed. As an exception to the manufacturing provisions, the statute prescribes that, where manufacture has taken place outside the United States or Canada, a maximum of 2000 copies of the foreign edition may be imported into the United States without affecting the copyright owners' rights. For this purpose, the Copyright Office will issue an Import Statement upon request and payment of a fee of $3 at the time of registration or at any later time. For further information about import statements, write for Form IS.

8 SPACE 8: Reproduction for Use of Blind or Physically Handicapped Individuals

General Instructions: One of the major programs of the Library of Congress is to provide Braille editions and special recordings of works for the exclusive use of the blind and physically handicapped. In an effort to simplify and speed up the copyright licensing procedures that are a necessary part of this program, section 710 of the copyright statute provides for the establishment of a voluntary licensing system to be tied in with copyright registration. Copyright Office regulations provide that you may grant a license for such reproduction and distribution solely for the use of persons who are certified by competent authority as unable to read normal printed material as a result of physical limitations. The license is entirely voluntary, nonexclusive, and may be terminated upon 90 days notice.

How to Grant the License: If you wish to grant it, check one of the three boxes in space 8. Your check in one of these boxes, together with your signature in space 10, will mean that the Library of Congress can proceed to reproduce and distribute under the license without further paperwork. For further information, write for Circular R63.

9,10,11 SPACE 9, 10, 11: Fee, Correspondence, Certification, Return Address

Deposit Account: If you maintain a Deposit Account in the Copyright Office, identify it in space 9. Otherwise leave the space blank and send the fee of $10 with your application and deposit.

Correspondence (space 9): This space should contain the name, address, area code, and telephone number of the person to be consulted if correspondence about this application becomes necessary.

Certification (space 10): The application cannot be accepted unless it bears the date and the **handwritten signature** of the author or other copyright claimant, or of the owner of exclusive right(s), or of the duly authorized agent of the author, claimant, or owner of exclusive right(s).

Address for Return of Certificate (space 11): The address box must be completed legibly since the certificate will be returned in a window envelope.

FORM SE
UNITED STATES COPYRIGHT OFFICE

REGISTRATION NUMBER

U

EFFECTIVE DATE OF REGISTRATION

| Month | Day | Year |

DO NOT WRITE ABOVE THIS LINE. IF YOU NEED MORE SPACE, USE A SEPARATE CONTINUATION SHEET.

1

TITLE OF THIS SERIAL ▼

Volume ▼   Number ▼   Date on Copies ▼   Frequency of Publication ▼

PREVIOUS OR ALTERNATIVE TITLES ▼

2

a

NAME OF AUTHOR ▼

DATES OF BIRTH AND DEATH
Year Born ▼   Year Died ▼

Was this contribution to the work a "work made for hire"?
☐ Yes
☐ No

AUTHOR'S NATIONALITY OR DOMICILE
Name of Country
OR { Citizen of ▶
Domiciled in ▶

WAS THIS AUTHOR'S CONTRIBUTION TO THE WORK
Anonymous?   ☐ Yes ☐ No
Pseudonymous? ☐ Yes ☐ No
If the answer to either of these questions is "Yes," see detailed instructions.

NATURE OF AUTHORSHIP Briefly describe nature of the material created by this author in which copyright is claimed. ▼
☐ Collective Work   Other:

NOTE
Under the law, the "author" of a "work made for hire" is generally the employer, not the employee (see instructions). For any part of this work that was "made for hire" check "Yes" in the space provided, give the employer (or other person for whom the work was prepared) as "Author" of that part, and leave the space for dates of birth and death blank.

b

NAME OF AUTHOR ▼

DATES OF BIRTH AND DEATH
Year Born ▼   Year Died ▼

Was this contribution to the work a "work made for hire"?
☐ Yes
☐ No

AUTHOR'S NATIONALITY OR DOMICILE
Name of country
OR { Citizen of ▶
Domiciled in ▶

WAS THIS AUTHOR'S CONTRIBUTION TO THE WORK
Anonymous?   ☐ Yes ☐ No
Pseudonymous? ☐ Yes ☐ No
If the answer to either of these questions is "Yes," see detailed instructions.

NATURE OF AUTHORSHIP Briefly describe nature of the material created by this author in which copyright is claimed. ▼
☐ Collective Work   Other:

c

NAME OF AUTHOR ▼

DATES OF BIRTH AND DEATH
Year Born ▼   Year Died ▼

Was this contribution to the work a "work made for hire"?
☐ Yes
☐ No

AUTHOR'S NATIONALITY OR DOMICILE
Name of Country
OR { Citizen of ▶
Domiciled in ▶

WAS THIS AUTHOR'S CONTRIBUTION TO THE WORK
Anonymous?   ☐ Yes ☐ No
Pseudonymous? ☐ Yes ☐ No
If the answer to either of these questions is "Yes," see detailed instructions.

NATURE OF AUTHORSHIP Briefly describe nature of the material created by this author in which copyright is claimed. ▼
☐ Collective Work   Other:

3

YEAR IN WHICH CREATION OF THIS ISSUE WAS COMPLETED This information must be given in all cases.
◄ Year

DATE AND NATION OF FIRST PUBLICATION OF THIS PARTICULAR ISSUE
Complete this information ONLY if this work has been published.
Month ▶   Day ▶   Year ▶
◄ Nation

4

See instructions before completing this space.

COPYRIGHT CLAIMANT(S) Name and address must be given even if the claimant is the same as the author given in space 2.▼

TRANSFER If the claimant(s) named here in space 4 are different from the author(s) named in space 2, give a brief statement of how the claimant(s) obtained ownership of the copyright.▼

DO NOT WRITE HERE
OFFICE USE ONLY

APPLICATION RECEIVED

ONE DEPOSIT RECEIVED

TWO DEPOSITS RECEIVED

REMITTANCE NUMBER AND DATE

MORE ON BACK ► • Complete all applicable spaces (numbers 5-11) on the reverse side of this page
• See detailed instructions   • Sign the form at line 10

DO NOT WRITE HERE
Page 1 of_____pages

EXAMINED BY _____

CHECKED BY _____

☐ CORRESPONDENCE
  Yes

☐ DEPOSIT ACCOUNT
  FUNDS USED

FORM SE

FOR
COPYRIGHT
OFFICE
USE
ONLY

DO NOT WRITE ABOVE THIS LINE. IF YOU NEED MORE SPACE, USE A SEPARATE CONTINUATION SHEET.

PREVIOUS REGISTRATION   Has registration for this issue, or for an earlier version of this particular issue, already been made in the Copyright Office?

☐ **Yes**   ☐ **No**   If your answer is "Yes," why is another registration being sought? (Check appropriate box) ▼

a. ☐ This is the first published version of an issue previously registered in unpublished form.

b. ☐ This is the first application submitted by this author as copyright claimant.

c. ☐ This is a changed version of this issue, as shown by space 6 on this application.

If your answer is "Yes," give: **Previous Registration Number** ▼   **Year of Registration** ▼

5

DERIVATIVE WORK OR COMPILATION   Complete both space 6a & 6b for a derivative work; complete only 6b for a compilation.

a.   Preexisting Material   Identify any preexisting work or works that this work is based on or incorporates. ▼

b.   Material Added to This Work   Give a brief, general statement of the material that has been added to this work and in which copyright is claimed.▼

See instructions
before completing
this space.

6

MANUFACTURERS AND LOCATIONS   If this is a published work consisting preponderantly of nondramatic literary material in English, the law may require that the copies be manufactured in the United States or Canada for full protection. If so, the names of the manufacturers who performed certain processes, and the places where these processes were performed **must** be given. See instructions for details.

Names of Manufacturers ▼   **Places of Manufacture** ▼

7

REPRODUCTION FOR USE OF BLIND OR PHYSICALLY HANDICAPPED INDIVIDUALS   A signature on this form at space 10, and a check in one of the boxes here in space 8, constitutes a non-exclusive grant of permission to the Library of Congress to reproduce and distribute solely for the blind and physically handicapped and under the conditions and limitations prescribed by the regulations of the Copyright Office: (1) copies of the work identified in space 1 of this application in Braille (or similar tactile symbols); or (2) phonorecords embodying a fixation of a reading of that work; or (3) both.

a ☐ Copies and Phonorecords   b ☐ Copies Only   c ☐ Phonorecords Only

See instructions.

8

DEPOSIT ACCOUNT   If the registration fee is to be charged to a Deposit Account established in the Copyright Office, give name and number of Account.

Name ▼   Account Number ▼

9

CORRESPONDENCE   Give name and address to which correspondence about this application should be sent.   Name/Address/Apt/City/State/Zip ▼

Area Code & Telephone Number ▶

Be sure to
give your
daytime phone
◀ number.

CERTIFICATION*   I, the undersigned, hereby certify that I am the

Check one ▶

☐ author
☐ other copyright claimant
☐ owner of exclusive right(s)
☐ authorized agent of _____

of the work identified in this application and that the statements made
by me in this application are correct to the best of my knowledge.

Name of author or other copyright claimant, or owner of exclusive right(s) ▲

10

Typed or printed name and date ▼ If this is a published work, this date must be the same as or later than the date of publication given in space 3.

_____ date ▶ _____

Handwritten signature (X) ▼

**MAIL
CERTIFI-
CATE TO**

Name ▼

Number/Street/Apartment Number ▼

City/State/ZIP ▼

**Certificate
will be
mailed in
window
envelope**

Have you:
• Completed all necessary spaces?
• Signed your application in space 10?
• Enclosed check or money order for $10 payable to *Register of Copyrights*?
• Enclosed your deposit material with the application and fee?
MAIL TO: Register of Copyrights, Library of Congress, Washington, D.C. 20559.

11

* 17 U.S.C. § 506(e): Any person who knowingly makes a false representation of a material fact in the application for copyright registration provided for by section 409, or in any written statement filed in connection with the application, shall be fined not more than $2,500.

☆U.S. GOVERNMENT PRINTING OFFICE: 1988—202-133/60,013

March 1988—20,000

Filling Out Application Form PA

Detach and read these instructions before completing this form. Make sure all applicable spaces have been filled in before you return this form.

BASIC INFORMATION

When to Use This Form: Use Form PA for registration of published or unpublished works of the performing arts. This class includes works prepared for the purpose of being "performed" directly before an audience or indirectly "by means of any device or process." Works of the performing arts include: (1) musical works, including any accompanying words; (2) dramatic works, including any accompanying music; (3) pantomimes and choreographic works; and (4) motion pictures and other audiovisual works.

Deposit to Accompany Application: An application for copyright registration must be accompanied by a deposit consisting of copies or phonorecords representing the entire work for which registration is to be made. The following are the general deposit requirements as set forth in the statute:

Unpublished Work: Deposit one complete copy (or phonorecord).

Published Work: Deposit two complete copies (or phonorecords) of the best edition.

Work First Published Outside the United States: Deposit one complete copy (or phonorecord) of the first foreign edition.

Contribution to a Collective Work: Deposit one complete copy (or phonorecord) of the best edition of the collective work.

Motion Pictures: Deposit *both* of the following: (1) a separate written description of the contents of the motion picture; and (2) for a published work, one complete copy of the best edition of the motion picture; or, for an unpublished work, one complete copy of the motion picture or identifying material. Identifying material may be either an audiorecording of the entire soundtrack or one frame enlargement or similar visual print from each 10-minute segment.

The Copyright Notice: For published works, the law provides that a copyright notice in a specified form "shall be placed on all publicly distributed copies from which the work can be visually perceived." Use of the copyright notice is the responsibility of the copyright owner and does not require advance permission from the Copyright Office. The required form of the notice for copies generally consists of three elements: (1) the symbol "©", or the word "Copyright," or the abbreviation "Copr."; (2) the year of first publication; and (3) the name of the owner of copyright. For example: "© 1981 Constance Porter." The notice is to be affixed to the copies "in such manner and location as to give reasonable notice of the claim of copyright."

For further information about copyright registration, notice, or special questions relating to copyright problems, write:

Information and Publications Section, LM-455
Copyright Office
Library of Congress
Washington, D.C. 20559

PRIVACY ACT ADVISORY STATEMENT Required by the Privacy Act of 1974 (P.L. 93-579)
The authority for requesting this information is title 17, U.S.C., secs. 409 and 410. Furnishing the requested information is voluntary. But if the information is not furnished, it may be necessary to delay or refuse registration and you may not be entitled to certain relief, remedies, and benefits provided in chapters 4 and 5 of title 17, U.S.C.
The principal uses of the requested information are the establishment and maintenance of a public record and the examination of the application for compliance with legal requirements.
Other routine uses include public inspection and copying, preparation of public indexes, preparation of public catalogs of copyright registrations, and preparation of search reports upon request.
NOTE: No other advisory statement will be given in connection with this application. Please keep this statement and refer to it if we communicate with you regarding this application.

LINE-BY-LINE INSTRUCTIONS

1 SPACE 1: Title

Title of This Work: Every work submitted for copyright registration must be given a title to identify that particular work. If the copies or phonorecords of the work bear a title (or an identifying phrase that could serve as a title), transcribe that wording *completely* and *exactly* on the application. Indexing of the registration and future identification of the work will depend on the information you give here. If the work you are registering is an entire "collective work" (such as a collection of plays or songs), give the overall title of the collection. If you are registering one or more individual contributions to a collective work, give the title of each contribution, followed by the title of the collection. Example: "'A Song for Elinda' in *Old and New Ballads for Old and New People*."

Previous or Alternative Titles: Complete this space if there are any additional titles for the work under which someone searching for the registration might be likely to look, or under which a document pertaining to the work might be recorded.

Nature of This Work: Briefly describe the general nature or character of the work being registered for copyright. Examples: "Music"; "Song Lyrics"; "Words and Music"; "Drama"; "Musical Play"; "Choreography"; "Pantomime"; "Motion Picture"; "Audiovisual Work."

2 SPACE 2: Author(s)

General Instructions: After reading these instructions, decide who are the "authors" of this work for copyright purposes. Then, unless the work is a "collective work," give the requested information about every "author" who contributed any appreciable amount of copyrightable matter to this version of the work. If you need further space, request additional Continuation Sheets. In the case of a collective work, such as a songbook or a collection of plays, give information about the author of the collective work as a whole.

Name of Author: The fullest form of the author's name should be given. Unless the work was "made for hire," the individual who actually created the work is its "author." In the case of a work made for hire, the statute provides

that "the employer or other person for whom the work was prepared is considered the author."

What is a "Work Made for Hire"? A "work made for hire" is defined as: (1) "a work prepared by an employee within the scope of his or her employment"; or (2) "a work specially ordered or commissioned for use as a contribution to a collective work, as a part of a motion picture or other audiovisual work, as a translation, as a supplementary work, as a compilation, as an instructional text, as a test, as answer material for a test, or as an atlas, if the parties expressly agree in a written instrument signed by them that the work shall be considered a work made for hire." If you have checked "Yes" to indicate that the work was "made for hire," you must give the full legal name of the employer (or other person for whom the work was prepared). You may also include the name of the employee along with the name of the employer (for example: "Elster Music Co., employer for hire of John Ferguson").

"Anonymous" or "Pseudonymous" Work: An author's contribution to a work is "anonymous" if that author is not identified on the copies or phonorecords of the work. An author's contribution to a work is "pseudonymous" if that author is identified on the copies or phonorecords under a fictitious name. If the work is "anonymous" you may: (1) leave the line blank; or (2) state "anonymous" on the line; or (3) reveal the author's identity. If the work is "pseudonymous" you may: (1) leave the line blank; or (2) give the pseudonym and identify it as such (for example: "Huntley Haverstock, pseudonym"); or (3) reveal the author's name, making clear which is the real name and which is the pseudonym (for example: "Judith Barton, whose pseudonym is Madeline Elster"). However, the citizenship or domicile of the author **must** be given in all cases.

Dates of Birth and Death: If the author is dead, the statute requires that the year of death be included in the application unless the work is anonymous or pseudonymous. The author's birth date is optional, but is useful as a form of identification. Leave this space blank if the author's contribution was a "work made for hire."

Author's Nationality or Domicile: Give the country of which the author is a citizen, or the country in which the author is domiciled. Nationality or domicile **must** be given in all cases.

Nature of Authorship: Give a brief general statement of the nature of this particular author's contribution to the work. Examples: "Words"; "Co-Author of Music"; "Words and Music"; "Arrangement"; "Co-Author of Book and Lyrics"; "Dramatization"; "Screen Play"; "Compilation and English Translation"; "Editorial Revisions."

3 SPACE 3: Creation and Publication

General Instructions: Do not confuse "creation" with "publication." Every application for copyright registration must state "the year in which creation of the work was completed." Give the date and nation of first publication only if the work has been published.

Creation: Under the statute, a work is "created" when it is fixed in a copy or phonorecord for the first time. Where a work has been prepared over a period of time, the part of the work existing in fixed form on a particular date constitutes the created work on that date. The date you give here should be the year in which the author completed the particular version for which registration is now being sought, even if other versions exist or if further changes or additions are planned.

Publication: The statute defines "publication" as "the distribution of copies or phonorecords of a work to the public by sale or other transfer of ownership, or by rental, lease, or lending"; a work is also "published" if there has been an "offering to distribute copies or phonorecords to a group of persons for purposes of further distribution, public performance, or public display." Give the full date (month, day, year) when, and the country where, publication first occurred. If first publication took place simultaneously in the United States and other countries, it is sufficient to state "U.S.A."

4 SPACE 4: Claimant(s)

Name(s) and Address(es) of Copyright Claimant(s): Give the name(s) and address(es) of the copyright claimant(s) in this work even if the claimant is the same as the author. Copyright in a work belongs initially to the author of the work (including, in the case of a work made for hire, the employer or other person for whom the work was prepared). The copyright claimant is either the author of the work or a person or organization to whom the copyright initially belonging to the author has been transferred.

Transfer: The statute provides that, if the copyright claimant is not the author, the application for registration must contain "a brief statement of how the claimant obtained ownership of the copyright." If any copyright claimant named in space 4 is not an author named in space 2, give a brief, general statement summarizing the means by which that claimant obtained ownership of the copyright. Examples: "By written contract"; "Transfer of all rights by author"; "Assignment"; "By will." Do not attach transfer documents or other attachments or riders.

5 SPACE 5: Previous Registration

General Instructions: The questions in space 5 are intended to find out whether an earlier registration has been made for this work and, if so, whether there is any basis for a new registration. As a general rule, only one basic copyright registration can be made for the same version of a particular work.

Same Version: If this version is substantially the same as the work covered by a previous registration, a second registration is not generally possible unless: (1) the work has been registered in unpublished form and a second registration is now being sought to cover this first published edition; or (2) someone other than the author is identified as copyright claimant in the earlier registration, and the author is now seeking registration in his or her own name. If either of these two exceptions apply, check the appropriate box and give the

earlier registration number and date. Otherwise, do not submit Form PA; instead, write the Copyright Office for information about supplementary registration or recordation of transfers of copyright ownership.

Changed Version: If the work has been changed, and you are now seeking registration to cover the additions or revisions, check the last box in space 5, give the earlier registration number and date, and complete both parts of space 6 in accordance with the instructions below.

Previous Registration Number and Date: If more than one previous registration has been made for the work, give the number and date of the latest registration.

6 SPACE 6: Derivative Work or Compilation

General Instructions: Complete space 6 if this work is a "changed version," "compilation," or "derivative work," and if it incorporates one or more earlier works that have already been published or registered for copyright, or that have fallen into the public domain. A "compilation" is defined as "a work formed by the collection and assembling of preexisting materials or of data that are selected, coordinated, or arranged in such a way that the resulting work as a whole constitutes an original work of authorship." A "derivative work" is "a work based on one or more preexisting works." Examples of derivative works include musical arrangements, dramatizations, translations, abridgments, condensations, motion picture versions, or "any other form in which a work may be recast, transformed, or adapted." Derivative works also include works "consisting of editorial revisions, annotations, or other modifications" if these changes, as a whole, represent an original work of authorship.

Preexisting Material (space 6a): Complete this space and space 6b for derivative works. In this space identify the preexisting work that has been recast, transformed, or adapted. For example, the preexisting material might be: "French version of Hugo's 'Le Roi s'amuse'." Do not complete this space for compilations.

Material Added to This Work (space 6b): Give a brief, general statement of the additional new material covered by the copyright claim for which registration is sought. In the case of a derivative work, identify this new material. Examples: "Arrangement for piano and orchestra"; "Dramatization for television"; "New film version"; "Revisions throughout; Act III completely new." If the work is a compilation, give a brief, general statement describing both the material that has been compiled and the compilation itself. Example: "Compilation of 19th Century Military Songs."

7,8,9 SPACE 7, 8, 9: Fee, Correspondence, Certification, Return Address

Deposit Account: If you maintain a Deposit Account in the Copyright Office, identify it in space 7. Otherwise leave the space blank and send the fee of $10 with your application and deposit.

Correspondence (space 7): This space should contain the name, address, area code, and telephone number of the person to be consulted if correspondence about this application becomes necessary.

Certification (space 8): The application cannot be accepted unless it bears the date and the handwritten signature of the author or other copyright claimant, or of the owner of exclusive right(s), or of the duly authorized agent of the author, claimant, or owner of exclusive right(s).

Address for Return of Certificate (space 9): The address box must be completed legibly since the certificate will be returned in a window envelope.

MORE INFORMATION

How To Register a Recorded Work: If the musical or dramatic work that you are registering has been recorded (as a tape, disk, or cassette), you have choose either copyright application Form PA or Form SR, Performing Arts or Sound Recordings, depending on the purpose of the registration.

Form PA should be used to register the underlying musical or dramatic work. Form SR has been developed specifically to register a "sound recording" as defined by the Copyright Act—a work resulting from the "fixation of a series of sounds," separate and distinct from the underlying musical or dramatic work. Form SR should be used when the copyright claim is limited to the sound recording itself. (In one instance, Form SR may also be used to file for a copyright registration for both kinds of works—see (4) below.) Therefore:

(1) File Form PA if you are seeking to register the musical or dramatic work, not the "sound recording," even though what you deposit for copyright purposes may be in the form of a phonorecord.

(2) File Form PA if you are seeking to register the audio portion of an audiovisual work, such as a motion picture soundtrack; these are considered integral parts of the audiovisual work.

(3) File Form SR if you are seeking to register the "sound recording" itself, that is, the work that results from the fixation of a series of musical, spoken, or other sounds, but not the underlying musical or dramatic work.

(4) File Form SR if you are the copyright claimant for both the underlying musical or dramatic work and the sound recording, and you prefer to register both on the same form.

(5) File both forms PA and SR if you are the copyright claimant for the underlying work and sound recording differ, or you prefer to have separate registration for them.

"Copies" and "Phonorecords": To register for copyright, you are required to deposit "copies" or "phonorecords." These are defined as follows:

Musical compositions may be embodied (fixed) in "copies," objects from which a work can be read or visually perceived, directly or with the aid of a machine or device, such as manuscripts, books, sheet music, film, and videotape. They may also be fixed in "phonorecords," objects embodying fixations of sounds, such as tapes and phonograph disks, commonly known as phonograph records. For example, a song (the work to be registered) can be reproduced in sheet music ("copies") or phonograph records ("phonorecords"), or both.

189

FORM PA
UNITED STATES COPYRIGHT OFFICE

REGISTRATION NUMBER

PA   PAU

EFFECTIVE DATE OF REGISTRATION

Month   Day   Year

DO NOT WRITE ABOVE THIS LINE. IF YOU NEED MORE SPACE, USE A SEPARATE CONTINUATION SHEET.

1   TITLE OF THIS WORK ▼

PREVIOUS OR ALTERNATIVE TITLES ▼

NATURE OF THIS WORK ▼ See instructions

2
a

NAME OF AUTHOR ▼

DATES OF BIRTH AND DEATH ▼
Year Born ▼   Year Died ▼

Was this contribution to the work a "work made for hire"?
☐ Yes
☐ No

AUTHOR'S NATIONALITY OR DOMICILE
Name of Country
OR { Citizen of ▶_____
Domiciled in ▶_____

WAS THIS AUTHOR'S CONTRIBUTION TO THE WORK
Anonymous? ☐ Yes ☐ No
Pseudonymous? ☐ Yes ☐ No
If the answer to either of these questions is "Yes," see detailed instructions.

NATURE OF AUTHORSHIP Briefly describe nature of the material created by this author in which copyright is claimed. ▼

NOTE

Under the law, the "author" of a "work made for hire" is generally the employer, not the employee (see instructions). For any part of this work that was "made for hire" check "Yes" in the space provided, give the employer (or other person for whom the work was prepared) as "Author" of that part, and leave the space for dates of birth and death blank.

b

NAME OF AUTHOR ▼

DATES OF BIRTH AND DEATH
Year Born ▼   Year Died ▼

Was this contribution to the work a "work made for hire"?
☐ Yes
☐ No

AUTHOR'S NATIONALITY OR DOMICILE
Name of country
OR { Citizen of ▶_____
Domiciled in ▶_____

WAS THIS AUTHOR'S CONTRIBUTION TO THE WORK
Anonymous? ☐ Yes ☐ No
Pseudonymous? ☐ Yes ☐ No
If the answer to either of these questions is "Yes," see detailed instructions.

NATURE OF AUTHORSHIP Briefly describe nature of the material created by this author in which copyright is claimed. ▼

c

NAME OF AUTHOR ▼

DATES OF BIRTH AND DEATH
Year Born ▼   Year Died ▼

Was this contribution to the work a "work made for hire"?
☐ Yes
☐ No

AUTHOR'S NATIONALITY OR DOMICILE
Name of Country
OR { Citizen of ▶_____
Domiciled in ▶_____

WAS THIS AUTHOR'S CONTRIBUTION TO THE WORK
Anonymous? ☐ Yes ☐ No
Pseudonymous? ☐ Yes ☐ No
If the answer to either of these questions is "Yes," see detailed instructions.

NATURE OF AUTHORSHIP Briefly describe nature of the material created by this author in which copyright is claimed. ▼

3

YEAR IN WHICH CREATION OF THIS WORK WAS COMPLETED This information must be given in all cases.
◀ Year

DATE AND NATION OF FIRST PUBLICATION OF THIS PARTICULAR WORK
Complete this information ONLY if this work has been published.
Month ▶_____ Day ▶_____ Year ▶_____
◀ Nation

4

COPYRIGHT CLAIMANT(S) Name and address must be given even if the claimant is the same as the author given in space 2.▼

See instructions before completing this space.

TRANSFER If the claimant(s) named here in space 4 are different from the author(s) named in space 2, give a brief statement of how the claimant(s) obtained ownership of the copyright.▼

APPLICATION RECEIVED

ONE DEPOSIT RECEIVED

TWO DEPOSITS RECEIVED

REMITTANCE NUMBER AND DATE

DO NOT WRITE HERE — OFFICE USE ONLY

MORE ON BACK ▶ • Complete all applicable spaces (numbers 5-9) on the reverse side of this page.
• See detailed instructions. • Sign the form at line 8.

DO NOT WRITE HERE

Page 1 of ___ pages

190

EXAMINED BY	FORM PA
CHECKED BY	
☐ CORRESPONDENCE Yes	FOR COPYRIGHT OFFICE USE ONLY
☐ DEPOSIT ACCOUNT FUNDS USED	

DO NOT WRITE ABOVE THIS LINE. IF YOU NEED MORE SPACE, USE A SEPARATE CONTINUATION SHEET.

PREVIOUS REGISTRATION Has registration for this work, or for an earlier version of this work, already been made in the Copyright Office?
☐ **Yes** ☐ **No** If your answer is "Yes," why is another registration being sought? (Check appropriate box) ▼

☐ This is the first published edition of a work previously registered in unpublished form.

☐ This is the first application submitted by this author as copyright claimant.

☐ This is a changed version of the work, as shown by space 6 on this application.

If your answer is "Yes," give: **Previous Registration Number** ▼   **Year of Registration** ▼

5

DERIVATIVE WORK OR COMPILATION Complete both space 6a & 6b for a derivative work; complete only 6b for a compilation.
a. Preexisting Material Identify any preexisting work or works that this work is based on or incorporates. ▼

b. Material Added to This Work Give a brief, general statement of the material that has been added to this work and in which copyright is claimed.▼

See instructions before completing this space.

6

DEPOSIT ACCOUNT If the registration fee is to be charged to a Deposit Account established in the Copyright Office, give name and number of Account.
Name ▼   **Account Number** ▼

7

CORRESPONDENCE Give name and address to which correspondence about this application should be sent.   Name/Address/Apt/City/State/Zip ▼

Area Code & Telephone Number ▶

Be sure to give your daytime phone ◀ number.

CERTIFICATION* I, the undersigned, hereby certify that I am the
Check only one ▼

☐ author

☐ other copyright claimant

☐ owner of exclusive right(s)

☐ authorized agent of _____
Name of author or other copyright claimant, or owner of exclusive right(s) ▲

of the work identified in this application and that the statements made
by me in this application are correct to the best of my knowledge.

Typed or printed name and date ▼ If this is a published work, this date must be the same as or later than the date of publication given in space 3.

_____ **date** ▶ _____

Handwritten signature (X) ▼

8

MAIL CERTIFI-CATE TO	Name ▼	Have you: • Completed all necessary spaces? • Signed your application in space 8?
Certificate will be mailed in window envelope	Number/Street/Apartment Number ▼	• Enclosed check or money order for $10 payable to *Register of Copyrights*? • Enclosed your deposit material with the application and fee?
	City/State/ZIP ▼	**MAIL TO:** Register of Copyrights, Library of Congress, Washington, D.C. 20559

9

* 17 U.S.C. § 506(e): Any person who knowingly makes a false representation of a material fact in the application for copyright registration provided for by section 409, or in any written statement filed in connection with the application, shall be fined not more than $2,500.

☆U.S. GOVERNMENT PRINTING OFFICE: 1987:181-531/60,000

July 1987-100,000

Filling Out Application Form VA

Detach and read these instructions before completing this form. Make sure all applicable spaces have been filled in before you return this form.

BASIC INFORMATION

When to Use This Form: Use Form VA for copyright registration of published or unpublished works of the visual arts. This category consists of "pictorial, graphic, or sculptural works," including two-dimensional and three-dimensional works of fine, graphic, and applied art, photographs, prints and art reproductions, maps, globes, charts, technical drawings, diagrams, and models.

What Does Copyright Protect? Copyright in a work of the visual arts protects those pictorial, graphic, or sculptural elements that, either alone or in combination, represent an "original work of authorship." The statute declares: "In no case does copyright protection for an original work of authorship extend to any idea, procedure, process, system, method of operation, concept, principle, or discovery, regardless of the form in which it is described, explained, illustrated, or embodied in such work."

Works of Artistic Craftsmanship and Designs: "Works of artistic craftsmanship" are registrable on Form VA, but the statute makes clear that protection extends to "their form" and not to "their mechanical or utilitarian aspects." The "design of a useful article" is considered copyrightable "only if, and only to the extent that, such design incorporates pictorial, graphic, or sculptural features that can be identified separately from, and are capable of existing independently of, the utilitarian aspects of the article."

Labels and Advertisements: Works prepared for use in connection with the sale or advertisement of goods and services are registrable if they contain "original work of authorship." Use Form VA if the copyrightable material in the work you are registering is mainly pictorial or graphic; use Form TX if it consists mainly of text. NOTE: Words and short phrases such as names, titles, and slogans cannot be protected by copyright, and the same is true of standard symbols, emblems, and other commonly used graphic designs that are in the public domain. When used commercially, material of that sort can sometimes be protected under state laws of unfair competition or under the Federal trademark laws. For information about trademark registration, write to the Commissioner of Patents and Trademarks, Washington, D.C. 20231.

Deposit to Accompany Application: An application for copyright registration must be accompanied by a deposit consisting of copies representing the entire work for which registration is to be made.

Unpublished Work: Deposit one complete copy.

Published Work: Deposit two complete copies of the best edition.

Work First Published Outside the United States: Deposit one complete copy of the first foreign edition.

Contribution to a Collective Work: Deposit one complete copy of the best edition of the collective work.

The Copyright Notice: For published works, the law provides that a copyright notice in a specified form "shall be placed on all publicly distributed copies from which the work can be visually perceived." Use of the copyright notice is the responsibility of the copyright owner and does not require advance permission from the Copyright Office. The required form of the notice for copies generally consists of three elements: (1) the symbol "©", or the word "Copyright," or the abbreviation "Copr."; (2) the year of first publication; and (3) the name of the owner of copyright. For example: "© 1981 Constance Porter." The notice is to be affixed to the copies "in such manner and location as to give reasonable notice of the claim of copyright."

For further information about copyright registration, notice, or special questions relating to copyright problems, write:

Information and Publications Section, LM-455
Copyright Office, Library of Congress, Washington, D.C. 20559

PRIVACY ACT ADVISORY STATEMENT Required by the Privacy Act of 1974 (P.L. 93-579)

The authority for requesting this information is title 17, U.S.C., secs. 409 and 410. Furnishing the requested information is voluntary. But if the information is not furnished, it may be necessary to delay or refuse registration and you may not be entitled to certain relief, remedies, and benefits provided in chapters 4 and 5 of title 17, U.S.C.

The principal uses of the requested information are the establishment and maintenance of a public record and the examination of the application for compliance with legal requirements.

Other routine uses include public inspection and copying, preparation of public indexes, preparation of public catalogs of copyright registrations, and preparation of search reports upon request.

NOTE: No other advisory statement will be given in connection with this application. Please keep this statement and refer to it if we communicate with you regarding this application.

LINE-BY-LINE INSTRUCTIONS

1 SPACE 1: Title

Title of This Work: Every work submitted for copyright registration must be given a title to identify that particular work. If the copies of the work bear a title (or an identifying phrase that could serve as a title), transcribe that wording *completely* and *exactly* on the application. Indexing of the registration and future identification of the work will depend on the information you give here.

Previous or Alternative Titles: Complete this space if there are any additional titles for the work under which someone searching for the registration might be likely to look, or under which a document pertaining to the work might be recorded.

Publication as a Contribution: If the work being registered is a contribution to a periodical, serial, or collection, give the title of the contribution in the "Title of This Work" space. Then, in the line headed "Publication as a Contribution," give information about the collective work in which the contribution appeared.

Nature of This Work: Briefly describe the general nature or character of the pictorial, graphic, or sculptural work being registered for copyright. Examples: "Oil Painting"; "Charcoal Drawing"; "Etching"; "Sculpture"; "Map"; "Photograph"; "Scale Model"; "Lithographic Print"; "Jewelry Design"; "Fabric Design."

2 SPACE 2: Author(s)

General Instructions: After reading these instructions, decide who are the "authors" of this work for copyright purposes. Then, unless the work is a "collective work," give the requested information about every "author" who contributed any appreciable amount of copyrightable matter to this version of the work. If you need further space, request additional Continuation Sheets. In the case of a collective work, such as a catalog of paintings or collection of cartoons by various authors, give information about the author of the collective work as a whole.

Name of Author: The fullest form of the author's name should be given. Unless the work was "made for hire," the individual who actually created the work is its "author." In the case of a work made for hire, the statute provides that "the employer or other person for whom the work was prepared is considered the author."

What is a "Work Made for Hire"? A "work made for hire" is defined as: (1) "a work prepared by an employee within the scope of his or her employment"; or (2) "a work specially ordered or commissioned for use as a contribution to a collective work, as a part of a motion picture or other audiovisual work, as a translation, as a supplementary work, as a compilation, as an instructional text, as a test, as answer material for a test, or as an atlas, if the parties expressly agree in a written instrument signed by them that the work shall be considered a work made for hire." If you have checked "Yes" to indicate that the work was "made for hire," you must give the full legal name of the employer (or other person for whom the work was prepared). You may also include the name of the employee along with the name of the employer (for example: "Elster Publishing Co., employer for hire of John Ferguson").

"Anonymous" or "Pseudonymous" Work: An author's contribution to a work is "anonymous" if that author is not identified on the copies or phonorecords of the work. An author's contribution to a work is "pseudonymous" if that author is identified on the copies or phonorecords under a fictitious name. If the work is "anonymous" you may: (1) leave the line blank; or (2) state "anonymous" on the line; or (3) reveal the author's identity. If the work is "pseudonymous" you may: (1) leave the line blank; or (2) give the pseudonym and identify it as such (for example: "Huntley Haverstock, pseudonym"); or (3) reveal the author's name, making clear which is the real name and which is the pseudonym (for example: "Henry Leek, whose pseudonym is Priam Farrel"). However, the citizenship or domicile of the author **must** be given in all cases.

Dates of Birth and Death: If the author is dead, the statute requires that the year of death be included in the application unless the work is anonymous or pseudonymous. The author's birth date is optional, but is useful as a form of identification. Leave this space blank if the author's contribution was a "work made for hire."

Author's Nationality or Domicile: Give the country of which the author is a citizen, or the country in which the author is domiciled. Nationality or domicile **must** be given in all cases.

Nature of Authorship: Give a brief general statement of the nature of this particular author's contribution to the work. Examples: "Painting"; "Photograph"; "Silk Screen Reproduction"; "Co-author of Cartographic Material"; "Technical Drawing"; "Text and Artwork."

3 SPACE 3: Creation and Publication

General Instructions: Do not confuse "creation" with "publication." Every application for copyright registration must state "the year in which creation of the work was completed." Give the date and nation of first publication only if the work has been published.

Creation: Under the statute, a work is "created" when it is fixed in a copy or phonorecord for the first time. Where a work has been prepared over a period of time, the part of the work existing in fixed form on a particular date constitutes the created work on that date. The date you give here should be the year in which the author completed the particular version for which registration is now being sought, even if other versions exist or if further changes or additions are planned.

Publication: The statute defines "publication" as "the distribution of copies or phonorecords of a work to the public by sale or other transfer of ownership, or by rental, lease, or lending"; a work is also "published" if there has been an "offering to distribute copies or phonorecords to a group of persons for purposes of further distribution, public performance, or public display." Give the full date (month, day, year) when, and the country where, publication first occurred. If first publication took place simultaneously in the United States and other countries, it is sufficient to state "U.S.A."

4 SPACE 4: Claimant(s)

Name(s) and Address(es) of Copyright Claimant(s): Give the name(s) and address(es) of the copyright claimant(s) in this work even if the claimant is the same as the author. Copyright in a work belongs initially to the author of the work (including, in the case of a work made for hire, the employer or other person for whom the work was prepared). The copyright claimant is either the author of the work or a person or organization to whom the copyright initially belonging to the author has been transferred.

Transfer: The statute provides that, if the copyright claimant is not the author, the application for registration must contain "a brief statement of how the claimant obtained ownership of the copyright." If any copyright claimant named in space 4 is not an author named in space 2, give a brief, general statement summarizing the means by which that claimant obtained ownership of the copyright. Examples: "By written contract"; "Transfer of all rights by author"; "Assignment"; "By will." Do not attach transfer documents or other attachments or riders.

5 SPACE 5: Previous Registration

General Instructions: The questions in space 5 are intended to find out whether an earlier registration has been made for this work and, if so, whether there is any basis for a new registration. As a rule, only one basic copyright registration can be made for the same version of a particular work.

Same Version: If this version is substantially the same as the work covered by a previous registration, a second registration is not generally possible unless: (1) the work has been registered in unpublished form and a second registration is now being sought to cover this first published edition; or (2) some-

one other than the author is identified as copyright claimant in the earlier registration, and the author is now seeking registration in his or her own name. If either of these two exceptions apply, check the appropriate box and give the earlier registration number and date. Otherwise, do not submit Form VA; instead, write the Copyright Office for information about supplementary registration or recordation of transfers of copyright ownership.

Changed Version: If the work has been changed, and you are now seeking registration to cover the additions or revisions, check the last box in space 5, give the earlier registration number and date, and complete both parts of space 6 in accordance with the instructions below.

Previous Registration Number and Date: If more than one previous registration has been made for the work, give the number and date of the latest registration.

6 SPACE 6: Derivative Work or Compilation

General Instructions: Complete space 6 if this work is a "changed version," "compilation," or "derivative work," and if it incorporates one or more earlier works that have already been published or registered for copyright, or that have fallen into the public domain. A "compilation" is defined as "a work formed by the collection and assembling of preexisting materials or of data that are selected, coordinated, or arranged in such a way that the resulting work as a whole constitutes an original work of authorship." A "derivative work" is "a work based on one or more preexisting works." Examples of derivative works include reproductions of works of art, sculptures based on drawings, lithographs based on paintings, maps based on previously published sources, or "any other form in which a work may be recast, transformed, or adapted." Derivative works also include works "consisting of editorial revisions, annotations, or other modifications" if these changes, as a whole, represent an original work of authorship.

Preexisting Material (space 6a): Complete this space **and** space 6b for derivative works. In this space identify the preexisting work that has been recast, transformed, or adapted. Examples of preexisting material might be "Grunewald Altarpiece"; or "19th century quilt design." Do not complete this space for compilations.

Material Added to This Work (space 6b): Give a brief, general statement of the **additional** new material covered by the copyright claim for which registration is sought. In the case of a derivative work, identify this new material. Examples: "Adaptation of design and additional artistic work"; "Reproduction of painting by photolithography"; "Additional cartographic material"; "Compilation of photographs." If the work is a compilation, give a brief, general statement describing both the material that has been compiled and the compilation itself. Example: "Compilation of 19th Century Political Cartoons."

7,8,9 SPACE 7, 8, 9: Fee, Correspondence, Certification, Return Address

Deposit Account: If you maintain a Deposit Account in the Copyright Office, identify it in space 7. Otherwise leave the space blank and send the fee of $10 with your application and deposit.

Correspondence (space 7): This space should contain the name, address, area code, and telephone number of the person to be consulted if correspondence about this application becomes necessary.

Certification (space 8): The application cannot be accepted unless it bears the date and the **handwritten signature** of the author or other copyright claimant, or of the owner of exclusive right(s), or of the duly authorized agent of the author, claimant, or owner of exclusive right(s).

Address for Return of Certificate (space 9): The address box must be completed legibly since the certificate will be returned in a window envelope.

MORE INFORMATION

Form of Deposit for Works of the Visual Arts

Exceptions to General Deposit Requirements: As explained on the reverse side of this page, the statutory deposit requirements (generally one copy for unpublished works and two copies for published works) will vary for particular kinds of works of the visual arts. The copyright law authorizes the Register of Copyrights to issue regulations specifying "the administrative classes into which works are to be placed for purposes of deposit and registration, and the nature of the copies or phonorecords to be deposited in the various classes specified." For particular classes, the regulations may require or permit "the deposit of identifying material instead of copies or phonorecords," or "the deposit of only one copy or phonorecord where two would normally be required."

What Should You Deposit? The detailed requirements with respect to the kind of deposit to accompany an application on Form VA are contained in the Copyright

Office Regulations. The following does not cover all of the deposit requirements, but is intended to give you some general guidance.

For an Unpublished Work, the material deposited should represent the entire copyrightable content of the work for which registration is being sought.

For a Published Work, the material deposited should generally consist of two complete copies of the best edition. Exceptions: (1) For certain types of works, one complete copy may be deposited instead of two. These include greeting cards, postcards, stationery, labels, advertisements, scientific drawings, and globes; (2) For most three-dimensional sculptural works, and for certain two-dimensional works, the Copyright Office Regulations require deposit of identifying material (photographs or drawings in a specified form) rather than copies; and (3) Under certain circumstances, for works published in five copies or less or in limited, numbered editions, the deposit may consist of one copy or of identifying reproductions.

FORM VA
UNITED STATES COPYRIGHT OFFICE

REGISTRATION NUMBER

VA   VAU

EFFECTIVE DATE OF REGISTRATION

Month   Day   Year

DO NOT WRITE ABOVE THIS LINE. IF YOU NEED MORE SPACE, USE A SEPARATE CONTINUATION SHEET.

1

TITLE OF THIS WORK ▼   NATURE OF THIS WORK ▼ See instructions

PREVIOUS OR ALTERNATIVE TITLES ▼

PUBLICATION AS A CONTRIBUTION If this work was published as a contribution to a periodical, serial, or collection, give information about the collective work in which the contribution appeared.   **Title of Collective Work ▼**

If published in a periodical or serial give: Volume ▼   Number ▼   Issue Date ▼   On Pages ▼

2

a

NAME OF AUTHOR ▼   DATES OF BIRTH AND DEATH
Year Born ▼   Yea. Died ▼

Was this contribution to the work a "work made for hire"?
☐ Yes   ☐ No

AUTHOR'S NATIONALITY OR DOMICILE
Name of Country
OR { Citizen of ▶_____
Domiciled in ▶_____

WAS THIS AUTHOR'S CONTRIBUTION TO THE WORK
Anonymous?   ☐ Yes ☐ No
Pseudonymous?   ☐ Yes ☐ No
If the answer to either of these questions is "Yes," see detailed instructions.

NOTE

Under the law, the "author" of a "work made for hire" is generally not the employer, not the employee (see instructions). For any part of this work that was "made for hire" check "Yes" in the space provided, give the employer (or other person for whom the work was prepared) as "Author" of that part, and leave the space for dates of birth and death blank.

NATURE OF AUTHORSHIP Briefly describe nature of the material created by this author in which copyright is claimed. ▼

b

NAME OF AUTHOR ▼   DATES OF BIRTH AND DEATH
Year Born ▼   Year Died ▼

Was this contribution to the work a "work made for hire"?
☐ Yes   ☐ No

AUTHOR'S NATIONALITY OR DOMICILE
Name of country
OR { Citizen of ▶_____
Domiciled in ▶_____

WAS THIS AUTHOR'S CONTRIBUTION TO THE WORK
Anonymous?   ☐ Yes ☐ No
Pseudonymous?   ☐ Yes ☐ No
If the answer to either of these questions is "Yes," see detailed instructions.

NATURE OF AUTHORSHIP Briefly describe nature of the material created by this author in which copyright is claimed. ▼

c

NAME OF AUTHOR ▼   DATES OF BIRTH AND DEATH
Year Born ▼   Year Died ▼

Was this contribution to the work a "work made for hire"?
☐ Yes   ☐ No

AUTHOR'S NATIONALITY OR DOMICILE
Name of Country
OR { Citizen of ▶_____
Domiciled in ▶_____

WAS THIS AUTHOR'S CONTRIBUTION TO THE WORK
Anonymous?   ☐ Yes ☐ No
Pseudonymous?   ☐ Yes ☐ No
If the answer to either of these questions is "Yes," see detailed instructions.

NATURE OF AUTHORSHIP Briefly describe nature of the material created by this author in which copyright is claimed. ▼

3

YEAR IN WHICH CREATION OF THIS WORK WAS COMPLETED This information must be given in all cases.   ◀ Year

DATE AND NATION OF FIRST PUBLICATION OF THIS PARTICULAR WORK
Complete this information Month ▶_____ Day ▶_____ Year ▶_____
ONLY if this work has been published.   ◀ Nation

4

See instructions before completing this space.

COPYRIGHT CLAIMANT(S) Name and address must be given even if the claimant is the same as the author given in space 2.▼

TRANSFER If the claimant(s) named here in space 4 are different from the author(s) named in space 2..give a brief statement of how the claimant(s) obtained ownership of the copyright.▼

APPLICATION RECEIVED

ONE DEPOSIT RECEIVED

TWO DEPOSITS RECEIVED

REMITTANCE NUMBER AND DATE

DO NOT WRITE HERE OFFICE USE ONLY

MORE ON BACK ▶ • Complete all applicable spaces (numbers 5-9) on the reverse side of this page.
• See detailed instructions.   • Sign the form at line 8.

DO NOT WRITE HERE
Page 1 of_____pages_

EXAMINED BY		FORM VA
CHECKED BY		

☐ CORRESPONDENCE Yes

☐ DEPOSIT ACCOUNT FUNDS USED

FOR COPYRIGHT OFFICE USE ONLY

DO NOT WRITE ABOVE THIS LINE. IF YOU NEED MORE SPACE, USE A SEPARATE CONTINUATION SHEET.

PREVIOUS REGISTRATION Has registration for this work, or for an earlier version of this work, already been made in the Copyright Office?
☐ **Yes** ☐ **No** If your answer is "Yes," why is another registration being sought? (Check appropriate box) ▼
☐ This is the first published edition of a work previously registered in unpublished form.
☐ This is the first application submitted by this author as copyright claimant.
☐ This is a changed version of the work, as shown by space 6 on this application.
If your answer is "Yes," give: **Previous Registration Number** ▼   **Year of Registration** ▼

5

DERIVATIVE WORK OR COMPILATION Complete both space 6a & 6b for a derivative work; complete only 6b for a compilation.
a. **Preexisting Material** Identify any preexisting work or works that this work is based on or incorporates. ▼

b. **Material Added to This Work** Give a brief, general statement of the material that has been added to this work and in which copyright is claimed.▼

6

See instructions before completing this space.

DEPOSIT ACCOUNT If the registration fee is to be charged to a Deposit Account established in the Copyright Office, give name and number of Account.
Name ▼   **Account Number** ▼

7

CORRESPONDENCE Give name and address to which correspondence about this application should be sent.   Name/Address/Apt/City/State/Zip ▼

Area Code & Telephone Number ▶

Be sure to give your daytime phone ◀ number.

CERTIFICATION* I, the undersigned, hereby certify that I am the
Check only one ▼
☐ author
☐ other copyright claimant
☐ owner of exclusive right(s)
☐ authorized agent of_____
         Name of author or other copyright claimant, or owner of exclusive right(s) ▲

of the work identified in this application and that the statements made
by me in this application are correct to the best of my knowledge.

Typed or printed name and date ▼ If this is a published work, this date must be the same as or later than the date of publication given in space 3.
_____ date ▶ _____

Handwritten signature (X) ▼

8

MAIL CERTIFI-CATE TO	Name ▼	Have you: • Completed all necessary spaces? • Signed your application in space 8?
Certificate will be mailed in window envelope	Number/Street/Apartment Number ▼	• Enclosed check or money order for $10 payable to *Register of Copyrights*? • Enclosed your deposit material with the application and fee?
	City/State/ZIP ▼	**MAIL TO:** Register of Copyrights, Library of Congress, Washington, D.C. 20559.

9

* 17 U.S.C. § 506(e): Any person who knowingly makes a false representation of a material fact in the application for copyright registration provided for by section 409, or in any written statement filed in connection with the application, shall be fined not more than $2,500.

U.S. GOVERNMENT PRINTING OFFICE: 1987—181—531/60,009   August 1987—60,000

195

Filling Out Application Form SR

Detach and read these instructions before completing this form. Make sure all applicable spaces have been filled in before you return this form.

BASIC INFORMATION

When to Use This Form: Use Form SR for copyright registration of published or unpublished sound recordings. It should be used where the copyright claim is limited to the sound recording itself, and it may also be used where the same copyright claimant is seeking simultaneous registration of the underlying musical, dramatic, or literary work embodied in the phonorecord.

With one exception, "sound recordings" are works that result from the fixation of a series of musical, spoken, or other sounds. The exception is for the audio portions of audiovisual works, such as a motion picture soundtrack or an audio cassette accompanying a filmstrip; these are considered a part of the audiovisual work as a whole.

Deposit to Accompany Application: An application for copyright registration of a sound recording must be accompanied by a deposit consisting of phonorecords representing the entire work for which registration is to be made.

Unpublished Work: Deposit one complete phonorecord.

Published Work: Deposit two complete phonorecords of the best edition, together with "any printed or other visually perceptible material" published with the phonorecords.

Work First Published Outside the United States: Deposit one complete phonorecord of the first foreign edition.

Contribution to a Collective Work: Deposit one complete phonorecord of the best edition of the collective work.

The Copyright Notice: For published sound recordings, the law provides that a copyright notice in a specified form "shall be placed on all publicly distributed phonorecords of the sound recording." Use of the copyright notice is the responsibility of the copyright owner and does not require advance permission from the Copyright Office. The required form of the notice for phonorecords of sound recordings consists of three elements: (1) the symbol "℗" (the letter "P" in a circle); (2) the year of first publication of the sound recording; and (3) the name of the owner of copyright. For example: "℗ 1981 Rittenhouse Record Co." The notice is to be "placed on the surface of the phonorecord, or on the label or container, in such manner and location as to give reasonable notice of the claim of copyright." For further information about copyright, write: Information and Publications Section, LM-455
Copyright Office, Library of Congress, Washington, D.C. 20559

LINE-BY-LINE INSTRUCTIONS

1 SPACE 1: Title

Title of This Work: Every work submitted for copyright registration must be given a title to identify that particular work. If the phonorecords or any accompanying printed material bear a title (or an identifying phrase that could serve as a title), transcribe that wording completely and exactly on the application. Indexing of the registration and future identification of the work may depend on the information you give here.

Nature of Material Recorded: Indicate the general type or character of the works or other material embodied in the recording. The box marked "Literary" should be checked for nondramatic spoken material of all sorts, including narration, interviews, panel discussions, and training material. If the material recorded is not musical, dramatic, or literary in nature, check "Other" and briefly describe the type of sounds fixed in the recording. For example: "Sound Effects"; "Bird Calls"; "Crowd Noises."

Previous or Alternative Titles: Complete this space if there are any additional titles for the work under which someone searching for the registration might be likely to look, or under which a document pertaining to the work might be recorded.

2 SPACE 2: Author(s)

General Instructions: After reading these instructions, decide who are the "authors" of this work for copyright purposes. Then, unless the work is a "collective work," give the requested information about every "author" who contributed any appreciable amount of copyrightable matter to this version of the work. If you need further space, request additional Continuation Sheets. In the case of a collective work, such as a collection of previously published or registered sound recordings, give information about the author of the collective work as a whole. If you are submitting this Form SR to cover the recorded musical, dramatic, or literary work as well as the sound recording itself, it is important for space 2 to include full information about the various authors of all of the material covered by the copyright claim, making clear the nature of each author's contribution.

Name of Author: The fullest form of the author's name should be given. Unless the work was "made for hire," the individual who actually created the work is its "author." In the case of a work made for hire, the statute provides that "the employer or other person for whom the work was prepared is considered the author."

What is a "Work Made for Hire"? A "work made for hire" is defined as: (1) "a work prepared by an employee within the scope of his or her employment"; or (2) "a work specially ordered or commissioned for use as a contribution to a collective work, as a part of a motion picture or other audiovisual work, as a translation, as a supplementary work, as a compilation, as an instructional text, as a test, as answer material for a test, or as an atlas, if the parties expressly agree in a written instrument signed by them that the work shall be considered a work made for hire." If you have checked "Yes" to indicate that the work was "made for hire," you must give the full legal name of the employer (or other person for whom the work was prepared). You may also include the name of the employee along with the name of the employer (for example: "Elster Record Co., employer for hire of John Ferguson").

"Anonymous" or "Pseudonymous" Work: An author's contribution to a work is "anonymous" if that author is not identified on the copies or phonorecords of the work. An author's contribution to a work is "pseudonymous" if that author is identified on the copies or phonorecords under a fictitious name. If the work is "anonymous" you may: (1) leave the line blank; or (2) state "anonymous" on the line; or (3) reveal the author's identity. If the work is "pseudonymous" you may: (1) leave the line blank; or (2) give the pseudonym and identify it as such (for example: "Huntley Haverstock, pseudonym"); or (3) reveal the author's name, making clear which is the real name and which is the pseudonym (for example: "Judith Barton, whose pseudonym is Madeline Elster"). However, the citizenship or domicile of the author must be given in all cases.

Dates of Birth and Death: If the author is dead, the statute requires that the year of death be included in the application unless the work is anonymous or pseudonymous. The author's birth date is optional, but is useful as a form of identification. Leave this space blank if the author's contribution was a "work made for hire."

Author's Nationality or Domicile: Give the country of which the author is a citizen, or the country in which the author is domiciled. Nationality or domicile must be given in all cases.

Nature of Authorship: Give a brief general statement of the nature of this particular author's contribution to the work. If you are submitting this Form SR to cover both the sound recording and the underlying musical, dramatic, or literary work, make sure that the precise nature of each author's contribution is reflected here. Examples where the authorship pertains to the recording: "Sound Recording"; "Performance and Recording"; "Compilation and Remixing of Sounds." Examples where the authorship pertains to both the recording and the underlying work: "Words, Music, Performance, Recording"; "Arrangement of Music and Recording"; "Compilation of Poems and Reading."

196

3 SPACE 3: Creation and Publication

General Instructions: Do not confuse "creation" with "publication." Every application for copyright registration must state "the year in which creation of the work was completed." Give the date and nation of first publication only if the work has been published.

Creation: Under the statute, a work is "created" when it is fixed in a copy or phonorecord for the first time. Where a work has been prepared over a period of time, the part of the work existing in fixed form on a particular date constitutes the created work on that date. The date you give here should be the year in which the author completed the particular version for which registration is now being sought, even if other versions exist or if further changes or additions are planned.

Publication: The statute defines "publication" as "the distribution of copies or phonorecords of a work to the public by sale or other transfer of ownership, or by rental, lease, or lending"; a work is also "published" if there has been an "offering to distribute copies or phonorecords to a group of persons for purposes of further distribution, public performance, or public display." Give the full date (month, day, year) when, and the country where, publication first occurred. If first publication took place simultaneously in the United States and other countries, it is sufficient to state "U.S.A."

4 SPACE 4: Claimant(s)

Name(s) and Address(es) of Copyright Claimant(s): Give the name(s) and address(es) of the copyright claimant(s) in this work even if the claimant is the same as the author. Copyright in a work belongs initially to the author of the work (including, in the case of a work made for hire, the employer or other person for whom the work was prepared). The copyright claimant is either the author of the work or a person or organization to whom the copyright initially belonging to the author has been transferred.

Transfer: The statute provides that, if the copyright claimant is not the author, the application for registration must contain "a brief statement of how the claimant obtained ownership of the copyright." If any copyright claimant named in space 4 is not an author named in space 2, give a brief, general statement summarizing the means by which that claimant obtained ownership of the copyright. Examples: "By written contract"; "Transfer of all rights by author"; "Assignment"; "By will." Do not attach transfer documents or other attachments or riders.

5 SPACE 5: Previous Registration

General Instructions: The questions in space 5 are intended to find out whether an earlier registration has been made for this work and, if so, whether there is any basis for a new registration. As a rule, only one basic copyright registration can be made for the same version of a particular work.

Same Version: If this version is substantially the same as the work covered by a previous registration, a second registration is not generally possible unless: (1) the work has been registered in unpublished form and a second registration is now being sought to cover this first published edition; or (2) someone other than the author is identified as copyright claimant in the earlier registration, and the author is now seeking registration in his or her own name. If either of these two exceptions apply, check the appropriate box and give the earlier registration number and date. Otherwise, do not submit Form SR; instead, write the Copyright Office for information about supplementary registration or recordation of transfers of copyright ownership.

Changed Version: If the work has been changed, and you are now seeking registration to cover the additions or revisions, check the last box in space 6, give the earlier registration number and date, and complete both parts of space 6 in accordance with the instructions below.

Previous Registration Number and Date: If more than one previous registration has been made for the work, give the number and date of the latest registration.

6 SPACE 6: Derivative Work or Compilation

General Instructions: Complete space 6 if this work is a "changed version," "compilation," or "derivative work," and if it incorporates one or more earlier works that have already been published or registered for copyright, or that have fallen into the public domain, or sound recordings that were fixed before February 15, 1972. A "compilation" is defined as "a work formed by the collection and assembling of preexisting materials or of data that are selected, coordinated, or arranged in such a way that the resulting work as a whole constitutes an original work of authorship." A "derivative work" is "a work based on one or more preexisting works." Examples of derivative works include recordings reissued with substantial editorial revisions or abridgments of the recorded sounds, and recordings republished with new recorded material, or "any other form in which a work may be recast, transformed, or adapted." Derivative works also include works "consisting of editorial revisions, annotations, or other modifications" if these changes, as a whole, represent an original work of authorship.

Preexisting Material (space 6a): Complete this space and space 6b for derivative works. In this space identify the preexisting work that has been recast, transformed, or adapted. For example, the preexisting material might be: "1970 recording by Sperryville Symphony of Bach Double Concerto." Do not complete this space for compilations.

Material Added to This Work (space 6b): Give a brief, general statement of the additional new material covered by the copyright claim for which registration is sought. In the case of a derivative work, identify this new material. Examples: "Recorded performances on bands 1 and 3"; "Remixed sounds from original multitrack sound sources"; "New words, arrangement, and additional sounds." If the work is a compilation, give a brief, general statement describing both the material that has been compiled and the compilation itself. Example: "Compilation of 1938 Recordings by various swing bands."

7,8,9 SPACE 7, 8, 9: Fee, Correspondence, Certification, Return Address

Deposit Account: If you maintain a Deposit Account in the Copyright Office, identify it in space 7. Otherwise leave the space blank and send the fee of $10 with your application and deposit.

Correspondence (space 7): This space should contain the name, address, area code, and telephone number of the person to be consulted if correspondence about this application becomes necessary.

Certification (space 8): The application cannot be accepted unless it bears the date and the **handwritten signature** of the author or other copyright claimant, or of the owner of exclusive right(s), or of the duly authorized agent of the author, claimant, or owner of exclusive right(s).

Address for Return of Certificate (space 9): The address box must be completed legibly since the certificate will be returned in a window envelope.

MORE INFORMATION

"Works": "Works" are the basic subject matter of copyright; they are what authors create and copyright protects. The statute draws a sharp distinction between the "work" and "any material object in which the work is embodied."

"Copies" and "Phonorecords": These are the two types of material objects in which "works" are embodied. In general, "copies" are objects from which a work can be read or visually perceived, directly or with the aid of a machine or device, such as manuscripts, books, sheet music, film, and videotape. "Phonorecords" are objects embodying fixations of sounds, such as audio tapes and phonograph disks. For example, a song (the "work") can be reproduced in sheet music ("copies") or phonograph disks ("phonorecords"), or both.

"Sound Recordings": These are "works," not "copies" or "phonorecords." "Sound recordings" are "works" that result from the fixation of a series of musical, spoken, or other sounds, but not including the sounds accompanying a motion picture or other audiovisual work." Example: When a record company issues a new release, the release will typically involve two distinct "works": the "musical work" that has been recorded, and the "sound recording" as a separate work in itself. The material objects that the record company sends out are "phonorecords": physical reproductions of both the "musical work" and the "sound recording."

Should You File More Than One Application?

If your work consists of a recorded musical, dramatic, or literary work, and both that "work," and the sound recording as a separate "work," are eligible for registration, the application form you should file depends on the following:

File Only Form SR if: The copyright claimant is the same for both the musical, dramatic, or literary work and for the sound recording, and you are seeking a single registration to cover both of these "works."

File Only Form PA (or Form TX) if: You are seeking to register only the musical, dramatic, or literary work, not the sound recording. Form PA is appropriate for works of the performing arts; Form TX is for nondramatic literary works.

Separate Applications Should Be Filed on Form PA (or Form TX) and on Form SR if: (1) The copyright claimant for the musical, dramatic, or literary work is different from the copyright claimant for the sound recording; or (2) You prefer to have separate registrations for the musical, dramatic, or literary work and for the sound recording.

197

FORM SR
UNITED STATES COPYRIGHT OFFICE

REGISTRATION NUMBER

SR   SRU

EFFECTIVE DATE OF REGISTRATION

Month   Day   Year

DO NOT WRITE ABOVE THIS LINE. IF YOU NEED MORE SPACE, USE A SEPARATE CONTINUATION SHEET.

1

TITLE OF THIS WORK ▼

PREVIOUS OR ALTERNATIVE TITLES ▼

NATURE OF MATERIAL RECORDED ▼ See instructions.
☐ Musical ☐ Musical-Dramatic
☐ Dramatic ☐ Literary
☐ Other _____

2

a

NAME OF AUTHOR ▼

DATES OF BIRTH AND DEATH
Year Born ▼   Year Died ▼

Was this contribution to the work a "work made for hire"?
☐ Yes
☐ No

AUTHOR'S NATIONALITY OR DOMICILE
Name of Country
OR { Citizen of ▶ _____
Domiciled in ▶ _____

WAS THIS AUTHOR'S CONTRIBUTION TO THE WORK
Anonymous? ☐ Yes ☐ No
Pseudonymous? ☐ Yes ☐ No
If the answer to either of these questions is "Yes," see detailed instructions.

NATURE OF AUTHORSHIP Briefly describe nature of the material created by this author in which copyright is claimed. ▼

NOTE
Under the law, the "author" of a "work made for hire" is generally the employer, not the employee (see instructions). For any part of this work that was "made for hire" check "Yes" in the space provided, give the employer (or other person for whom the work was prepared) as "Author" of that part, and leave the space for dates of birth and death blank.

b

NAME OF AUTHOR ▼

DATES OF BIRTH AND DEATH
Year Born ▼   Year Died ▼

Was this contribution to the work a "work made for hire"?
☐ Yes
☐ No

AUTHOR'S NATIONALITY OR DOMICILE
Name of country
OR { Citizen of ▶ _____
Domiciled in ▶ _____

WAS THIS AUTHOR'S CONTRIBUTION TO THE WORK
Anonymous? ☐ Yes ☐ No
Pseudonymous? ☐ Yes ☐ No
If the answer to either of these questions is "Yes," see detailed instructions.

NATURE OF AUTHORSHIP Briefly describe nature of the material created by this author in which copyright is claimed. ▼

c

NAME OF AUTHOR ▼

DATES OF BIRTH AND DEATH
Year Born ▼   Year Died ▼

Was this contribution to the work a "work made for hire"?
☐ Yes
☐ No

AUTHOR'S NATIONALITY OR DOMICILE
Name of Country
OR { Citizen of ▶ _____
Domiciled in ▶ _____

WAS THIS AUTHOR'S CONTRIBUTION TO THE WORK
Anonymous? ☐ Yes ☐ No
Pseudonymous? ☐ Yes ☐ No
If the answer to either of these questions is "Yes," see detailed instructions.

NATURE OF AUTHORSHIP Briefly describe nature of the material created by this author in which copyright is claimed. ▼

3

YEAR IN WHICH CREATION OF THIS WORK WAS COMPLETED This information must be given in all cases. ◀ Year

DATE AND NATION OF FIRST PUBLICATION OF THIS PARTICULAR WORK
Complete this information ONLY if this work has been published.
Month ▶ _____ Day ▶ _____ Year ▶ _____ ◀ Nation

4

See instructions before completing this space.

COPYRIGHT CLAIMANT(S) Name and address must be given even if the claimant is the same as the author given in space 2.▼

TRANSFER If the claimant(s) named here in space 4 are different from the author(s) named in space 2, give a brief statement of how the claimant(s) obtained ownership of the copyright.▼

APPLICATION RECEIVED

ONE DEPOSIT RECEIVED

TWO DEPOSITS RECEIVED

REMITTANCE NUMBER AND DATE

DO NOT WRITE HERE
OFFICE USE ONLY

MORE ON BACK ▶ • Complete all applicable spaces (numbers 5-9) on the reverse side of this page.
• See detailed instructions. • Sign the form at line 8.

DO NOT WRITE HERE
Page 1 of _____ pages

EXAMINED BY		FORM SR
CHECKED BY		
☐ CORRESPONDENCE Yes		FOR COPYRIGHT OFFICE USE ONLY
☐ DEPOSIT ACCOUNT FUNDS USED		

DO NOT WRITE ABOVE THIS LINE. IF YOU NEED MORE SPACE, USE A SEPARATE CONTINUATION SHEET.

PREVIOUS REGISTRATION Has registration for this work, or for an earlier version of this work, already been made in the Copyright Office?
☐ **Yes** ☐ **No** If your answer is "Yes," why is another registration being sought? (Check appropriate box) ▼
☐ This is the first published edition of a work previously registered in unpublished form.
☐ This is the first application submitted by this author as copyright claimant.
☐ This is a changed version of the work, as shown by space 6 on this application.
If your answer is "Yes," give: **Previous Registration Number** ▼   **Year of Registration** ▼

5

DERIVATIVE WORK OR COMPILATION Complete both space 6a & 6b for a derivative work; complete only 6b for a compilation.
a. Preexisting Material Identify any preexisting work or works that this work is based on or incorporates. ▼

See instructions before completing this space.

b. Material Added to This Work Give a brief, general statement of the material that has been added to this work and in which copyright is claimed. ▼

6

DEPOSIT ACCOUNT If the registration fee is to be charged to a Deposit Account established in the Copyright Office, give name and number of Account.
Name ▼   **Account Number** ▼

7

CORRESPONDENCE Give name and address to which correspondence about this application should be sent.   Name/Address/Apt/City/State/Zip ▼

Be sure to give your daytime phone number

Area Code & Telephone Number ▶

CERTIFICATION* I, the undersigned, hereby certify that I am the
Check one ▼
☐ author
☐ other copyright claimant
☐ owner of exclusive right(s)
☐ authorized agent of_____
Name of author or other copyright claimant, or owner of exclusive right(s) ▲

of the work identified in this application and that the statements made
by me in this application are correct to the best of my knowledge.

Typed or printed name and date ▼ If this is a published work, this date must be the same as or later than the date of publication given in space 3.

_____ date ▶ _____

Handwritten signature (X) ▼

8

MAIL CERTIFI-CATE TO	Name ▼	**Have you:** • Completed all necessary spaces? • Signed your application in space 8?
Certificate will be mailed in window envelope	Number/Street/Apartment Number ▼	• Enclosed check or money order for $10 payable to *Register of Copyrights?* • Enclosed your deposit material with the application and fee?
	City/State/ZIP ▼	**MAIL TO:** Register of Copyrights, Library of Congress, Washington, D.C. 20559.

9

* 17 U.S.C. § 506(e): Any person who knowingly makes a false representation of a material fact in the application for copyright registration provided for by section 409 or in any written statement filed in connection with the application, shall be fined not more than $2,500.
☆ U.S. GOVERNMENT PRINTING OFFICE: 1982-361-278/63

Sept. 1982—210,000

199

FORM RE

UNITED STATES COPYRIGHT OFFICE
LIBRARY OF CONGRESS
WASHINGTON, D.C. 20559

APPLICATION FOR
Renewal Registration

HOW TO REGISTER A RENEWAL CLAIM:

- **First:** Study the information on this page and make sure you know the answers to two questions:

  (1) What are the renewal time limits in your case?

  (2) Who can claim the renewal?

- **Second:** Turn this page over and read through the specific instructions for filling out Form RE. Make sure, before starting to complete the form, that the copyright is now eligible for renewal, that you are authorized to file a renewal claim, and that you have all of the information about the copyright you will need.

- **Third:** Complete all applicable spaces on Form RE, following the line-by-line instructions on the back of this page. Use typewriter, or print the information in dark ink.

- **Fourth:** Detach this sheet and send your completed Form RE to: Register of Copyrights, Library of Congress, Washington, D.C. 20559. Unless you have a Deposit Account in the Copyright Office, your application must be accompanied by a check or money order for $6, payable to: *Register of Copyrights*. Do not send copies, phonorecords, or supporting documents with your renewal application.

WHAT IS RENEWAL OF COPYRIGHT? For works originally copyrighted between January 1, 1950 and December 31, 1977, the statute now in effect provides for a first term of copyright protection lasting for 28 years, with the possibility of renewal for a second term of 47 years. If a valid renewal registration is made for a work, its total copyright term is 75 years (a first term of 28 years, plus a renewal term of 47 years). Example: For a work copyrighted in 1960, the first term will expire in 1988, but if renewed at the proper time the copyright will last through the end of 2035.

SOME BASIC POINTS ABOUT RENEWAL:

(1) There are strict time limits and deadlines for renewing a copyright.

(2) Only certain persons who fall into specific categories named in the law can claim renewal.

(3) The new copyright law does away with renewal requirements for works first copyrighted after 1977. However, copyrights that were already in their first copyright term on January 1, 1978 (that is, works originally copyrighted between January 1, 1950 and December 31, 1977) **still have to be renewed** in order to be protected for a second term.

TIME LIMITS FOR RENEWAL REGISTRATION: The new copyright statute provides that, in order to renew a copyright, the renewal application and fee must be received in the Copyright Office "within one year prior to the expiration of the copyright." It also provides that all terms of copyright will run through the end of the year in which they would otherwise expire. Since all copyright terms will expire on December 31st of their last year, all periods for renewal registration will run from December 31st of the 27th year of the copyright, and will end on December 31st of the following year.

To determine the time limits for renewal in your case:

(1) First, find out the date of original copyright for the work. (In the case of works originally registered in unpublished form, the date of copyright is the date of registration; for published works, copyright begins on the date of first publication.)

(2) Then add 28 years to the year the work was originally copyrighted.

Your answer will be the calendar year during which the copyright will be eligible for renewal, and December 31st of that year will be the renewal deadline. Example: a work originally copyrighted on April 19, 1957, will be eligible for renewal between December 31, 1984, and December 31, 1985.

WHO MAY CLAIM RENEWAL: Renewal copyright may be claimed only by those persons specified in the law. Except in the case of four specific types of works, the law gives the right to claim renewal to the individual author of the work, regardless of who owned the copyright during the original term. If the author is dead, the statute gives the right to claim renewal to certain of the author's beneficiaries (widow and children, executors, or next of kin, depending on the circumstances). The present owner (proprietor) of the copyright is entitled to claim renewal only in four specified cases, as explained in more detail on the reverse of this page.

CAUTION: Renewal registration is possible only if an acceptable application and fee are **received** in the Copyright Office during the renewal period and before the renewal deadline. If an acceptable application and fee are not received before the renewal deadline, the work falls into the public domain and the copyright cannot be renewed. The Copyright Office has no discretion to extend the renewal time limits.

200

INSTRUCTIONS FOR COMPLETING FORM RE

SPACE 1: RENEWAL CLAIM(S)

• *General Instructions:* In order for this application to result in a valid renewal, space 1 must identify one or more of the persons who are entitled to renew the copyright under the statute. Give the full name and address of each claimant, with a statement of the basis of each claim, using the wording given in these instructions.

• *Persons Entitled to Renew:*

A. The following persons may claim renewal in all types of works except those enumerated in Paragraph B. below:

1. The author, if living. State the claim as: *the author.*

2. The widow, widower, and/or children of the author, if the author is not living. State the claim as: *the widow (widower) of the author* . . . .
(Name of author)

and/or *the child (children) of the deceased author* . . . .
(Name of author)

3. The author's executor(s), if the author left a will and if there is no surviving widow, widower, or child. State the claim as: *the executor(s) of the author*
. . . .
(Name of author)

4. The next of kin of the author, if the author left no will and if there is no surviving widow, widower, or child. State the claim as: *the next of kin of the deceased author* . . . . *there being no will.*
(Name of author)

B. In the case of the following four types of works, the proprietor (owner of the copyright at the time of renewal registration) may claim renewal:

1. Posthumous work (a work as to which no copyright assignment or other contract for exploitation has occurred during the author's lifetime). State the claim as: *proprietor of copyright in a posthumous work.*

2. Periodical, cyclopedic, or other composite work. State the claim as: *proprietor of copyright in a composite work.*

3. "Work copyrighted by a corporate body otherwise than as assignee or licensee of the individual author." State the claim as: *proprietor of copyright in a work copyrighted by a corporate body otherwise than as assignee or licensee of the individual author.* (This type of claim is considered appropriate in relatively few cases.)

4. Work copyrighted by an employer for whom such work was made for hire. State the claim as: *proprietor of copyright in a work made for hire.*

SPACE 2: WORK RENEWED

• *General Instructions:* This space is to identify the particular work being renewed. The information given here should agree with that appearing in the certificate of original registration.

• *Title:* Give the full title of the work, together with any subtitles or descriptive wording included with the title in the original registration. In the case of a musical composition, give the specific instrumentation of the work.

• *Renewable Matter:* Copyright in a new version of a previous work (such as an arrangement, translation, dramatization, compilation, or work republished with new matter) covers only the additions, changes, or other new material appearing for the first time in that version. If this work was a new version, state in general the new matter upon which copyright was claimed.

• *Contribution to Periodical, Serial, or other Composite Work:* Separate renewal registration is possible for a work published as a contribution to a periodical, serial, or other composite work, whether the contribution was copyrighted independently or as part of the larger work in which it appeared. Each contribution published in a separate issue ordinarily requires a separate renewal registration. However, the new law provides an alternative, permitting groups of periodical contributions by the same individual author to be combined under a single renewal application and fee in certain cases.

If this renewal application covers a single contribution, give all of the requested information in space 2. If you are seeking to renew a group of contributions, include a reference such as "See space 5" in space 2 and give the requested information about all of the contributions in space 5.

SPACE 3: AUTHOR(S)

• *General Instructions:* The copyright secured in a new version of a work is independent of any copyright protection in material published earlier. The only "authors" of a new version are those who contributed copyrightable matter to it. Thus, for renewal purposes, the person who wrote the original version on

which the new work is based cannot be regarded as an "author" of the new version, unless that person also contributed to the new matter.

• *Authors of Renewable Matter:* Give the full names of all authors who contributed copyrightable matter to this particular version of the work.

SPACE 4: FACTS OF ORIGINAL REGISTRATION

• *General Instructions:* Each item in space 4 should agree with the information appearing in the original registration for the work. If the work being renewed is a single contribution to a periodical or composite work that was not separately registered, give information about the particular issue in which the contribution appeared. You may leave this space blank if you are completing space 5.

• *Original Registration Number:* Give the full registration number, which is a series of numerical digits, preceded by one or more letters. The registration

number appears in the upper right hand corner of the certificate of registration.

• *Original Copyright Claimant:* Give the name in which ownership of the copyright was claimed in the original registration.

• *Date of Publication or Registration:* Give only one date. If the original registration gave a publication date, it should be transcribed here; otherwise the registration was for an unpublished work, and the date of registration should be given.

SPACE 5: GROUP RENEWALS

• *General Instructions:* A single renewal registration can be made for a group of works if **all** of the following statutory conditions are met: (1) all of the works were written by the same author, who is named in space 3 and who is or was an individual (not an employer for hire); (2) all of the works were first published as contributions to periodicals (including newspapers) and were copyrighted on their first publication; (3) the renewal claimant or claimants, and the basis of claim or claims, as stated in space 1, is the same for all of the works; (4) the renewal application and fee are "received not more than 28 or less than 27 years after the 31st day of December of the calendar year in which all of the works were first published"; and (5) the renewal application identifies each work separately, including the periodical containing it and the date of first publication.

Time Limits for Group Renewals: To be renewed as a group, all of the contributions must have been first published during the same calendar year. For example, suppose six contributions by the same author were published on April 1, 1960, July 1, 1960, November 1, 1960, February 1, 1961, July 1, 1961, and March 1, 1962. The three 1960 copyrights can be combined and renewed at any time during 1988, and the two 1961 copyrights can be renewed as a group during 1989, but the 1962 copyright must be renewed by itself, in 1990.

Identification of Each Work: Give all of the requested information for each contribution. The registration number should be that for the contribution itself if it was separately registered, and the registration number for the periodical issue if it was not.

SPACES 6, 7 AND 8: FEE, MAILING INSTRUCTIONS, AND CERTIFICATION

• *Deposit Account and Mailing Instructions (Space 6):* If you maintain a Deposit Account in the Copyright Office, identify it in space 6. Otherwise, you will need to send the renewal registration fee of $6 with your form. The space headed "Correspondence" should contain the name and address of the person to be consulted if correspondence about the form becomes necessary.

• *Certification (Space 7):* The renewal application is not acceptable unless it bears the handwritten signature of the renewal claimant or the duly authorized agent of the renewal claimant.

• *Address for Return of Certificate (Space 8):* The address box must be completed legibly, since the certificate will be returned in a window envelope.

FORM RE

UNITED STATES COPYRIGHT OFFICE

REGISTRATION NUMBER

EFFECTIVE DATE OF RENEWAL REGISTRATION

....
(Month)   (Day)   (Year)

DO NOT WRITE ABOVE THIS LINE.   FOR COPYRIGHT OFFICE USE ONLY

1 Renewal Claimant(s)	RENEWAL CLAIMANT(S), ADDRESS(ES), AND STATEMENT OF CLAIM: (See Instructions)
	1 Name .... Address .... Claiming as .... (Use appropriate statement from instructions)
	2 Name .... Address .... Claiming as .... (Use appropriate statement from instructions)
	3 Name .... Address .... Claiming as .... (Use appropriate statement from instructions)

2 Work Renewed	TITLE OF WORK IN WHICH RENEWAL IS CLAIMED:
	RENEWABLE MATTER:
	CONTRIBUTION TO PERIODICAL OR COMPOSITE WORK: Title of periodical or composite work: .... If a periodical or other serial, give: Vol. .... No. .... Issue Date ....

3 Author(s)	AUTHOR(S) OF RENEWABLE MATTER:

4 Facts of Original Registration	ORIGINAL REGISTRATION NUMBER:	ORIGINAL COPYRIGHT CLAIMANT:
	....	
	ORIGINAL DATE OF COPYRIGHT:	

• If the original registration for this work was made in published form, give: } OR { • If the original registration for this work was made in unpublished form, give:

DATE OF PUBLICATION: ....
(Month)   (Day)   (Year)

DATE OF REGISTRATION: ....
(Month)   (Day)   (Year)

202

	EXAMINED BY:	RENEWAL APPLICATION RECEIVED:	FOR COPYRIGHT OFFICE USE ONLY
	CHECKED BY:		
	DEPOSIT ACCOUNT FUNDS USED: ☐	REMITTANCE NUMBER AND DATE:	

DO NOT WRITE ABOVE THIS LINE. FOR COPYRIGHT OFFICE USE ONLY

RENEWAL FOR GROUP OF WORKS BY SAME AUTHOR: To make a single registration for a group of works by the same individual author published as contributions to periodicals (see instructions), give full information about each contribution. If more space is needed, request continuation sheet (Form RE/CON). — **(5) Renewal for Group of Works**

1
Title of Contribution: . . . .
Title of Periodical: . . . . Vol. . . . . No. . . . . . . Issue Date . . . .
Date of Publication: . . . . Registration Number: . . . .
(Month) (Day) (Year)

2
Title of Contribution: . . . .
Title of Periodical: . . . . Vol. . . . . No. . . . . . . Issue Date . . . .
Date of Publication: . . . . Registration Number: . . . .
(Month) (Day) (Year)

3
Title of Contribution: . . . .
Title of Periodical: . . . . Vol. . . . . No. . . . . . . Issue Date . . . .
Date of Publication: . . . . Registration Number: . . . .
(Month) (Day) (Year)

4
Title of Contribution: . . . .
Title of Periodical: . . . . Vol. . . . . No. . . . . . . Issue Date . . . .
Date of Publication: . . . . Registration Number: . . . .
(Month) (Day) (Year)

5
Title of Contribution: . . . .
Title of Periodical: . . . . Vol. . . . . No. . . . . . . Issue Date . . . .
Date of Publication: . . . . Registration Number: . . . .
(Month) (Day) (Year)

6
Title of Contribution: . . . .
Title of Periodical: . . . . Vol. . . . . No. . . . . . . Issue Date . . . .
Date of Publication: . . . . Registration Number: . . . .
(Month) (Day) (Year)

7
Title of Contribution: . . . .
Title of Periodical: . . . . Vol. . . . . No. . . . . . . Issue Date . . . .
Date of Publication: . . . . Registration Number: . . . .
(Month) (Day) (Year)

DEPOSIT ACCOUNT: (If the registration fee is to be charged to a Deposit Account established in the Copyright Office, give name and number of Account.)
Name: . . . .
Account Number: . . . .

CORRESPONDENCE: (Give name and address to which correspondence about this application should be sent.)
Name: . . . .
Address: . . . . (Apt.)
. . . .
(City) (State) (ZIP)

(6) Fee and Correspondence

CERTIFICATION: I, the undersigned, hereby certify that I am the: (Check one)
☐ renewal claimant ☐ duly authorized agent of: . . . .
(Name of renewal claimant)
of the work identified in this application, and that the statements made by me in this application are correct to the best of my knowledge.
Handwritten signature: (X) . . . .
Typed or printed name: . . . .
Date: . . . .

(7) Certification (Application must be signed)

. . . .
(Name)
. . . .
(Number, Street and Apartment Number)
. . . .
(City) (State) (ZIP code)

MAIL CERTIFICATE TO
(Certificate will be mailed in window envelope)

(8) Address for Return of Certificate

FORM CA

UNITED STATES COPYRIGHT OFFICE
LIBRARY OF CONGRESS
WASHINGTON, D.C. 20559

Application for
Supplementary Copyright Registration

To Correct or Amplify Information Given in the
Copyright Office Record of an Earlier Registration

What is "Supplementary Copyright Registration"? Supplementary registration is a special type of copyright registration provided for in section 408(d) of the copyright law.

Purpose of Supplementary Registration. As a rule, only one basic copyright registration can be made for the same work. To take care of cases where information in the basic registration turns out to be incorrect or incomplete, the law provides for "the filing of an application for supplementary registration, to correct an error in a copyright registration or to amplify the information given in a registration."

Earlier Registration Necessary. Supplementary registration can be made only if a basic copyright registration for the same work has already been completed.

Who May File. Once basic registration has been made for a work, any author or other copyright claimant, or owner of any exclusive right in the work, who wishes to correct or amplify the information given in the basic registration, may submit Form CA.

Please Note:

- Do not use Form CA to correct errors in statements on the copies or phonorecords of the work in question, or to reflect changes in the content of the work. If the work has been changed substantially, you should consider making an entirely new registration for the revised version to cover the additions or revisions.

- Do not use Form CA as a substitute for renewal registration. For works originally copyrighted between January 1, 1950 and December 31, 1977, registration of a renewal claim within strict time limits is necessary to extend the first 28-year copyright term to the full term of 75 years. This cannot be done by filing Form CA.

- Do not use Form CA as a substitute for recording a transfer of copyright or other document pertaining to rights under a copyright. Recording a document under section 205 of the statute gives all persons constructive notice of the facts stated in the document and may have other important consequences in cases of infringement or conflicting transfers. Supplementary registration does not have that legal effect.

How to Apply for Supplementary Registration:

First: Study the information on this page to make sure that filing an application on Form CA is the best procedure to follow in your case.

Second: Turn this page over and read through the specific instructions for filling out Form CA. Make sure, before starting to complete the form, that you have all of the detailed information about the basic registration you will need.

Third: Complete all applicable spaces on this form, following the line-by-line instructions on the back of this page. Use typewriter, or print the information in dark ink.

Fourth: Detach this sheet and send your completed Form CA to: Register of Copyrights, Library of Congress, Washington, D.C. 20559. Unless you have a Deposit Account in the Copyright Office, your application must be accompanied by a non-refundable filing fee in the form of a check or money order for $10 payable to: *Register of Copyrights.* Do not send copies, phonorecords, or supporting documents with your application, since they cannot be made part of the record of a supplementary registration.

What Happens When a Supplementary Registration is Made? When a supplementary registration is completed, the Copyright Office will assign it a new registration number in the appropriate registration category, and issue a certificate of supplementary registration under that number. The basic registration will not be expunged or cancelled, and the two registrations will both stand in the Copyright Office records. The supplementary registration will have the effect of calling the public's attention to a possible error or omission in the basic registration, and of placing the correct facts or the additional information on official record. Moreover, if the person on whose behalf Form CA is submitted is the same as the person identified as copyright claimant in the basic registration, the Copyright Office will place a note referring to the supplementary registration in its records of the basic registration.

PLEASE READ DETAILED INSTRUCTIONS ON REVERSE

Please read the following line-by-line instructions carefully and refer to them while completing Form CA.

INSTRUCTIONS
For Completing FORM CA (Supplementary Registration)

PART A: BASIC INSTRUCTIONS

• **General Instructions:** The information in this part identifies the basic registration to be corrected or amplified. Each item must agree exactly with the information as it already appears in the basic registration (even if the purpose of filing Form CA is to change one of these items).

• **Title of Work:** Give the title as it appears in the basic registration, including previous or alternative titles if they appear.

• **Registration Number:** This is a series of numerical digits, pre-ceded by one or more letters. The registration number appears in the upper right hand corner of the certificate of registration.

• **Registration Date:** Give the year when the basic registration was completed.

• **Name(s) of Author(s) and Name(s) of Copyright Claimant(s):** Give all of the names as they appear in the basic registration.

PART B: CORRECTION

• **General Instructions:** Complete this part **only** if information in the basic registration was incorrect at the time that basic registration was made. Leave this part blank and complete Part C, instead, if your purpose is to add, update, or clarify information rather than to rectify an actual error.

• **Location and Nature of Incorrect Information:** Give the line number and the heading or description of the space in the basic registration where the error occurs (for example: "Line number 3 . . . Citizenship of author").

• **Incorrect Information as it Appears in Basic Registration:** Transcribe the erroneous statement exactly as it appears in the basic registration.

• **Corrected Information:** Give the statement as it should have appeared.

• **Explanation of Correction (Optional):** If you wish, you may add an explanation of the error or its correction.

PART C. AMPLIFICATION

• **General Instructions:** Complete this part if you want to provide any of the following: (1) additional information that could have been given but was omitted at the time of basic registration; (2) changes in facts, such as changes of title or address of claimant, that have oc-curred since the basic registration; or (3) explanations clarifying infor-mation in the basic registration.

• **Location and Nature of Information to be Amplified:** Give the line number and the heading or description of the space in the basic registration where the information to be amplified appears.

• **Amplified Information:** Give a statement of the added, updated, or explanatory information as clearly and succinctly as possible.

• **Explanation of Amplification (Optional):** If you wish, you may add an explanation of the amplification.

PARTS D, E, F, G: CONTINUATION, FEE, MAILING INSTRUCTIONS AND CERTIFICATION

• **Continuation (Part D):** Use this space if you do not have enough room in Parts B or C.

• **Deposit Account and Mailing Instructions (Part E):** If you main-tain a Deposit Account in the Copyright Office, identify it in Part E. Otherwise, you will need to send the non-refundable filing fee of $10 with your form. The space headed "Correspondence" should contain the name and address of the person to be consulted if correspondence about the form becomes necessary.

• **Certification (Part F):** The application is not acceptable unless it bears the handwritten signature of the author, or other copyright clai-mant, or of the owner of exclusive right(s), or of the duly authorized agent of such author, claimant, or owner.

• **Address for Return of Certificate (Part G):** The address box must be completed legibly, since the certificate will be returned in a window envelope.

FORM CA
UNITED STATES COPYRIGHT OFFICE

REGISTRATION NUMBER

| TX | TXU | PA | PAU | VA | VAU | SR | SRU | RE |

Effective Date of Supplementary Registration

....

MONTH   DAY   YEAR

DO NOT WRITE ABOVE THIS LINE. FOR COPYRIGHT OFFICE USE ONLY

(A) Basic Instructions

TITLE OF WORK:

REGISTRATION NUMBER OF BASIC REGISTRATION: | YEAR OF BASIC REGISTRATION:

NAME(S) OF AUTHOR(S): | NAME(S) OF COPYRIGHT CLAIMANT(S):

(B) Correction

LOCATION AND NATURE OF INCORRECT INFORMATION IN BASIC REGISTRATION:
Line Number .... Line Heading or Description ....

INCORRECT INFORMATION AS IT APPEARS IN BASIC REGISTRATION:

CORRECTED INFORMATION:

EXPLANATION OF CORRECTION: (Optional)

(C) Amplification

LOCATION AND NATURE OF INFORMATION IN BASIC REGISTRATION TO BE AMPLIFIED:
Line Number .... Line Heading or Description ....

AMPLIFIED INFORMATION:

EXPLANATION OF AMPLIFIED INFORMATION: (Optional)

	EXAMINED BY: . . . . CHECKED BY:	FORM CA RECEIVED:	FOR COPYRIGHT OFFICE USE ONLY
	CORRESPONDENCE: ☐ YES	REMITTANCE NUMBER AND DATE:	
	REFERENCE TO THIS REGISTRATION ADDED TO BASIC REGISTRATION: ☐ YES ☐ NO	DEPOSIT ACCOUNT FUNDS USED: ☐	

DO NOT WRITE ABOVE THIS LINE. FOR COPYRIGHT OFFICE USE ONLY

CONTINUATION OF: (Check which) ☐ PART B OR ☐ PART C

D

Continuation

DEPOSIT ACCOUNT: If the registration fee is to be charged to a Deposit Account established in the Copyright Office, give name and number of Account:

Name . . . . Account Number . . . .

CORRESPONDENCE: Give name and address to which correspondence should be sent:

Name . . . . Apt. No. . . . .

Address . . . .
(Number and Street)   (City)   (State)   (ZIP Code)

E

**Deposit
Account and
Mailing
Instructions**

CERTIFICATION ✱ I, the undersigned, hereby certify that I am the: (Check one)

☐ author ☐ other copyright claimant ☐ owner of exclusive right(s) ☐ authorized agent of: . . . .
(Name of author or other copyright claimant, or owner of exclusive right(s))
of the work identified in this application and that the statements made by me in this application are correct to the best of my knowledge.

Handwritten signature: (X) . . . .

Typed or printed name. . . . .

Date: . . . .

✱ 17 USC §506(e) FALSE REPRESENTATION—Any person who knowingly makes a false representation of a material fact in the application for copyright registration provided for by section 409, or in any written statement filed in connection with the application, shall be fined not more than $2,500.

F

**Certification
(Application
must be
signed)**

**MAIL
CERTIFICATE
TO**

. . . .
(Name)
. . . .
(Number, Street and Apartment Number)
. . . .
(City)   (State)   (ZIP code)

(Certificate will
be mailed in
window envelope)

G

**Address for
Return of
Certificate**

April 1987—20,000   ☆U.S. GOVERNMENT PRINTING OFFICE: 1987—181-531/40,022

THIS FORM:

- Can be used solely as an adjunct to a basic application for copyright registration.
- Is not acceptable unless submitted together with Form TX, Form PA, or Form VA.
- Is acceptable only if the group of works listed on it all qualify for a single copyright registration under 17 U.S.C. § 408 (c)(2).

FORM GR/CP

UNITED STATES COPYRIGHT OFFICE
LIBRARY OF CONGRESS
WASHINGTON, D.C. 20559

ADJUNCT APPLICATION
for Copyright Registration for a
Group of Contributions to Periodicals

WHEN TO USE FORM GR/CP: Form GR/CP is the appropriate adjunct application form to use when you are submitting a basic application on Form TX, Form PA, or Form VA, for a group of works that qualify for a single registration under section 408(c)(2) of the copyright statute.

WHEN DOES A GROUP OF WORKS QUALIFY FOR A SINGLE REGISTRATION UNDER 17 U.S.C. §408 (c)(2)? The statute provides that a single copyright registration for a group of works can be made if **all** of the following conditions are met:

(1) All of the works are by the same author, who is an individual (not an employer for hire); and

(2) All of the works were first published as contributions to periodicals (including newspapers) within a twelve-month period; and

(3) Each of the contributions as first published bore a separate copyright notice, and the name of the owner of copyright in the work (or an abbreviation or alternative designation of the owner) was the same in each notice; and

(4) One copy of the entire periodical issue or newspaper section in which each contribution was first published must be deposited with the application; and

(5) The application must identify each contribution separately, including the periodical containing it and the date of its first publication.

How to Apply for Group Registration:

First: Study the information on this page to make sure that all of the works you want to register together as a group qualify for a single registration.

Second: Turn this page over and read through the detailed instructions for group registration. Decide which form you should use for the basic registration (Form TX for nondramatic literary works; or Form PA for musical, dramatic, and other works of the performing arts; or Form VA for pictorial and graphic works). Be sure that you have all of the information you need before you start filling out both the basic and the adjunct application forms.

Third: Complete the basic application form, following the detailed instructions accompanying it **and the special instructions on the reverse of this page**.

Fourth: Complete the adjunct application on Form GR/CP and mail it, together with the basic application form and the required copy of each contribution, to: Register of Copyrights, Library of Congress, Washington, D.C. 20559. Unless you have a Deposit Account in the Copyright Office, your application and copies must be accompanied by a check or money order for $10, payable to: *Register of Copyrights.*

208

PROCEDURE FOR GROUP REGISTRATION

TWO APPLICATION FORMS MUST BE FILED

When you apply for a single registration to cover a group of contributions to periodicals, you must submit two application forms:

(1) A basic application on either Form TX, or Form PA, or Form VA. It must contain all of the information required for copyright registration except the titles and information concerning publication of the contributions.

(2) An adjunct application on Form GR/CP. The purpose of this form is to provide separate identification for each of the contributions and to give information about their first publication, as required by the statute.

WHICH BASIC APPLICATION FORM TO USE

The basic application form you choose to submit should be determined by the nature of the contributions you are registering. As long as they meet the statutory qualifications for group registration (outlined on the reverse of this page), the contributions can be registered together even if they are entirely different in nature, type, or content. However, you must choose which of three forms is generally the most appropriate on which to submit your basic application:

Form TX: for nondramatic literary works consisting primarily of text. Examples are fiction, verse, articles, news stories, features, essays, reviews, editorials, columns, quizzes, puzzles, and advertising copy.

Form PA: for works of the performing arts. Examples are music, drama, choreography, and pantomimes.

Form VA: for works of the visual arts. Examples are photographs, drawings, paintings, prints, art reproductions, cartoons, comic strips, charts, diagrams, maps, pictorial ornamentation, and pictorial or graphic material published as advertising.

If your contributions differ in nature, choose the form most suitable for the majority of them. However, if any of the contributions consists preponderantly of nondramatic text matter in English, you should file Form TX for the entire group. This is because Form TX is the only form containing spaces for information about the manufacture of copies, which the statute requires to be given for certain works.

REGISTRATION FEE FOR GROUP REGISTRATION

The fee for registration of a group of contributions to periodicals is $10, no matter how many contributions are listed on Form GR/CP. Unless you maintain a Deposit Account in the Copyright Office, the registration fee must accompany your application forms and copies. Make your remittance payable to: *Register of Copyrights.*

WHAT COPIES SHOULD BE DEPOSITED FOR GROUP REGISTRATION?

The application forms you file for group registration must be accompanied by one complete copy of each contribution listed in Form GR/CP, exactly as the contribution was first published in a periodical. The deposit must consist of the entire issue of the periodical containing the contribution; or, if the contribution was first published in a newspaper, the deposit should consist of the entire section in which the contribution appeared. Tear sheets or proof copies are not acceptable for deposit.

COPYRIGHT NOTICE REQUIREMENTS

For published works, the law provides that a copyright notice in a specified form "shall be placed on all publicly distributed copies from which the work can be visually perceived." The required form of the notice generally consists of three elements: (1) the symbol "©", or the word "Copyright", or the abbreviation "Copr."; (2) the year of first publication of the work; and (3) the name of the owner of copyright in the work, or an abbreviation or alternative form of the name. For example: "© 1978 Samuel Craig".

Among the conditions for group registration of contributions to periodicals, the statute establishes two requirements involving the copyright notice:

(1) Each of the contributions as first published must have borne a separate copyright notice; and

(2) "The name of the owner of copyright in the work, or an abbreviation by which the name can be recognized, or a generally known alternative designation of the owner" must have been the same in each notice.

HOW TO FILL OUT THE BASIC APPLICATION FORM WHEN APPLYING FOR GROUP REGISTRATION

In general, the instructions for filling out the basic application (Form TX, Form PA, or Form VA) apply to group registrations. In addition, please observe the following specific instructions:

Space 1 (Title): Do not give information concerning any of the contributions in space 1 of the basic application. Instead, in the block headed "Title of this Work", state: "See Form GR/CP, attached". Leave the other blocks in space 1 blank.

Space 2 (Author): Give the name and other information concerning the author of all of the contributions listed in Form GR/CP. To qualify for group registration, all of the contributions must have been written by the same individual author.

Space 3 (Creation and Publication): In the block calling for the year of creation, give the year of creation of the last of the contributions to be completed. Leave the block calling for the date and nation of first publication blank.

Space 4 (Claimant): Give all of the requested information, which must be the same for all of the contributions listed on Form GR/CP.

Other spaces: Complete all of the applicable spaces, and be sure that the form is signed in the certification space.

HOW TO FILL OUT FORM GR/CP

PART A: IDENTIFICATION OF APPLICATION

• **Identification of Basic Application:** Indicate, by checking one of the boxes, which of the basic application forms (Form TX, or Form PA, or Form VA) you are filing for registration.

• **Identification of Author and Claimant:** Give the name of the individual author exactly as it appears in line 2 of the basic application, and give the name of the copyright claimant exactly as it appears in line 4. These must be the same for all of the contributions listed in Part B of Form GR/CP.

PART B: REGISTRATION FOR GROUP OF CONTRIBUTIONS

• **General Instructions:** Under the statute, a group of contributions to periodicals will qualify for a single registration only if the application "identifies each work separately, including the periodical containing it and its date of first publication." Part B of the Form GR/CP provides lines enough to list 19 separate contributions; if you need more space, use additional Forms GR/CP. If possible, list the contributions in the order of their publication, giving the earliest first. Number each line consecutively.

• **Important:** All of the contributions listed on Form GR/CP must have been published within a single twelve-month period. This does not mean that all of the contributions must have been published during the same calendar year, but it does mean that, to be grouped in a single application, the earliest and latest contributions must not have been published more than twelve months apart. Example: Contributions published on April 1, 1978, July 1, 1978, and March 1, 1979, could be grouped together, but a contribution published on April 15, 1979, could not be registered with them as part of the group.

• **Title of Contribution:** Each contribution must be given a title that is capable of identifying that particular work and of distinguishing it from others. If the contribution as published in the periodical bears a title (or an identifying phrase that could serve as a title), transcribe its wording completely and exactly.

• **Identification of Periodical:** Give the over-all title of the periodical in which the contribution was first published, together with the volume and issue number (if any) and the issue date.

• **Pages:** Give the number of the page of the periodical issue on which the contribution appeared. If the contribution covered more than one page, give the inclusive pages, if possible.

• **First Publication:** The statute defines "publication" as "the distribution of copies or phonorecords of a work to the public by sale or other transfer of ownership, or by rental, lease, or lending"; a work is also "published" if there has been an "offering to distribute copies or phonorecords to a group of persons for purposes of further distribution, public performance, or public display." Give the full date (month, day, and year) when, and the country where, publication of the periodical issue containing the contribution first occurred. If first publication took place simultaneously in the United States and other countries, it is sufficient to state "U.S.A."

NOTE: The advantage of group registration is that it allows any number of works published within a twelve-month period to be registered "on the basis of a single deposit, application, and registration fee." On the other hand, group registration may also have disadvantages under certain circumstances. If infringement of a published work begins before the work has been registered, the copyright owner can still obtain the ordinary remedies for copyright infringement (including injunctions, actual damages and profits, and impounding and disposition of infringing articles). However, in that situation—where the copyright in a published work is infringed before registration is made—the owner cannot obtain special remedies (statutory damages and attorney's fees) unless registration was made within three months after first publication of the work.

ADJUNCT APPLICATION
for
Copyright Registration for a
Group of Contributions to Periodicals

- Use this adjunct form only if your are making a single registration for a group of contributions to periodicals, and you are also filing a basic application on Form TX, Form PA, or Form VA. Follow the instructions, attached.
- Number each line in Part B consecutively. Use additional Forms GR/CP if you need more space.
- Submit this adjunct form with the basic application form. Clip (do not tape or staple) and fold all sheets together before submitting them.

FORM GR/CP

UNITED STATES COPYRIGHT OFFICE

REGISTRATION NUMBER

TX   PA   VA

EFFECTIVE DATE OF REGISTRATION

(Month)   (Day)   (Year)

FORM GR/CP RECEIVED

Page _____ of _____ pages

DO NOT WRITE ABOVE THIS LINE. FOR COPYRIGHT OFFICE USE ONLY

(A)

Identification of Application

IDENTIFICATION OF BASIC APPLICATION:
- This application for copyright registration for a group of contributions to periodicals is submitted as an adjunct to an application filed on:

(Check which)

☐ Form TX   ☐ Form PA   ☐ Form VA

IDENTIFICATION OF AUTHOR AND CLAIMANT: (Give the name of the author and the name of the copyright claimant in all of the contributions listed in Part B of this form. The names should be the same as the names given in spaces 2 and 4 of the basic application.)

Name of Author: ....

Name of Copyright Claimant: ....

(B)

Registration For Group of Contributions

COPYRIGHT REGISTRATION FOR A GROUP OF CONTRIBUTIONS TO PERIODICALS: (To make a single registration for a group of works by the same individual author, all first published as contributions to periodicals within a 12-month period (see instructions), give full information about each contribution. If more space is needed, use additional Forms GR/CP.)

☐ Title of Contribution: ....
Title of Periodical: .... Vol...... No...... Issue Date........ Pages........
Date of First Publication: .... (Month) (Day) (Year) Nation of First Publication .... (Country)

☐ Title of Contribution: ....
Title of Periodical: .... Vol...... No...... Issue Date........ Pages........
Date of First Publication: .... (Month) (Day) (Year) Nation of First Publication .... (Country)

☐ Title of Contribution: ....
Title of Periodical: .... Vol...... No...... Issue Date........ Pages........
Date of First Publication: .... (Month) (Day) (Year) Nation of First Publication .... (Country)

☐ Title of Contribution: ....
Title of Periodical: .... Vol...... No...... Issue Date........ Pages........
Date of First Publication: .... (Month) (Day) (Year) Nation of First Publication .... (Country)

☐ Title of Contribution: ....
Title of Periodical: .... Vol...... No...... Issue Date........ Pages........
Date of First Publication: .... (Month) (Day) (Year) Nation of First Publication .... (Country)

☐ Title of Contribution: ....
Title of Periodical: .... Vol...... No...... Issue Date........ Pages........
Date of First Publication: .... (Month) (Day) (Year) Nation of First Publication .... (Country)

☐ Title of Contribution: ....
Title of Periodical: .... Vol...... No...... Issue Date........ Pages........
Date of First Publication: .... (Month) (Day) (Year) Nation of First Publication .... (Country)

		FOR COPYRIGHT OFFICE USE ONLY

DO NOT WRITE ABOVE THIS LINE. FOR COPYRIGHT OFFICE USE ONLY

☐ Title of Contribution: ....
Title of Periodical: .... Vol..... No..... Issue Date......... Pages........
Date of First Publication:.............................. Nation of First Publication...........................
(Month)   (Day)   (Year)   (Country)

Ⓑ
Continued

☐ Title of Contribution: ....
Title of Periodical: .... Vol..... No..... Issue Date......... Pages........
Date of First Publication:.............................. Nation of First Publication...........................
(Month)   (Day)   (Year)   (Country)

☐ Title of Contribution: ....
Title of Periodical: .... Vol..... No..... Issue Date......... Pages........
Date of First Publication:.............................. Nation of First Publication...........................
(Month)   (Day)   (Year)   (Country)

☐ Title of Contribution: ....
Title of Periodical: .... Vol..... No..... Issue Date......... Pages........
Date of First Publication:.............................. Nation of First Publication...........................
(Month)   (Day)   (Year)   (Country)

☐ Title of Contribution: ....
Title of Periodical: .... Vol..... No..... Issue Date......... Pages........
Date of First Publication:.............................. Nation of First Publication...........................
(Month)   (Day)   (Year)   (Country)

☐ Title of Contribution: ....
Title of Periodical: .... Vol..... No..... Issue Date......... Pages........
Date of First Publication:.............................. Nation of First Publication...........................
(Month)   (Day)   (Year)   (Country)

☐ Title of Contribution: ....
Title of Periodical: .... Vol..... No..... Issue Date......... Pages........
Date of First Publication:.............................. Nation of First Publication...........................
(Month)   (Day)   (Year)   (Country)

☐ Title of Contribution: ....
Title of Periodical: .... Vol..... No..... Issue Date......... Pages........
Date of First Publication:.............................. Nation of First Publication...........................
(Month)   (Day)   (Year)   (Country)

☐ Title of Contribution: ....
Title of Periodical: .... Vol..... No..... Issue Date......... Pages........
Date of First Publication:.............................. Nation of First Publication...........................
(Month)   (Day)   (Year)   (Country)

☐ Title of Contribution: ....
Title of Periodical: .... Vol..... No..... Issue Date......... Pages........
Date of First Publication:.............................. Nation of First Publication...........................
(Month)   (Day)   (Year)   (Country)

☐ Title of Contribution: ....
Title of Periodical: .... Vol..... No..... Issue Date......... Pages........
Date of First Publication:.............................. Nation of First Publication...........................
(Month)   (Day)   (Year)   (Country)

☐ Title of Contribution: ....
Title of Periodical: .... Vol..... No..... Issue Date......... Pages........
Date of First Publication:.............................. Nation of First Publication...........................
(Month)   (Day)   (Year)   (Country)

∴ U.S. GOVERNMENT PRINTING OFFICE: 1978—261-022/12   Apr. 1978—300,000

APPENDIX D

SAMPLE DESKTOP PUBLISHING CONTRACTS

SAMPLE BOOK PUBLISHING CONTRACT

PUBLISHING CONTRACT

THIS PUBLISHING CONTRACT is made on _____ , 19_____ , between _____ (Full name of publisher), Publisher, residing at _____ (Address of publisher), and _____ (Full name of author), Author, residing at _____ (Address of author).

1.   The Author agrees to deliver an original and one copy of the Manuscript which is tentatively titled _____ (Tentative title of work), referred to as the Work, to the Publisher on or before _____ ,19_____.

The Work is described as _____ (Here provide a detailed description of the work, including subject matter, word length, outline if possible, and overall description).

If the Author fails to deliver the Manuscript and any necessary related materials within _____ days of the Manuscript due date, the Publisher may terminate this contract and the Author agrees to repay any money advanced.

2. Within _____ days of receipt of the Manuscript, the Publisher agrees to notify the Author if the Publisher finds the Manuscript unsatisfactory in form or content. The Publisher also agrees to provide the Author with a list of necessary changes. The Author agrees to make the changes within _____ days. If the Publisher still reasonably rejects the Manuscript as unsatisfactory, the Publisher may terminate this contract and the Author agrees to repay any money advanced.

3. With the delivery of the Manuscript, the Author also agrees to provide the Publisher with any necessary permissions to include material copyrighted by others. The Author is responsible for any payments necessary to obtain such permissions.

4. With the delivery of the Manuscript, the Author agrees to provide to the Publisher the following additional related items necessary for publication:_____ (Here detail any additional items required for the publication. For example: photographs, illustrations, drawings, charts, table of contents, prefix, forward, introduction, bibliography, appendices, glossary, index, etc).

5. The Author grants the Publisher the rights listed below, for the entire term of the copyright of the Work in _____ (Here detail the geographic limits of the rights granted. For example: the United States of America and Canada, or the entire World, etc.), :

    A. Book Trade Edition Rights: The exclusive right to print, publish, and sell hardcover or softcover editions of the Work for distribution through normal book trade channels;

B. Mass Market Book Reprint Rights: The exclusive right to print, publish, and sell or license others to print, publish, and sell mass market softcover editions of the Work;

C. Book Club Rights: The exclusive right to license others to print, publish, and sell book club editions of the Work;

D. General Publication Rights: The exclusive right to print, publish, and sell or license others to print, publish, and sell condensations, abridgements, Braille editions, or selections from the Work for inclusion in anthologies, compilations, digests, newspapers, magazines, or textbooks;

E. Direct Mail Rights: The exclusive right to sell or license others to sell the work through direct mail or coupon advertising;

F. First Book Serialization Rights: The exclusive right, prior to initial publication, to publish or license others to publish the work or portions of the Work;

G. Dramatic Rights: The exclusive right to use or license others to use the work or portions of the Work in any stage presentation;

H. Movie Rights: The exclusive right to use or license other to use the work or portions of the work in any motion picture presentation;

I. Television or Radio Rights: The exclusive right to use or license others to use the work or portions of the work in any television or radio presentation.

J. Translation Rights: The exclusive right to translate or license others to translate the work or portions of the work into any foreign languages and print, publish, and sell such translations of the work.

K. Publicity Rights: The exclusive right to use the work or any portion of the work in any manner for the purposes of promoting the sales of the work;

6.   Any rights not specifically granted to the Publisher shall remain with the Author. The Author agrees not to exercise any retained rights in such a manner as to adversely affect to value of the rights granted to the Publisher.

7.   The Publisher shall pay to the Author as an advance against any money to be paid to the Author under this contract the amount of $_____ to be paid one-half upon signing this contract and one-half upon delivery of a satisfactory manuscript. This amount is not repayable unless the Author fails to deliver a satisfactory manuscript within the time allowed.

8.   The Publisher agrees to pay the Author a royalty on the retail price of every copy sold by the Publisher (less any returns and a _____ percent reserve for returns), as follows:

A. _____ Percent (___%) up to and including _____ copies;

B. _____ Percent (___%) up to and including _____ copies;

C. _____ Percent (___%) for sales over _____ copies;

D. ____ Percent (___%) of the amount received for sales by direct mail;

E. _____ Percent (____%) of the amount received for sales
of _____ (elementary, junior high school, etc.)
textbook editions;

F. _____ Percent (____%) of the amount received for sales
on which the publisher granted a discount of greater
than _____ percent to the purchaser;

G. _____ Percent (____%) of the amount received for any
licenses of _____ rights granted by the
Publisher under this contract.

9.   The Author agrees to proofread, correct and promptly
      return all proofs of the work to the Publisher and to pay in
      cash for any changes required by the Author which are not
      printer's errors.

      The Author also agrees to provide necessary revisions of
      the Work in order to keep the Work up-to-date. Such
      revisions shall not be required more often than once every
      two years.

10.   The style, format, design, layout, advertising, promotion
      and price of the published work shall be in the sole
      discretion of the Publisher. However, no editorial changes
      in the manuscript, which materially alter the meaning of the
      text, will be made without the consent of the Author, unless
      the Publisher reasonably believes that the Work or portions
      of the Work are in violation of any of the Author's
      Warranties regarding the Work.

11.   The Author agrees to be reasonably available for promotion
      of the Work in the _____ (geographic) area for radio,
      television, and newspaper interviews. If the Publisher
      desires the Author to promote the book outside of this area
      and the Author consents, the Publisher agrees to pay the
      cost of transportation, meals, and lodging for the Author to
      attend any such promotional engagements.

12. The Publisher agrees to provide the Author with ____ copies of the published Work free of charge and to sell the Author any amount of additional copies at a 50% discount.

   The Publisher may distribute a reasonable number of books for promotional purposes without cost and without payment of royalty to the Author.

13. The Publisher and Author agree to attempt to compromise any dispute over any terms in this contract. If unable to mutually agree within a reasonable time, they agree to submit the dispute to a professional mediator to be mutually agreed upon, with the cost of the mediation to be equally shared.

14. The Author warrants that:

   A. The Work is the sole creation of the Author;

   B. The Author is the sole owner of the rights granted under this contract;

   C. The Work does not infringe upon the copyright of any other work;

   D. The Work is original and unpublished;

   E. The Work is not in the Public Domain;

   F. The Work is not obscene, libelous, and does not invade the privacy of any person;

   G. All statements of fact in the Work are true and based upon reasonable research.

15. If there is ever a claim based upon an alleged violation of any of the Author's warranties, the Publisher has the right to defend against the claim, but will not settle any claim without the reasonable consent of the Author. The Author

agrees to indemnify the Publisher for 50% of any losses under any such claim, except for any claim of copyright infringement for which the Author agrees to indemnify the Publisher in full.

Publisher agrees to arrange for Author to be a named insured under any publisher liability insurance policy.

16.   The Publisher agrees that, within one year from the receipt of a satisfactory manuscript of the Work, the work will be published at Publisher's sole expense. If Publisher fails to do so, unless prevented by conditions beyond Publisher's control, the Author may terminate this Contract.

17.   The Publisher agrees to register the copyright of the Work in the name of the Author in the United States and include a sufficient copyright notice on all copies of the Work distributed to the public.

18.   The Publisher agrees to provide the Author with a _____ accounting of all monies due. Payment of all royalties due shall be made within 30 days of such accounting.

The Publisher agrees that the Author shall have the right, on 48-hour notice, to examine the Publisher's accounting books and records which relate to the Work.

19.   The Author agrees that during the duration of the contract he or she will not edit, prepare, publish, or sell any material based on the Work which would interfere with the Publisher's sale of the Work.

20.   The Work will be considered "out-of-print" when the Publisher fails to sell _____ copies during any calendar year. When the work is out-of-print, all rights granted to the Publisher will revert to the Author, except those rights the Publisher has already licensed to others.

21. The Author agrees to submit his or her next work to the Publisher before submitting it to any other publisher. The Publisher agrees to make a decision on publication of the new work within six months of receipt. If a decision is made to publish the new work, the Author and Publisher agree to negotiate a publishing contract for the new work. If the Author and Publisher are, in good faith, unable to arrive at an acceptable contract within 30 days from the decision-to-publish date, the Author is free to submit the manuscript elsewhere.

22. This contract shall be interpreted according to the laws of the state of the Publisher's residence. This contract shall be binding upon the heirs, representatives and assigns of the Author and Publisher, but no assignment of this contract will be binding on either party without the written consent of the other. Time is of the essence in this contract.

    This contract is the complete agreement between the Author and Publisher. No modification or waiver of any terms will be valid unless in writing and signed by both parties.

This Contract is signed by the parties on the date first written above.

_____
Signature of Publisher
(Typewritten Name of Publisher)

_____
Signature of Author
(Typewritten Name of Author)
(Author's Social Security Number)

SAMPLE MAGAZINE ARTICLE CONTRACT

PUBLISHING CONTRACT

THIS PUBLISHING CONTRACT is made on _____, 19_____ , between _____ (Full name of publisher), Publisher, residing at _____ (Address of publisher), and _____ (Full name of author), Author, residing at _____ (Address of author).

1.   The Author agrees to deliver an original and one copy of the Manuscript which is tentatively titled _____ (Tentative title of work), referred to as the Work, to the Publisher on or before _____, 19_____.

   The Work is described as _____ (Here provide a detailed description of the work, including subject matter, word length, outline if possible, and overall description).

   If the Author fails to deliver the Manuscript within _____ days of the Manuscript due date, the Publisher may terminate this contract.

2.   Within _____ days of receipt of the Manuscript, the Publisher agrees to notify the Author if the Publisher finds the Manuscript unsatisfactory in form or content. The Publisher also agrees to provide the Author with a list of necessary changes. The Author agrees to make the changes within _____ days. If the Publisher still reasonably rejects the Manuscript as unsatisfactory, the Publisher may terminate this contract.

3.   The Author grants the Publisher the first North American Serial Rights in the Work. Any rights not specifically granted to the Publisher shall remain with the Author. The Author agrees not to exercise any retained rights in such a manner as to adversely affect to value of the rights granted to the Publisher.

4. The Publisher shall pay to the Author upon acceptance of the Manuscript the amount of $_____.

5. The style, format, design, layout, and any required editorial changes of the published work shall be in the sole discretion of the Publisher.

6. The Author warrants that:

    A. The Work is the sole creation of the Author;

    B. The Author is the sole owner of the rights granted under this contract;

    C. The Work does not infringe upon the copyright of any other work;

    D. The Work is original and has not been published before;

    E. The Work is not in the Public Domain;

    F. The Work is not obscene, libelous, and does not invade the privacy of any person;

    G. All statements of fact in the Work are true and based upon reasonable research.

7. The Publisher agrees to register the copyright of the Work in the name of the Author in the United States and include a sufficient copyright notice on all copies of the Work distributed to the public.

8. The Publisher agrees that, within one year from the receipt of a satisfactory manuscript of the Work, the work will be published at Publisher's sole expense. If Publisher fails to do so, unless prevented by conditions beyond the Publisher's control, the Author may terminate this Contract.

9.   This Contract is the complete agreement between the Author and Publisher. No modification or waiver of any terms will be valid unless in writing and signed by both parties.

This Contract is signed by the parties on the date first written above.

_____

Signature of Publisher
(Typewritten Name of Publisher)

_____

Signature of Author
(Typewritten Name of Author)
(Author's Social Security Number)

SAMPLE LETTER AGREEMENT

Desktop Publishing Company
123 Fifth Avenue
New York, NY 10000

Ms. Ima Writer
789 Main Street
Smalltown, MI 40000

Dear Ms. Writer:

With regard to your submission entitled "The Joy of Desktop Publishing", we are interested in publishing the piece in our September issue of THE JOURNAL OF DESKTOP PUBLISHING RELATIONSHIPS.

We will pay you $250.00 for the First United States Serial Rights for this article.

You warrant that you are the sole author of the work and you have not sold it elsewhere; that it does not infringe upon any copyright; that it has not been published before; and that it contains no material which violates any law.

We will have the right and sole discretion to edit the work as we may need. We will obtain a copyright for the work in your name and publish the appropriate copyright notice.

If we do not publish the work within 1 year, all rights to the work will revert to you and you may retain the payment.

You will not write or have published any other similar work dealing with the same subject matter within 1 year of your acceptance of this agreement.

If you agree with these terms, please sign one copy of this letter where indicated and return it to us. Your check for payment will be forwarded to you immediately. Please retain the other copy of this letter for your personal records.

Thank you very much.

Sincerely,

Desktop Publishing Company

William Desktop, Publisher

Agreed to and accepted on
_____, 19_____

_____
Ima Writer

BIBLIOGRAPHY

Adler, Bill. *Inside Publishing*. Bobbs-Merrill, 1982,

American Law Institute-American Bar Association. *The Copyright Act of 1976*. American Law Institute-American Bar Association, 1977.

Bailey, Herbert S. *The Art and Science of Book Publishing.* University of Texas Press, 1970.

Balkin, Richard. *A Writer's Guide to Book Publishing.* Hawthorn Books, 1977.

Bunnin, Brad, and Peter Beren. *Author Law and Strategies.* Nolo Press, 1983

Bureau of National Affairs. *Media Law Reporter.* Bureau of National Affairs, 1980-

Bush, George P. *Technology and Copyright: Sources and Materials.* Lomond Books, 1979.

Chickering, Robert B., and Susan Hartman. *How to Register a Copyright and Protect Your Creative Work.* Charles Scribner's Sons, 1980.

Commerce Clearing House. *Copyright Law Reporter.* Commerce Clearing House, 1980-.

Copyright Society of the U.S.A. *Bulletin.* New York University Law Center, 1953- (Bi-monthly).

Copyright Society of the U.S.A. *Studies on Copyright.* Bobbs-Merrill Co., 1983.

Crawford, Tad. *The Writer's Legal Guide.* Hawthorn Books, 1977.

Dessauer, John. *Book Publishing, What it is, What it Does.* R. R. Bowker, 1976.

Greenfield, Howard. *Books: From Writer to Reader.* Crown Publishing, 1976.

Henn, Harry G. *Copyright Primer.* Practising Law Institute, 1979.

Hirsch, E. G. *Copyright it Yourself.* Whitehall Co., 1979.

Hurst, Walter E. *Copyright: How to Register Your Copyright & Introduction to New and Historic Copyright Law.* Seven Arts Press, 1977.

Johnston, Donald F. *Copyright Handbook.* R. R. Bowker, 1978.

Kaplan, Benjamin, and Ralph S. Brown, Jr. *Cases on Copyright, Unfair Competition, and Other Topics Bearing on the Protection of Literary, Musical, and Artistic Works.* Foundation Press, 1978.

Kupferman, Theodore R., and Matthew Foner (Eds.) *Universal Copyright Convention Analyzed*. Federal Legal Publications, 1955.

Latman, Alan. *The Copyright Law: Howell's Copyright Law Revised and the 1976 Act.* Bureau of National Affairs, 1979.

Latman, Alan, and Ralph Gorman. *Copyright for the Eighties: Cases and Materials.* Michie Bobbs-Merrill, 1981.

Lindey, Alexander. *Lindey on Entertainment, Publishing, and the Art; Agreements and the Law.* Clark Boardman, 1980-.

Metcalf, Slade R. *Rights and Liabilities of Publishers, Broadcasters, and Reporters.* Shepards/McGraw-Hill, 1983.

Nimmer, Melville B. *Cases and Materials on Copyright and Other Aspects of Law Pertaining to Literary, Musical, and Artistic Works.* West Publishing Co., 1979

Nimmer, Melville B. *Nimmer on Copyright.* M. Bender, 1982.

Patent, Trademark, and Copyright Journal. Bureau of National Affairs, 1970- (weekly).

Patterson, Lyman Ray. *Copyright in Historical Perspective.* Vanderbilt University Press, 1968.

Polking, Kirk, and Leonard S. Meranus (Eds.) *Law and the Writer.* Writer's Digest Books, 1978.

Ringer, Barbara. *The demonology of copyright.* R. R. Bowker, 1974.

Sandford, Bruce W. *Synopsis of the Law of Libel and the Right of Privacy.* World Almanac Publications, 1981.

Sack, Robert D. *Libel, Slander, and Related Problems.* Practising Law Institute, 1980.

Shatzkin, Leonard. *In Cold Type.* Houghton-Mifflin, 1982.

Stuart, Sally E. and Woody Young. *Copyright Not Copycat: A Writer's Guide to Copyright.* Joy Publishing, 1987.

United Nations Educational, Scientific, and Cultural Organization. Copyright Division. *Copyright Bulletin.* 1967- (Quarterly).

Weinstein, David A. *How To Protect Your Creative Work.* John Wiley and Sons, Inc., 1987.

Wincor, Richard. *Copyright, Patents, and Trademarks: The Protection of Intellectual and Industrial Property.* Oceana Publications, 1980.

Wittenberg, Phillip. *The Protection of Literary Property.* The Writer, Inc., 1978.

GLOSSARY OF LEGAL AND PUBLISHING TERMS

ACTUAL DAMAGES: Damages which have actually occurred, and which may be monetarily compensated for.

ACTUAL MALICE: Actual knowledge of the falsity of a libelous statement or reckless disregard for the truth or falsity of the statement.

ASSIGNMENT: The transfer of ownership in property, either in whole or in part.

AUTHOR: The *creator*, through some intellectual effort, of copyrightable material.

BASIC REGISTRATION: The original copyright registration for a particular work.

BASIS: For tax purposes, the full cost of an asset.

BENEFICIARY: A person who has or will receive a benefit.

BEST EDITION: The most suitable edition of a work for Library of Congress purposes.

BY-LAWS: The internal rules of operation for a corporation.

CAPITAL EXPENDITURES: For tax purposes, those expenses which are considered investments in the business.

CERTIFICATE OF RECORDATION: A Copyright Office certificate stating that a document has been officially recorded with the Copyright Office.

CIVIL LAWSUIT: A lawsuit based on a private wrong, as opposed to a public wrong or criminal act.

CO-AUTHOR: A person who has acted jointly with another to create a work.

COLLABORATION: To work jointly with others to create a work.

COLLECTION/COLLECTIVE WORK: A work consisting of independent works compiled or assembled into a collective whole work.

COMMISSIONED WORK: A work specially ordered or requested as a contribution to a *collective work*, if the parties agree in writing that the work will be a *"work-for-hire"*.

COMPILATION: A work consisting of pre-existing materials compiled or assembled into a new *collective* whole, including any collective works.

COMPULSORY LICENSE: A license to exercise one of the rights of copyright without permission of the owner, but with a payment of a *royalty* fee.

CONSIDERATION: In contract law, a mutually bargained-for exchange of something of value.

CONTRACT: An agreement between two or more parties which is enforceable by law.

CONTRIBUTION TO A COLLECTIVE WORK: A complete independent work, compiled and assembled with others to form a *collective work*.

COPYRIGHT: The five exclusive right under the Copyright Act of 1976: the right to make copies, make variations, publicly perform, publicly display, or distribute copies of works of creation.

CORPORATION: A business owned by one or more shareholders and incorporated under the laws of any state.

COSTS: The expenses of bringing or defending a lawsuit. A court award of "costs" in a case to either party does not, generally, include payment for attorney's fees.

CREATOR: The person who is the author of a work.

DAMAGES: Monetary compensation asked for in a law suit by a person or entity which has suffered a loss or injury due to a unlawful, reckless, or negligent act of another.

DEFAMATION: A false statement which tends to damage the business or personal reputation of another.

DEPRECIATION: For tax purposes, an accounting principle which allows a business to recover a proportionate yearly percentage of the cost of an asset as a deductions against expenses.

DERIVATIVE WORK: A variation of a pre-existing work; as an adaptation, translation, abridgement, editorial revision, etc.

DISTRIBUTE: To make copies available for sale or rental to the public.

DRAMATIC WORK: A literary composition which tells a story through action and dialogue.

ENJOIN: To require a person or entity, with a court-ordered *injunction*, to stop a certain action, or to prevent a certain action.

EXCLUSIVE LICENSE: Permission given for one person to do an act with the agreement that no other person will be given similar permission.

EXCLUSIVE RIGHTS: A right which only the owner can legally exercise.

FAIR COMMENT: In libel law, a statement made in the good faith belief that it is true, even though the statement is, in fact, false.

FAIR USE: An exception to the full rights of copyright which allows use of a work without permission or payment of a royalty fee in certain instances; such as teaching, criticism, research, etc.

FIRST PUBLICATION: The initial distribution of a work to the public for sale or rental.

INFRINGEMENT OF COPYRIGHT: The violation of one of the five exclusive rights of copyright.

INJUNCTION: A court-ordered writ which orders a person or entity to stop a certain action, or not begin a certain action.

LIBEL: A written or broadcast false statement which tends to damage the business or personal reputation of another.

LIBEL PER SE: Certain forms of libel which have been determined to be defamatory on their face.

LICENSE: To authorize another to exercise a right.

LIMITED PARTNERSHIP: A hybrid type of partnership in which "limited" partners enjoy limited legal liability, and "general" partners are fully liable for the debts of the partnership.

LITERARY WORK: A work expressed in words or numbers, regardless of its form.

MISAPPROPRIATION: The unauthorized use of another's name or likeness for commercial gain and without compensation.

MITIGATION: Not a justification, excuse, of defense to a legal charge; but rather circumstances which tend to lessen the severity of the charge or lessen the liability of the one charged.

NEGLIGENCE: Failure to act as a reasonable person.

PARTNERSHIP: A business owned and operated by two or more persons or organizations.

PERIODICAL: A publication which is issued at recurring intervals.

PLAGIARISM: To copy another's work and claim it as one's own.

PLAINTIFF: A person or entity who files a law suit in court against another.

PRIMA FACIE: Legally sufficient "on its face" to prove a fact or an issue, unless disproved by stronger evidence.

PUBLIC DOMAIN: Material not protected by copyright, belonging to the general public; material which may be copied or used without permission or payment of royalty.

PUBLICATION: In copyright--the distribution of a copy of a work to the public for sale or rental/ In libel--the transmission of a statement to another party.

REGISTRATION: The action of filing a claim or ownership to a copyright.

ROYALTY: Payment made to the owner of a copyright for permission to exercise certain or all rights under the copyright.

"S" CORPORATION: A hybrid corporation for tax purposes which is operated like a corporation, but is taxed essentially like a partnership.

SERIAL: A publication which is published in a series of issues, as a magazine, journal, newspaper, newsletter, etc.

SLANDER: Oral or spoken *defamation*; false statements which tend to damage the personal or business reputation of another.

SOLE PROPRIETORSHIP: A business owned and operated by one person.

STATUTORY DAMAGES: An amount determined by a court, under the Copyright Act of 1976, to be just compensation for any injuries caused by copyright infringement.

STIPULATION: An agreement, usually written, by which both sides to an issue reach an understanding on any matter.

SUBSIDIARY RIGHTS: All rights exercisable under a copyright subsequent to the initial publication of the work.

TANGIBLE FORM: A form which has a physical presence, and may be read or viewed.

UNPUBLISHED: A work which has not been intentionally distributed to the public for sale or rental.

WILLFUL: An intentional act, as opposed to a inadvertent or negligent act.

WORK FOR HIRE: A work prepared by an employee within the scope of his or her employment; or a *commissioned* work.

INDEX

237